Generation Y

THRIVING *and surviving* WITH GENERATION Y AT WORK

Peter Sheahan

Hardie Grant Books

First published in 2005
Reprinted in 2005, 2006 (three times), 2007 (twice) by
Hardie Grant Books
85 High Street
Prahran, Victoria 3181, Australia
www.hardiegrant.com.au

National Library of Australia Cataloguing-in-Publication Data:
Sheahan, Peter.
Generation Y: thriving (and surviving) with Generation Y at work.
Includes index.
ISBN 13 978 1 74066 317 5.
ISBN 10 1 74066 317 9.
1. Young adults – Employment – Australia.
2. Intergenerational relations – Australia. 3. Personnel management – Australia. 4. Supervision of employees.
I.Title.
658.30084

Cover and text design by Phil Campbell
Layout by Pauline Haas, bluerinse setting
Printed and bound in Australia by Griffin Press

10 9 8 7

Peter Sheahan is obsessed with TALENT. He is on a one-way mission to develop the best of tomorrow's business leaders, ensuring that organisations and individuals know how to leverage talent for profit. A screaming example of what it takes to be successful in the 'free agent nation', he was the New South Wales MBN Young Entrepreneur of the Year in 2003.

Peter has delivered more than 1,500 presentations to over 165,000 people and consults to organisations that want to attract, manage and engage the best of Generation Y. His clients include Westpac, Panasonic and The Department of Education Science and Training.

For more information please visit <www.petersheahan.com>

'Written by a Generation Yer, this book provides a refreshingly honest and eye-opening read for those of us who may be grappling to understand the mindset of this unique post-modern generation. Peter Sheahan helps us to appreciate and meet the changing dynamics of young talent within our workforce today.

He provides practical, commonsense advice and solutions to winning the war for young talent; addressing head-on the challenges of attracting, managing and holding on to this new breed of talent, as well as ensuring we utilise the enormous potential that they bring to our organisations.

Peter Sheahan's take on what makes this generation tick and how to deal with them makes the challenge they present infinitely less daunting! This is balanced by the fact that he is realistic about their characteristics and failings – along with their specific development needs.

Generation Y is essential reading for all who seek to engage with this wonderful group of future leaders.'

James Millar – CEO, Ernst & Young

'In *Generation Y*, Peter Sheahan compellingly captures what it is to be born of that generation and offers practical guidance on how to recruit, manage and motivate Generation Yers.

As the voice of management in this country, the Australian Institute of Management listens to aspiring and professional managers at all levels. From this perspective, Peter's book is imperative reading.

From money to mood swings, Peter takes you inside the mind of Generation Y and stays true to his engaging, provocative style.'

C Barker FAIM – National Director,
Australian Institute of Management

'Peter Sheahan answers the question "Y You Should Care" about demographic and generational workforce changes. A must for all employers, recruiters (and parents!).'

Sheryle Moon – Director, Recruitment and Staffing Solutions Australasia, Manpower

'Reading this book on Generation Y is just like hearing Peter give one of his sensational presentations. And who better to give us an insight into Generation Y but one of their own! I have been privileged to witness first-hand the impact that he has on young people at schools and am delighted that he has taken this one step further by providing parents and employers with a "tool box" of tips to make life less complicated when dealing with and understanding the younger generation. For my mind, this is critical stuff if you want to be an employer of choice for Generation Y.'

Margaret Beerworth – Director, CPA Australia

'Generation Y is more than a cohort of the population born between 1978 and 1994 – it represents an attitude of mind which will increasingly pervade all generations as E information and communications technologies become ubiquitous.

Peter Sheahan, a Generation Yer himself, in a fast, direct, iconoclastic style, defines the expectations and actions of his generation with insights and anecdotes that changed my perceptions. The primary audience for the book is top management, HR executives and all those whose business success is dependent on attracting, motivating and retaining lively, innovative minds. However, understanding the values and lifestyles of Generation Y will be of equal relevance to cities, their planners and all those involved with shaping the expression of our environment.

The style is fast, direct, fresh and relevant. I could not put the book down and now I have I am beginning to see a new way to conceive the city and my business.'

John Worthington – Co-founder of DEGW and Graham Willis Professor, School of Architecture, University of Sheffield

'This book is the bible for people who need to recruit and manage Generation Y.'

Margaret Kirby – Managing Director, The I Group

Contents

Acknowledgments

With thanks to the tens of thousands of Generation Yers who have let me into their lives and minds, this book is for you. Together we will make the workplace an exciting place for talented people from all generations.

To my wife Sharon and daughter Maddy. You make the hard work worthwhile.

Special thanks to Emma Hogan, without whom this book would never have been written. One of the sharpest HR minds in Australia, Emma you kept this book on the rails.

To Mary Cunnane my friend and agent. It is one thing to write a book. It is another thing altogether to get it published. Thanks for believing in this project and for your commitment to getting it onto the shelves.

To the team at Hardie Grant. Thanks for all of your hard work, for meeting my near impossible deadline and most of all for putting up with me.

New World New Rules

It's unlike me to fall asleep in anything, least of all the orientation program for my first 'real' job (whatever that's supposed to mean). But there I was, sound asleep, awoken only by a sharp pain in my ribs. It was the elbow of my fellow recruit sitting next to me.

'Wake up, the speaker's looking at you.'

I'd begun to snore ever so slightly. Why? Well, I was bored. I'd dozed off thinking that in the interview they'd assured me their accounting firm was a vibrant and energetic place to work. Clearly, the orientation program did not match the promise. After just 24 hours I was tempted to make a career change, but I decided that just because the orientation program was boring, it didn't meant the job would be.

So I persevered. For eight days. That was it. I couldn't stand another minute. The final straw was when an accountant in my division handed me about 350 numbered pages and ask me to renumber them in green.

'But they're already numbered,' I said.

'Yes, but we need them numbered in green.'

'Why? What's wrong with black?'

'Nothing. We just need them numbered in green.'

'Yeah, but *why*?"

'Because.'

'"Because" is not an answer.'

'Listen, this is just the way we do things around here!'

And that was it. I left the papers on the desk, grabbed my meagre personal belongings and went to my manager's office. I thanked him, let him know that I appreciated the opportunity but had decided it wasn't for me.

'But you've only been here for eight days,' he said. 'No-one's ever left after just eight days.'

Well I just had, with my head held high, and in the knowledge that I'd set the record for the fastest person ever to leave the cadetship program at that particular international accounting firm. (For the record they're doing a much better job now and no longer exist in the same name or form as when I began my career there.)

The truth is it only takes a very short time to know whether you 'fit' somewhere or not. And there began my second career: a toilet cleaner in an Irish pub. As luck would have it, 12 months later I was the daytime manager of that hotel, and six months after that I was the general manager of a different Irish pub. Hardly an esteemed career by any stretch of the imagination, but a good start for a 19 year old. That pub had 30 staff, give or take 10%, most of whom were under the age of 25. They had plenty of skills, and lots of brains, but just didn't know how to sell themselves. I'd interview countless young people, their résumés terrible and out of date, their mobile phones going off *during* the interview. And if that weren't bad enough, they'd proceed to take the call, tell the person on the other end that they were in a job interview and then say they'd call them back! Others would front up wearing shorts and a T-shirt.

After 18 months running this business, I had my second career epiphany: someone has got to go into schools and teach students how to do this. 'This' being how to sell themselves to a prospective employer. I decided that it'd be my job to do it. I've since worked with more than 100,000 members of what I now call 'Generation Y', helping them to make the successful transition from school to work.

As I built my career, collated my research and spoke at venues around Australia, I couldn't help thinking about my eight days in the accounting firm. I realised that it wasn't just the students who were struggling with the transition from school to work – the companies they were going to work for were struggling just as much. They just didn't seem to understand the needs and expectations of this new generation of Australian workers. Friend after friend, client after client would relay to me stories of boring orientation programs, bad management and soaring attrition rates. And most of these stories related to my age group: Generation Y.

And that was epiphany number three. Someone needed to help organisations better attract, manage and engage Generation Y. After working with some of Australia's leading companies and reviewing the research for this book, I realised that Generation Y is not just about a demographic – it's about a mindset! A mindset which is permeating all ages and levels of the workforce. It may be starting with those born between 1978 and 1994, but their attitudes, demands and desires are spreading well beyond. Generation X are already making some of the same demands, and so will the Baby Boomers as they approach the end of their careers.

A flexible working week, the opportunity to do work that makes a difference, the absence of organisational loyalty and an unwillingness to put up with 'corporate slavery' are trends that are here to stay – people want a *life* and Generation Y are calling for it the loudest. When they don't get it, they talk with their feet, and this is the reason management and retention of Generation Y are two of the biggest issues facing business today.

Organisations can no longer afford to alienate or disengage staff. Firstly, we have truly moved into the knowledge economy, a world where the success of a business or organisation is directly related to the quality of the people in its employ. Add to this the emergence of an acute skills shortage and increased attrition in a time of high recruitment costs, and you have a serious challenge. And it is not a 'soft people' problem. It is affecting the ability of organisations to meet the needs of their stakeholders. And 'harder' still: it is having an impact on the bottom line.

The issues are not confined to Generation Y and workplace transformation. Consider the following factors affecting all businesses today:

> **An ageing workforce. In 2008 more Australians will leave the workforce than will enter it**
> **A skills shortage across multiple professions**
> **Flatter organisation structures and the demolition of the traditional vertical career path**
> **The changing nature of work itself. The demand for knowledge-based work, where creativity and innovation are key, as opposed to the efficient processing of resources**
> **Global competition**
> **Technology that not just changes the way we 'do' things, but has begun to change the very fabric of human society by changing the way we communicate**
> **A more transient workforce**

These factors are not confined to just one new age group, rather they represent a change in the way we live our lives, the type of products and services we produce and the way businesses make a profit. It is a new world with new rules, and Generation Y are geared not only to survive, but to thrive. They may seem to be the problem, but they are actually the solution.

In the 'Knowledge Age', businesses *need* to be 'talent-friendly'. **If you build a Generation Y–friendly organisation, you will build a talent-friendly organisation.**

The industrial business model was all about 'leveraging resources for profit'. The knowledge-based business model seeks to 'leverage *talent* for profit'. Leverage once came from efficiency in processing and economies of scale, now it comes from the full-scale engagement of the most talented people.

But how do you engage a generation that you barely understand?

The answer to that question is the premise of this book. It will give you in-depth, accurate insight into the mindset of Generation Y, which in turn will better equip you to attract, manage and engage not only this generation, but *all* generations.

Specifically, *Generation Y: Thriving (and Surviving) with Generation Y at Work* will:

> **Enable you to make better strategic decisions**
> **Give you an understanding of the wants and desires of Generation Y**
> **Detail specific strategies for all stages of the employment life cycle, from attracting through to exiting**
> **Open your eyes to the tremendous potential in your existing Generation Y talent pool**
> **Give you the tools to turn Generation Y talent into profit**

Who should read this book?

This book is targeted at anyone who deals with Generation Y. That includes senior managers, line managers, human resource professionals and trainers. It will also be of use to marketers and educators who seek to better understand the character traits and motivations of this generation. And no doubt, it will be of interest to Generation Y as well.

How should you read this book?

Generation Y: Thriving (and Surviving) with Generation Y at Work is broken into four parts. 'Part 1: Understanding Generation Y' will give you the insights you need into the mindset of this generation. Parts 2, 3 and 4 will give you the solutions you require to recruit, manage and retain your Generation Y workers. I suggest you resist the urge to skip straight to those 'how to' chapters because all businesses are different, and it is impossible to suggest solutions that will suit every business. However, if you empower yourself with an understanding of Generation Y, then you will be better able to adapt the solutions suggested in Parts 2, 3 and 4 to your organisation. You will also be equipped to better implement solutions to the following essential business activities covered in detail:

> **Recruiting**
> **Selecting**

- **Orientation**
- **Training**
- **Motivating**
- **Day-to-day managing**
- **Communicating**
- **Developing**
- **Retaining**
- **Exiting**

You will notice that at the end of every chapter in Part 1 there is an 'Executive Summary'. This chapter neatly encapsulates the character traits described in that chapter, providing a fast and easy later reference, or even a shortcut for those too busy to read the entire book.

At the end of each chapter in the 'how to' parts, there are directives, usually in the form of questions titled 'Your Quest!', which I recommend you complete after reading each chapter. Don't just read the book; make some changes to the way you do business as you go.

There are four major company case studies used:

- **Henry Davis York (Deborah Stonley – HR Manager) <www.hdy.com.au>**
- **Lion Nathan Australia (Linda Botter – HR Director, Strategy) <www.lion-nathan.com.au>**
- **Ford Australia (David Cvetkovski – HR Associate, Recruitment and Development) <www.ford.com.au>**
- **Marc Edward Agency (Edward Kaleel – Managing Director) <www.marcedward.com.au>**

All are exceptional employers of young talent and have generously given of their time and advice. That being said, the inclusion of their comments does not indicate that they support all the views and strategies put forward elsewhere in the book.

To be on a quest means to embark on a journey of discovery. I hope this book is but the beginning of your quest, and that as you apply the ideas and suggestions contained herein, you uncover the enormous potential of youth and that their fresh, enthusiastic outlook rubs off on the way we all do business. Most importantly, I hope that you use this information to improve not only the way you do business, but the experience you and your colleagues have at work. After all, we spend so much of our life at work, let's at least make it enjoyable. Better still: let's make a difference.

Enjoy!

Peter Sheahan

PS Never forget the power of youthful energy.

Part One

Understanding Generation Y

Introducing Generation Y

So who is Generation Y? Let's look first at how a generation is defined, and then I'll give you the run-down on whom and what the term 'Generation Y' actually represents.

Even though humans are formed from the same basic genetic material, we clearly do not all think or behave in the same way. It is the environment that surrounds us as we grow through our formative childhood and teenager years that shapes many of our character traits. It is logical, then, that groups of people born around the same time will have similar characteristics. Why? Because certain social, cultural, economic and technological environments remain relatively consistent for pockets of time. These 'pockets' can be used to define a generation. For example, those people born from 1946–1964 are defined as the Baby Boomer Generation. The Baby Boom refers to the spike in birth rates throughout that period.

It is the different perception of the world and the way it works, formed in response to our environment, that creates differences between one generation and another. These differences are usually referred to as a generation gap. People born in the late 70s, 80s and early 90s think differently from those born in the 60s and early 70s, who again are very different from those born before them. Just ask your grandparents, who lived through the Great Depression, about the way they view the world, people and money, and see just how different their opinions are from yours. The generation gap can be defined simply as the differences in outlook between generations.

It is not my intention to go into detail about all of the significant events that have been instrumental in the formation of the personality traits of this generation. Rather, many of these events will be revealed as we actually look at the character traits of Generation Y. More to the point, this book is designed to help you to understand, and to give you the practical 'how to' for dealing with, Generation Y.

No doubt you are already aware of the Baby Boomer generation and Generation X. Generation Y is the next wave of the population. You may have heard them referred to as:

- **Echo Boomers**
- **Generation Next**
- **Millennials**
- **Boomlets**
- **I Generation**
- **Net Generation**
- **Netizens**
- **Generation WHY**

Demographers refer to the period from 1978–1994 as an echo boom, where the birth rates around the developed world increased after the period of decline that defined Generation X. Although Australia's birth rates actually lagged a year or two behind those of the United States and Europe, our Generation Y is very similar. Currently, we define those born between 1978 and 1994 as being 'Generation Y'. Within Generation Y, it would be fair to say that due to the pace of change in technology and some of the recent world events, including September 11, there is likely to emerge a generation within a generation. It is possible that the definition of Generation Y will narrow as time goes on. The intensity of Generation Y's characteristics will also get stronger as those Generation Yers who are at school now begin to enter the workforce in the coming years. Or as I like to say, you ain't seen nothin' yet!

I promised not to go into a lengthy explanation of all the events that have influenced Generation Y, so instead the following table will give you a frame of reference for comparing the influences on the formation of the character traits of Baby Boomers, Generation X and Generation Y.

Influence	Baby Boomer	Generation X	Generation Y
Role Models	Men of Character	Men & Women of Character?	What is Character?
Television	*I Love Lucy*	*Happy Days*	*Jerry Springer*
Musical Icons	Elvis Presley	Madonna	Eminem
Music Mediums	LPs & EPs	Cassettes & CDs	Digital (iPods & MP3s)
Computer Games	Pong	Pacman	Counter Strike
Money	Earn it	It is not everything	Give it to me
Loyalty to Employer	Work my way to the top	Shortcut to the top	Give me Saturday off or I'll quit
Respecting your elders	Automatic	Is polite	Whatever!
Sex	After marriage	On the backseat	Online
Change	Resist it	Accept it	Want it
Technology	Ignorant of it	Comfortable	Feel it in their gut
Justice	Always prevails	Up to the courts	If you can afford it

This table is proof that the comment, 'I was just like that when I was a teenager back in the 1960s', which I hear all the time, is wrong. The world in 1960, compared to the world today, is so far apart you would scarcely believe it was the same place. It is simply impossible that teenagers today are like any teenage generations that have gone before. Social and environmental changes make this so. Sure, teenagers in the last 100 years have all been rebellious and have all differed from their parents' generation. Sure, there are some common themes for all humans as they pass through the 'rites of passage' that the teenage and early adult years bring. However, this does not make them the same. For example, consider the 'Australian Dream' of home ownership. According to research done by CPA Australia, 48% of Generation Y do not believe home ownership will be achievable for them in their lifetime. Australia is not the same place it was 20 years ago, and that is why Generation Y will not be like the teenagers of 20 years ago either.

As for those of you bitterly opposed to the process of pigeonholing an entire group of people into a definable generation, I agree, and so do Generation Y. Everyone's story is unique, and I firmly believe we have choices in regard to how we respond to our environment, and that, usually with help, we can rise above childhood conditioning and make independent choices. Making an attempt to at least define the underlying character traits of a generation, however, gives management, business, and community leaders a framework by which they can make intelligent decisions. And because I have worked with over 100,000 Generation Yers, researched many thousands more, and I am one myself, I can assure you there are some underlying characteristics of my generation. Even though individually we all differ in some way from this analysis, as a whole, such judgments are accurate.

Some research suggests that there is less of a generation gap than originally thought. However, in my experience, much of this research is based on 'values', and it does not necessarily look at the way a generation lives up to their 'values' in the work environment. For example, if you were to ask Generation Y if they value a 'good work ethic' many would reply with a resounding 'yes'. However, some further digging would reveal that a good work ethic for a Generation Yer has a very different meaning than it does for a Baby Boomer. Try a difference of about 30 hours per week. In reality my clients KNOW they have a problem. They do not need to do a survey to find out. They have high attrition, or a small talent pool, or poor performance or some other challenge that is affecting their company's bottom line. This is enough to signal to them that they have a problem, and it needs to be fixed. I will do my best here to bring together as much of that research as possible, and to make some practical sense out of it. My website <www.petersheahan.com> also posts the latest research and trends and relevant articles as they become available.

I should also note here, that we are focusing on the particular cohort of Generation Y that represents 'talent' in the workplace. There are plenty of other, probably less glamorous, characteristics of those Generation Yers who are representative of what I would call 'labour', not talent. This book is NOT designed to give you an insight into the mindset of the lowest common denominator. It is concerned with those Generation Yers who will be the target of professional organisations.

Street Smart

<Definition: Knowing how to survive modern urban life>

'I only respect people who respect me' – **Generation Yer**

You dump a member of Generation Y anywhere you like, give them a couple of dollars and they will find their way back. They have the resourcefulness to get places and, fortunately for business, to go places. They are mature in a way no other generation has been, and will find ways to get what they want, and do what needs to be done. They are not only the most educated generation ever, but they possess a different kind of smart. They are street smart. They know the way things go down, and are no longer naïve about the workings of the world and the intentions of businesses and other organisations. Why? The internet, of course, and a whole host of other influences. Let us look at exactly what it means to be street smart, how Generation Y got to be this way, and the implications this has for your business.

'They are not naïve at all. They are street smart and discerning.'

Linda Botter,
Lion Nathan Australia

To be street smart you need to see things as they really are. You understand that those who have the power, survive. You are very discriminatory about whom you trust and to whom you pay respect. On the street, respect is earned, and no title, age or even past experience will guarantee you will be respected. To survive, you have to know how everything works, be connected to the right people, and have access to whatever it is you need to ensure your survival. You do not procrastinate about things, because you know that there are two types of people on the street – the quick and the dead. Speed is of paramount importance, and you have a zero tolerance policy for both incompetence and propaganda. There are few things you haven't seen, heard about or know something about. You are opinionated and, in many ways, determined, because in order to survive you have to be. Your resourcefulness makes you both innovative and enterprising, as you will often be forced to make something out of nothing. You are always on the lookout for opportunity because you know that the competition is fierce, and you are fast to act upon it. And this, my friend, is Generation Y. Exciting, don't you think?

Mature and Resilient

Let's start with mature. We are talking about a generation that has had to deal with the emotional hardship of the disintegration of the family unit, namely divorce. According to the Australian Bureau of Statistics, 54% of all divorces in 1997 involved children under the age of 18. From a very young age, Generation Y, more than any other generation in our history, have had to juggle life's emotional challenges. Let's take at look at life from their perspective.

You live with Mum during the week and every other weekend, and you spend the remaining weekends at Dad's. Your Dad's new girlfriend thinks she is your mum, even though she is half the age of your real Mum, and your Mum's partner thinks he is Yoda and you are Luke Skywalker. For those whose parents are still together, statistics show us that there is a high chance that they both work, and if you ask a Generation Yer, this means there was little time for the kids, resulting in their being left to their own devices much of the time. And if this did not happen to you, it happened to your best friend, and you spent endless hours counselling him or her through the personal challenge. As a Generation Y teenager, you no longer have to just deal with the peer pressure to smoke and drink, or even smoke a joint, you now have ready access and sometimes regular exposure to peers using harder drugs like speed, ecstasy and many more. Add to that having to deal with the uncertainty of terrorism at a time when you were struggling to know why you even existed on this planet and whether you were of any value to it. Why would someone bomb a group of tourists enjoying a drink in one of your nation's favourite tourist spots, Bali? The older, adult section of the population had trouble figuring this out, let alone a teenager or someone in their early twenties.

Now I am not suggesting that Generation Y are the only generation who have had to deal with emotional challenges. Everyone has. It is just the type, the magnitude and the personal nature of so many of them that has made this generation particularly mature and adept at dealing with such challenges. The clear advantage for business is that due to their resilience, Generation Y employees will not be rocked to their foundations if the company turns a bad quarterly return. In fact, they probably won't be all that bothered (unless of course their remuneration is tied directly to that quarterly performance). If a major obstacle presents itself, they will not give up and turn away. Edward Kaleel of the Marc Edward Agency says 'Generation Y thrive when challenged', and considering he manages 1000s across Australia, he knows what he is talking about. When challenged, Generation Y will find a solution and press on. Be aware, though, if there is a barrage of bad news from direct supervisors or from head office, but the company seems disinterested in doing anything about it, Generation Y won't stay and watch the ship sink. They want to work with organisations that are proactively attempting to better themselves.

As mentioned earlier, those on the street see life as it really is. Generation Y stopped believing in Santa Claus a long time ago, and never for a minute thought life was really like it appears on *Playschool.* The extreme turnover of Generation Y staff is never because a job or a project was too challenging. It is usually caused by boredom and lack of a personal challenge. Generation Y think they are made of steel and will act like that in the face of adversity.

Educated and Fast Learners

Did you know that more than a third of Generation Y worked part-time while they were still at school? Not only that, but Generation Y are the most formally educated generation ever. Over 70% finish high school, of which 30% go on to university, and a further 40% get some other post-secondary training or qualification. Those who are at university are also staying longer. Despite what you may believe, an ACER (the Australian Council for Educational Research) reports show that over the past 30 years, literacy has stayed constant and numeracy has improved. David Cvetkovski at Ford Australia says 'compared to Gen X, their willingness to gain business knowledge and understanding has increased'.

However, an important point to note is that education has now changed. Outrageous as it may first sound, I have heard recruiters say, a little tongue in cheek I might add, that the Microsoft Certified Practitioner is worth more than an MBA. The world is changing at a rapid pace and the question is, will organisations be able to keep up? I know Generation Y will. Change is something that the Baby Boomers have resisted. Gen X have accepted change and have tried to adapt to it. Generation Y live for change. They do not know a world without it. They have never known a world without VCRs, laptop computers, video games, and multiple-channel colour televisions in every home. They have no experience of a workplace without networked computers and the internet. The eldest were born only a year before the CD was developed. Try this experiment. Ask the next teenager you meet (or employ) what the term 'you sound like a broken record' means, and see if they respond. Businesses will need to embrace members of Generation Y because of their ability to stay abreast of the phenomenal rate of technological and social change.

'In times of change the learner will inherit the earth, while the learned will find themselves well equipped to deal with a world that no longer exists.'

Eric Hoffer

Generation Y's love of change, and their ability to adapt to a constant state of flux, makes them extremely valuable in the process of innovation and achieving improved productivity. They will not resist the introduction of a new technology that can increase work efficiency. They will demand it. If there is a better system out there, they will know about it well before you do, and might even do some research on it and then come and tell you why the business needs it. I have heard managers refer to Generation Y as always looking for the easy way out. Always looking for a short cut. To which I respond, 'Great!' Isn't that the goal of efficiency? To find the fastest and easiest way to do something in order to free up time to do something else? Don't complain about it. Embrace it. Use it for what it is worth. In the past five years, the most popular conference speaker topic has been 'Change Management'. Well, here is a generation that doesn't need help managing it because they own it. It is a part of their work ethic and the culture they thrive in.

While this presents an obvious opportunity for business, there are also some warnings to be heeded. Where do you stop? When do you just say enough technology is enough? At some point, we have to stop looking for better ways to do things, and just do what needs to be done. This will be one of the keys to managing Generation Y in the workplace. Helping them get on with the job with the resources they have available. No business will be able to have the latest, the fastest, and the best of everything. Give me a break. Have you bought a laptop recently? You do your research, fully intending to buy within the week, but only after you have clearly thought through all the options and chosen the laptop that will best suit your needs. Then, by the time you get back to the store to make your purchase the sales rep informs you of a brand new product that has just come out which will do the job better. New technology becomes obsolete as fast as it is introduced. Get a system that works and then work it.

I can hear managers of Generation Y screaming, 'We know they are smart, but these guys think they know EVERYTHING!' With that I agree. There is no doubt that Generation Y think they know everything. The job of the manager or supervisor is to carefully 'manage' the ego of Generation Y staff, and to ensure they get the appropriate training they need to work in *your* business. The key lesson here is to understand that they will have no problem learning what you need them to learn, provided you can show them the rationale behind 'why' they need to learn it. The 'why' behind everything is so important because Generation Y are very practical.

Practical

One of the most commonly used terms I have found in research about this generation is 'pragmatic'. Generation Y are pragmatic. They are concerned only with what is relevant. If something has no practical application or value, then it is discarded. This has tremendous implications for managers, and the systems they have in place within the work environment. Generation Y will question everything. They will want to know why something needs to be done. What it achieves. Why they are the person to do it. This is such a definable trait of Generation Y that Eric Chester, a business consultant in the United States, has coined the term Generation WHY!

The reason for the questioning is probably because they have had such an overload of information that the only way to get by is to sift through all the rubbish and find the value. To focus only on what is relevant. In a recent conversation I had with Margaret Kirby, founder of the I Group and an expert in recruiting the younger Generation Xes and older Generation Yers, she said that Generation X tend to believe it when you say it, Baby Boomers accept it, whereas Generation Y, with their giant bullshit meter just say 'prove it'. And why wouldn't they? Consider the barrage of advertising directed at attracting the 'youth' dollar, which Generation Y has been subjected to for as long as they can remember. It is estimated that by age 12, they will be subjected to 22,000 ads per year, designed to sell directly to them.

I recently had a conversation with a Generation Yer, James, who works for a large Australian coffee shop chain.

I asked him whether he liked his job. His reply was far from convincing, so I inquired some more and dug a little deeper. It turned out that he loved working and making coffee, and he even quite liked his supervisor, but he hated the layout of the shop. When I asked him to explain, he unleashed on me a tutorial about how poorly designed the shop was and how the owner must have been an idiot, and that people who build coffee shops should ask the people who work in them how to best design them. He then went on to describe how he thought the store should be designed. I was so intrigued to see if he was right, that later in the week I drove to the franchise store in which he worked so I could observe. I watched for almost an hour as the customers came in and out, and I could not believe my eyes. He was right. If management did change the layout of the store and the way orders were processed, they would undoubtedly increase the efficiency of the shop and provide faster and more efficient service to the customer. James is fifteen. My experience with James is evidence of not just Generation Y's desire for practicality, but for their ability to think creatively and innovatively. What I call their ability to be enterprising.

Enterprising

Generation Y are enterprising and bear all the positive traits associated with it. They are creative, innovative and resourceful. They have to be. Competition is fierce, so Generation Y needs to be able to spot an opportunity when it arises. The pressure to succeed has gotten so high that we have created a generation of hypersensitive people who are constantly on the lookout for the next opportunity, the next job, or the next buck. This has both positive and negative implications for business.

The obvious benefits that come with having staff who are creative, innovative and resourceful is the development of good ideas and improved productivity. In fact, a recent Australian employer survey said the most important attribute required of graduates was creativity. Bring on Generation Y. Management guru Tom Peters, author of the international bestsellers *In Search of Excellence* and *Re-Imagine*, tells us that we must 'innovate or die'. His words not mine. Peters also says that business units need to adapt the 'Ready Fire Aim' mindset. In that order. Ready Fire Aim should be a Generation Y motto. They just do it. They don't muck around, and have little time for planning and strategising. This can be as much a problem as it is an asset to your company. Managers will need to keep Generation Y and their actions focused, and aligned to the strategic direction of the company. Or better still, educate Generation Y on the importance of strategy, and how crucial it is to long-term effective business, and they will do it themselves. Just don't use the word long-term (more on this later). Now, back to the positive.

Generation Y believe they can do anything, and if they don't immediately know how, they know they can easily find out. They will get on the computer and go to internet search engine Google, or log into a discussion board, chat room or the relevant blog (a website where experts on a particular topic post their ideas and information about a specific topic) and ask someone. Information about anything and everything is available on the net. Whereas the older manager fails to find the diamonds among the rough on the net, Generation Y have grown up honing their internet search skills, and they know where to get the best information. Add to this the ready access to information, and reasonable experience and education, and you have the makings of an extremely resourceful generation.

The most significant negative side effect of an opportunistic workforce is that they are always on the lookout for a better opportunity. Trust me, they are. Read: Better Job! The later chapters of the book, particularly Managing and Retaining, will address specific strategies to combat this.

Manipulative

Well, a negative trait had to arise somewhere in this first chapter on Generation Y being street smart. There will be little argument that these guys know how to manipulate. Let me give you an example. Recently, a friend of mine gave his mother his old computer because she needed it for her university course. He organised for his extremely tech-savvy Generation Y brother to take it to her and help her set it up. Just a few days later, when he went to visit his mother, he saw she had a 14-inch standard monitor, when he had actually given her a 17-inch flat screen. A little puzzled, he asked his brother what had happened to the monitor. His brother calmly explained that he did not think their mother needed a monitor that big so he had lent it to a 'friend' until he was able to save enough money to buy his own bigger monitor. His friend had swapped the flat screen, supposedly, for his 14-inch screen, which was now on their mother's desk. Some months later, my friend found out the truth. His brother had actually sold the monitor, bought a cheaper one for next to nothing, and kept the profit. What a scam.

Generation Y will twist and distort information to get what they want (sounds a bit like all human beings, actually). While this is a useful skill in a negotiation, you need to be very aware of it in the workplace. A common complaint among managers is that these new workers want all the money and all the perks, but want it all on their own terms.Not only that, they give no consideration to your needs as a manager or business owner, and expect you to bend to their every request. (I will give you some good examples of this in the chapter on Lifestyle Centred.) And if that's not enough, they often choose not to follow certain rules or policies that management have put in place, specifically rules or policies that you don't enforce. Generation Y are a very smart generation. If they see an easy beat, or a loophole, they will go after it and exploit it for all it is worth. As you will discover in the section on Managing Generation Y, it is essential to set clear guidelines, and to enforce them consistently, otherwise the incongruity will be discovered and then exploited. And one final point: Generation Y will test you to see if you are for real, and to see if you will keep them accountable.

A common complaint among managers is that these new workers want all the money and all the perks, but want it all on their own terms.

Executive Summary

Generation Y are street smart and they are also:

- Mature
- Resilient
- Fast Learners
- Practical
- Enterprising
- Manipulative

These personality traits represent opportunities for businesses:

- Generation Y will not be rocked by bad news, and will be capable of handling the inevitable chaos and change that surrounds business in the new millennium.
- Generation Y teams are a great place to trial new technologies because they will be open to new things, learn fast, and as such, will be the source of major improvements in productivity.
- Generation Y have a unique ability to see the practical side of things, and will be constantly on the lookout for better ways to do things. Managers who can effectively involve this generation in brainstorm sessions, and other idea-creation forums, stand to benefit greatly from this generation's creativity and practicality.
- Generation Y take action. They will not suffer from paralysis by analysis. Allow their action orientation to filter through to your teams and divisions.

They also represent challenges for businesses:

- Generation Y are obsessed with having the newest and fastest of anything technology related. Managers will need to draw the line somewhere and educate their Generation Y staff that at some point, they have to get the job done with the resources available.

- Generation Y can be perceived as thinking they know everything simply because they have read about or heard about something third-hand. They are not really supportive of the notion that experience is the most valuable knowledge. As such, managers will have a difficult time handling some of the ego in the workplace.
- Generation Y can be a little too short-term focused, and managers and supervisors need to communicate the importance of remaining focused on the strategic direction of the company, and following the set procedures for a given task.
- Managers need to be particularly astute when keeping Generation Y accountable for their actions. A good idea is to first ensure all rules or policies are practical and necessary, and then communicate very clearly the rule or policy, and the rationale behind it. If you are not going to enforce it, don't have it, and just as importantly, be consistent.

Aware

<Definition: conscious, having knowledge, being fully informed about current issues>

***'I am not going to work for them, they exploit workers in the third world'* – Generation Yer when asked about a particular organisation**

The differences are no longer those of race and gender, but of age. At least for Generation Y. They don't care what colour your skin is, where you or your family were born, the way you look, your sexual inclinations or anything else for that matter. Generation Y are a socially and culturally aware generation.

They are also environmentally aware, emotionally aware and in touch with who they are, what the state of the world is and what needs to be done about it. They are open in their communication and are willing to express their feelings. They will demand their point of view be heard, even if it means they have to set up a dedicated website to do it. They are determined to change the world for the better, and will stop at nothing to do it. Volunteering among their age group is at an all time high, with 27% of Generation Y being regularly involved in some sort of charitable work compared with only 17% of Generation X at the same age.

They are very social, and value personal connection and friendship, albeit occasionally in less traditional ways such as online. They are invaluable in the team environment, and in many ways thrive there.

Socially, Culturally and Environmentally Aware

Generation Y not only value diversity, they thrive on it. They are the least racist, most accepting generation to date. Young people are becoming more comfortable with their sexuality, whatever its kind. The same applies racially. Just make a visit to your local high school and check out the racial diversity that exists in the groups that hang out together at lunchtime. You won't hear a Generation Y say 'my Chinese friend', or 'my Lebanese friend', they will simply say 'my friend'.

The existence of recycling projects in homes and in schools has meant that Generation Y have grown up understanding the dynamics of nature and our role in preserving it. A survey released by the United States Roper Center for Public Opinion, at the University of Connecticut, found that by a ratio of 10 to 1, Generation Y believed they would have a more positive impact on the environment than their parents' generation have had.

'In interviews, Generation Y actually ask for specifics when it comes to our environmental programs. They are not willing to accept some PR stunt to look environmentally aware, they want to know if we are for real.'

David Cvetkovski,
Ford Australia

So what does this mean for your organisation? Thankfully, organisations are also becoming more socially, culturally and environmentally aware. But that 'awareness' had better be genuine, and not some public relations spin, because Generation Y have a bullshit meter on their foreheads that will ring loudly at any hint of insincerity. Generation Y will select their vocations and the organisations they will work for based on your proven commitment to embracing diversity, your commitment to community activities, and the way you and your products directly or indirectly treat people, their communities, and the environment at large.

Purposeful

These guys are not just aware, but dedicated to doing something about it. One of the researchers in my company has just returned from a month in Africa, working in refugee camps, teaching English and other subjects in the makeshift schools set up in these camps. His story is not uncommon.

Generation Y will put their money where their mouth is. They won't just sit back and talk about the problem, they want to be part of the solution. Economic historian William Howe and political scientist Neil Strauss were two of the earliest to research Generation Y, and they identified a civic-minded generation with a focus on community and rebuilding the world. Generation Y will not be on a mission to tear down the institutions that exist today. Instead, they would prefer to fix them up or create new ones that better meet the needs of society. What this means for employers is that in order to attract the best Generation Y talent, philanthropic and social projects will be as important to showcase as share price and market share.

There is a new kind of entrepreneur arising. It is called the socialpreneur, and describes those who are committed to creating businesses that contribute positively to the world. Youth-founded and -run organisations are perfect examples of what I am talking about. Youth Environment Society (YES) is a youth-run, non-profit organisation designed to give youth of Australia a voice in our community to deal with pressing environmental issues head-on. YES aims to gain sensible, sustainable results for a positively green future <www.yesworld.org.au>. If you want more examples of sites that are set up by youth or in which youth are actively involved, and which are based around social initiative, you will find plenty at <www.youth2youth.com.au/youthinfo.asp>. Also look up the Canadian Carl Kielburger, who at age 12, set up Free the Children, an international network allowing youth to help other youth. Or check out the Oak Tree Foundation, which is a non-profit organisation established in 2002 by Young Australian of the Year Hugh Evans to educate impoverished children in developing countries around the world.

Generation Y aren't just talking about being environmentally friendly, they truly mean it. And if organisations want to be regarded as employers of choice, they will need to do more than just talk about being environmentally friendly, and actually do something about it, too.

Corporations had better be ready. The damage that was done to Nike after the exposure of working conditions in their 'sweat shops' in third-world countries can have the same ramifications for your company if elements of your business seem unethical or exploitative. Not just from a sales point of view, but, equally as important, from a recruiting point of view. If you want to attract the best new talent, then you will have to convince Generation Y of the value your business contributes to the community. Generation Y will demand it. They will remember the brands that sponsored their talent quests and sporting competitions. They will remember who ripped their parents off or took advantage of them. They will remember and will retaliate with their feet. They will not want to work for such a company.

Employment branding will be buzz words of this decade. Being attractive to the limited talent pool will be essential for survival in the new business world, and the vision, purpose and activities of your organisation will be key determinants in the way Generation Y judge you as a potential employer. Don't think that some fancy mission statement and set of values will be sufficient. Generation Y have distinguished between an organisation's real values and its PR values. They will judge you not by what you say, but by what you do. This is how it is done on the street. They will see how your employees are treated, and how happy they look in their workplace. They will judge your credibility by the true culture that exists within your business. While they may initially be attracted to your name, they will be gone as fast as they arrived if you do not live up to your reputation. This will be one of the biggest challenges organisations face in recruiting the best talent: selling their purpose and their value to this new generation.

Generation Y's need for a purpose runs deeper than accepting what an organisation does at a macro level. The Higher Education Research Institute at the University of California, Los Angeles, has surveyed college freshmen in the United States for 35 years. They found that 97% of the class of 2000 thought 'doing work that allows me to have an impact on the world' was extremely important. If an employer wants genuine 'buy-in' from Generation Y, then they will need to provide a purpose, a reason for doing the 'work' at a micro level, not just macro. At Henry Davis York, Deborah Stonley explained that one of the most interesting parts of their induction program for Generation Y is the pro bono work they are asked to do. She says 'they love it, and want to be involved'.

Open, Accepting and Inclusive

We have already discussed the accepting nature of Generation Y. This is good news for you. It is well understood that synergy comes from diversity. Diversity of ideas, opinions and knowledge. The more you embrace difference, the more synergy your teams will generate. Bring on Generation Y, and your teams will never be the same again. They will want to hear different opinions and new ideas and will be keen to have their own ideas heard, too. Your job is to allow them to do so. Generation Y will contribute to conversations, team meetings and any other forums in which you involve them. A tremendous opportunity exists for organisations that are prepared to go out on a limb and incorporate Generation Y into their think tanks and decision-making processes. They truly have something unique and valuable to offer if only you will embrace them.

This openness extends to their personal life. Generation Y never knew the saying 'children should be seen, not heard'. They were taught to say what they thought and share their feelings. It was the Baby Boomers' open and permissive parenting style that has given rise to a new level of emotional intelligence. The Society of Research of Adolescence in 2002 stated 'many parents are adopting a more responsive and communicative style of parenting which facilitates the development of adolescent interpersonal skills'. There is little doubt that Generation Y are emotionally intelligent. Daniel Goleman, the pioneer of the concept of Emotional Intelligence, says that emotional intelligence gives rise to effective team work.

I have said it before: Generation Y will thrive in the team environment that is genuinely inclusive and open to their ideas and viewpoints. It is going to be a scary challenge for managers to provide a forum for genuine expression of employees' points of view, especially from people half their age. But they will have to. Generation Y will demand it. If you don't give it, they will either march into your office and just do it, or they will begin looking on www.seek.com.au for a company that will. While organisations claim to really 'get this', in practice, few ever truly 'do it'. Are you ready to be told how to run your business by someone more than half your age, with little or no experience, in a bluntly expressive style?

Connected

Generation Y are very sociable, and value personal connection and friendship. It amuses me to hear about how kids have lost the personal touch, with 'all these computers and gadgets they stay locked in their room playing for hours on end'. What you may not know is that many of these games they play are online and against others. The net, in many ways, is their medium for staying in touch. That and their mobile phone. The art of letter writing is lost, and will not make a comeback. Generation Y are so desperate to be 'connected' that even email is considered too slow. Instead, they have Instant Messaging. Sure I agree that a significant portion of Generation Y lack the necessary business etiquette and communications skills required to succeed in business, but this does not mean they are not a connected, communicative generation. Organisations may find they need to provide training in more traditional forms of communication such as verbal presentations, and the preparation of business proposals and documents, but I assure you, Generation Y will have no problems learning it.

'Relationships and being sociable are HUGE for Generation Y.'

David Cvetkovski,
Ford Australia

The real challenge here for business is controlling this. Generation Yers love working in teams and will want to work with their friends. Managers will have to be alert because there is a fine line between working in teams and overdoing it to the point that it becomes a social event. This is one of the paradoxes managers are beginning to face. Generation Y want to work out loud, with people they like, in a relaxed social atmosphere. The key is keeping it work, not play.

This desire to be connected, coupled with their awareness and purposeful nature, will make Generation Y particularly sensitive to corporate mindset, or as it is collectively called, 'culture'. Generation Y will not put up with what the Baby Boomers put up with. They will want to work in an environment that is fun and where they feel valued as an individual. This is all about the 'soft stuff'. But the 'soft stuff' is the 'big stuff'. And the better you do the 'soft stuff', the better the results in the 'hard stuff'. (Sorry, I got a little carried away there!)

> ***'Utilisation of Generation Y can be a challenge. They have many more distractions than older generations, like mobile phones, email, going out for coffee. They are an extremely social generation.'***
>
> Deborah Stonley, Henry Davis York

David Cvetkovski at Ford Australia gives an excellent example: 'In order to be more attractive to Generation Y, we have had to make some major changes, including to canteen facilities. In the past it was as though it was an unspoken law that you couldn't be seen relaxing over lunch in the canteen with your friends. Instead, you would get your lunch quietly and return to your desk. Not with Generation Y. They refused to buy into that law. They socialise with their friends and relax together. The best thing is they do it cross functionally and our communication between functions has improved as a result. Many teams no longer hold their weekly meetings in the conference rooms, but instead do it in the canteen over a latte. It has massively improved the communication here at Ford Australia.'

Marketers are beginning to tap into the connectedness of Generation Y as well. HR and managers could learn from them. With traditional advertising proving ineffective in this marketplace, the buzz in marketing circles is viral marketing. Getting the word of mouth happening, though with Generation Y it rarely spreads via word of mouth. It is usually word of SMS or word of instant messaging. So popular and powerful are these forms of techno communication that some marketers have even executed campaigns that had employees actually go online and visit chat rooms and make mention of some product they had recently seen (the one they are being paid to promote) in an attempt to begin the spread (like a virus) that has made Generation Y market penetration so valuable. What is the buzz out on the street about your company? What are you doing to ensure Generation Y talent know you are THE employer of choice? Some more ideas on this later.

Executive Summary

Generation Y are an aware generation. Culturally, socially, environmentally and emotionally aware. This is how they are in the workplace:

- Open
- Accepting
- Inclusive
- Team orientated
- Purposeful
- Social

These characteristics provide the following opportunities for your organisation:

- Generation Y will form teams that are more synergistic, more creative and more effective. That is, if you are able to embrace and value their ideas and input, and provide a forum through which they can express these ideas.
- Generation Y will be attracted to the social and community activities in which your organisation is involved. Make the most of these opportunities and make sure people know about them.

On the other hand, these characteristics will pose the following challenges:

- You will need to ensure that your organisation is not engaging, intentionally or unintentionally, in activities that may adversely affect your staff, your customers, their community or the environment.
- You will have to find ways to promote and market your social-mindedness in order to recruit and retain top Generation Y talent.
- Corporations will need to provide a forum for employees to express and share ideas, thoughts and feelings. (Like managers don't already have enough to do getting the job done!)

- The largest challenge of all is that, in reality, many Generation Y jobs will not need creative input or other such things. Managers will have to figure out ways to keep Generation Y motivated in the day-to-day reality of work. Considering that Generation Y are the ones that will fill most of the more mundane positions, it is little wonder that retention levels in these facets of businesses are so poor.
- You will have to make clear the distinction between work and play, while fostering a healthy, connected and friendly corporate culture.

Lifestyle Centred

<Definition: Focused on your personal way of life>

***'I want to be rich and successful, but I am not going to bust my gut to get it'* – Generation Yer**

Having been brought up by Baby Boomer parents, is it any surprise that Generation Y are lifestyle centred? They want all the success and all the money that a career offers, but unlike the Baby Boomers, they are not prepared to give their life to get it. Generation Y have seen their parents devote their life to the corporate machine only to see some of them chewed up and spat out again. Generation Y will not make the same mistake. They want success, but they want it on their terms.

They will go one of two ways with work. Work will serve as either a means to an end, or as an opportunity to make a difference. The former meaning they will work just for the money so they can support their real life, and the latter meaning work will be more than just an occupation. It will be their vocation or, better still, their 'occupassion'. (I love that word.) Or at least that is what they will want it to be.

Generation Y have been played up to their entire life, often with money and material things. As such, they are very materialistic, but are not wooed by it in the same ways their parents were. The bargaining power of money is lost. They know their value, and they know they have options, so paying them the right amount of money is just the first on their long list of demands. They will want flexible work hours and travel opportunities. They want exciting projects. And at worst, if work does not fit around their lifestyle they simply won't show. The problem for business is that an employee wanting and demanding these sorts of opportunities is no longer the exception. Organisations are being forced to provide some of these opportunities at work. In many ways this is a good thing, meaning the flexible hours and travel and such, but it does pose huge challenges for managers because you still have to keep Generation Y accountable for results, sometimes in environments over which you have no control and cannot supervise.

On the other hand, Generation Y will need to face the reality that they don't get paid for breathing. They need to add value to the business, and unless they can do this, they will not have a job. If they want these flexible hours and other perks like working from home, they will need to demonstrate that they can continue to deliver value under such conditions.

'They want success and to make a lot of money, but that is not the be all and end all for Generation Y.'

Linda Botter,
Lion Nathan Australia

To those Generation Yers who see work as merely a means to another end, they may well put up with the monotony of low-skill, repetitive jobs for just as many hours a week as is required to make enough money to maintain their lifestyle. But given their addiction to stimulation, and the desire within every human being to contribute, I can't see them staying in this frame of mind. Having said that, I think an opportunity exists in what are traditionally known as low-skill, repetitive jobs for companies to show people, of any generation, working in those positions that there is room to expand and to grow. The large supermarket chains are an excellent example. The scope to develop new skills and to move into different areas of the supermarket business is phenomenal, yet so few Generation Y workers see that potential.

Live for today has been the motto handed down by their parents. A motto reiterated by their idols and heroes. And a motto that is making Generation Y difficult to deal with. They make rash decisions, leave a job on a whim, and often can't see the use of investing time and energy today for a better result tomorrow. Which is something wisdom tells us is essential to personal and business success.

It is about More than just Money

We have already discovered that Generation Y want their work to have a purpose. They want their work to be more than just about making money. A recent Manpower Australia survey of call centre staff cited the following, in order, as the motivators for work:

- **Culture**
- **Team**
- **Management style**
- **Flexibility**
- **Conditions**
- **Salary**

The carrot and stick no longer works. The carrot, meaning if you just dangle enough future benefit and money in front of an employee, you will motivate them into action. Future benefit is not something Generation Y are motivated by. They want it now, not later. And as for the money, well, Generation Y have it embedded in their head that they are entitled to big money simply for breathing and that of course you are going to pay them a high salary. As for the stick, meaning Generation Y will be punished if they don't take the required action, well that won't work either. Go ahead and punish me, Generation Y will say. And then they won't show up the next day because they got a job, doing the same thing, for the same money, working with their friend at one of your main competitors.

Generation Y will want to negotiate on more than just money. I recently experienced this first-hand in my business. One of my sales staff wanted to renegotiate her employment contract. Let me give you some background. She was 18 years old, and prior to working for me she had no experience in an office environment, only retail. Like many employees in their first three months, there was no short-term return on investment for me. I was pumping the time and resources into training her. I even kept her predecessor in the position for an additional four weeks to train the new recruit properly. In the following two months, she really began producing results in the sales field, but left much to be desired in the administration side of things. No big deal, because I would rather have poor administration and lots of sales than no sales and perfect administration. Her job description started with about ten responsibilities but had to be culled to around seven after it was clear her talents did not lie in her ability to organise the office. This was outsourced. After barely five months she decided that her above-award wage did not make her feel 'valued' in her role and wanted to renegotiate. I am always open to conversation with my staff, and am a firm believer that people should be rewarded for the value they contribute to the business, not their age or even hours they work. She wanted more money (18% more) but only wanted to work three days instead of five. This equated to a 78% pay rise. When I asked her to justify her request she gave me reasons based on her performance in merely two of her areas of responsibility, completely discounting the other five she was still responsible for, and negating the fact that I had been forced to outsource a further three at a substantial cost to the business. But her demands did not stop there. She also wanted to be involved in the research side of the business, and to be made a part of the more 'businessy' (her words, not mine) activities.

To cut a long story short, she failed to see my side of the employment equation. The negotiation proceeded and a deal was done, but only after a very in-depth, and sometimes passionate, conversation about what her role was and what she was expected to produce in order to receive her current income let alone a higher one for less hours, with more autonomy and influence in the business. In other words, some education in my business's needs and my expectations was required before we could come to

To cut a long story short, she failed to see my side of the employment equation.

a mutually beneficial agreement. She now works fewer hours, for less overall money, but with an attractive bonus structure, and is doing a wonderful job. This is representative of one of the most difficult things about Generation Y in the workplace. They often fail to see the other side of the negotiation. A problem I was recently reminded of in a conversation with the director of a prestigious recruitment company. The director said that in her experience, Generation Y want the perks and the flexibility, but don't understand that they will still need to be kept accountable for their actions and that there are certain non-negotiable requirements for every position, most of all, the job description and performance outcomes.

The need for clear job descriptions and performance outcomes is more important than ever. Identify what is negotiable and what is not before you enter a conversation about work arrangements with someone from Generation Y. Be genuine. If it does not matter whether they are in the office on the fifth day of each week then use this as a negotiating tool. Don't be staunch just for the sake of it. But do stay firm on the points that are not negotiable. Don't lay all your cards on the table too early; keep some up your sleeve for later. You may need these as a clincher, or something to give as a performance bonus at some stage.

What if work has become a means to an end?

What do you do if the Generation Yers in your team are just there to make some money to support themselves on the weekend, and no matter what you say, they are still thinking 'car' instead of 'career'? An example of the kind of Generation Y I am talking about is a very bright student, from one of Sydney's top selective schools, who was in one of my workshops recently. He said, genuinely, that he just wanted to be a labourer, so he could make enough cash to surf. He also said he intended to only work nine months of the year, and travel around surfing for the remaining three months. If this is your staff, then you must find a way to make even the most mundane positions have some variety. At the very least, try to make it more fun. Think about the damage a staff member with that sort of attitude will do to your company's reputation. Most of the Generation Yers in the workforce are working on the front line, day in day out. Supermarkets, retailers, call centres and the like. You have to make these Generation Yers happy in their workplace because they are the people that represent your company to your customers. Sure your CEO may be the face in the press and the investment community, but he or she is not the one dealing with customer orders, customer complaints or customer inquiries. It is Generation Y that are doing this. They are in so many ways the face of your brand, and if they are not happy and enjoying themselves in their work, then your brand will suffer, make no mistake about it. The section on Managing Generation Y will detail numerous ways you can do this, but before you even get there, begin to think seriously about what you can do to improve your employees' experience in some of your more menial roles. This is not 'soft', this is about the bottom line. Happy and loyal staff means happy and loyal customers.

Happy and loyal staff means happy and loyal customers.

I hinted in the introduction to this chapter that even these nonchalant Generation Yers want purpose and meaning to their work, despite what they may demonstrate. You need to find ways to make their work more meaningful. To give them a more empowering metaphor for their work. Don't just try to make it more fun. Show them how it contributes to the overall performance of the company, or to the customer experience. Ensure they see the value of their role, and more importantly, show them that you value them in that role. If Generation Y workers in your company are being paid minimum wages and the actions of the company, regardless of what the propaganda in the weekly staff bulletin claims, indicates that there is no real intention to develop them, then why would they care about you and your company? They will not show any loyalty to the workplace, only to their desires. We must strive to show them the value of what they do and say things that demonstrate that the company appreciates them and what they do.

Materialistic

Generation Y are obsessed with having the latest, the newest, the fastest and the best, and they will pay for it. And they CAN actually pay for it. According to YouthSCAN survey 2001, the average Generation Y teenager makes $118 per week. Consider also that 87.7% of all working-age Generation Yers are in employment, including those still studying, and you will find that they have the means to satisfy some of their desires. As teenagers, Australian Bureau of Statistics research shows that 34% of Generation Y have jobs compared to 26% of Generation X at the same age. The Federal Government estimates that Generation Y consumers are worth in excess of $4 billion to the Australian economy each year.

Even with this amount of disposable income, these Generation Yers are not satisfied. According to research done by the University of Newcastle, more than 50% of Generation Yers they surveyed between the ages of 18 and 24 had credit card and personal loans debts totalling more than $14,000. And 25% had debts over $20,250. The same survey showed that 78% of Generation Yers had mobile phone debts, some even as high as $5000. Research by CPA Australia has shown similar things, with 70% of Generation Y saying they see saving as something they will do in the future, and with 76% of them having less than $10,000 saved. The CPA survey quoted 55% of Generation Y respondents as saying that having enough money to live on was their main concern today.

Generation Y want BOTH!

It seems like a contradiction to say that work is about more than just money for Generation Y, because it is. But it is not an either or thing. Generation Y want BOTH! They expect the money and the opportunity to make a difference, as well as variety and options in the workforce.

Is it any wonder though that they are so materialistic when research suggests they received four times more toys than their Baby Boomer parents. You may be familiar with the term 'chequebook parenting'. This refers to the inclination of parents to entertain their kids by giving them money and material items as opposed to giving them time. After all, Baby Boomers are busy. Research has shown that parents spend less time with their children now than they did only 30 years ago. Did you also know that less than 40% of Generation Y children were cared for in the family home before they started school? The remaining 60% plus were sent off to daycare centres, or left with a relative because both parents were working. This has been both out of financial necessity, and the welcomed desire of women to continue their careers. Add to this the rising divorce rate, which further increased the numbers of Generation Yers being cared for outside the family home. Hopefully, organisations will begin to truly create 'family friendly' work places, because Generation Y will demand that they do. In fact, many times it is cheaper to give Generation Y kids $25 to go off to the movies with their friends than it is to miss a weekend shift on double time and a half or arrange childcare during the school holidays. As a result, Generation Y have been able to use cash as a means to fund entertainment as opposed to making up some game in their front yards with all the other kids in the neighbourhood. This, and their own income stream, has given rise to Generation Y's materialistic nature. Add to that the materialistic nature of Western communities on the whole, and it is no wonder Generation Y are so focused on money and possessions.

... they are not thinking about a career when they begin on your cash registers. They are thinking 'car'.

For the teenage workers in the Generation Y age bracket, it is quite possible they are not thinking about a career when they begin on your cash registers. They are thinking 'car'. Or they are thinking a new top, the movies, or a new computer game. They are probably no different from any other teenager from any other generation in this respect. Regardless, we need to be aware of it, and its potential effects on work performance. As I have said, in whatever way possible, you as an employer need to make your entry-level position seem more like a stepping stone to bigger and better things, not just a means to an end. Be very careful not to create the 'sacrifice now for reward later' theme because Generation Y won't buy it.

This materialism also means, for those retailers among you, that there may be some distinct Generation Y motivators available to you such as store discounts, store credit points, bonuses paid in merchandise, and other such material things as opposed to having to pay your employees more money.

Be careful not to get the impression from this one point that money is the key motivator for Generation Y. It isn't. Providing compensation is 'fair' and that they can't get substantially more down the road doing the same thing, then you should be okay. More on this later.

Success Orientated

Well it is no surprise that Generation Y want to be successful. They have seen, and many will have experienced, what it is like to be poor. When we talk about people being poor, consider this. At times throughout the last decade, over 40% of Generation Y have lived in homes dependent on welfare. There are now second- and third-generation unemployed families. Sure there has always been poverty, and much more serious types of poverty than what we experience now in Australia, but the difference is that Generation Y know there is another option. I recently heard a futurist say that for the first time in history, the poor know they are poor. They know that this is not the only way life is. Generation Y have seen more to life, and naturally they want a part of it. The problem is they know nothing of the sacrifice that goes into getting it. Some have never known someone in full-time employment, and it is not like their successful idols are portrayed in the most conscientious light. No-one tells of the years of struggle and hard work that went into making Marshall Mathers the rapper Eminem. Nor do they talk about the training that made Anthony Mundine a supreme athlete. The media just take the bits they want, and the bits the marketing departments give them, to portray these stars in a less than pure way. Plus we have shows like *Australian*

Idol, Popstars and *Big Brother* where ordinary people are made famous through television. Where someone like Shannon Noll is ploughing fields on his farm one week and selling 300,000 singles the next. Wealth, success and stardom are plastered all over our television screens and throughout magazines. Of course Generation Y wants to be successful. They want more and they want it now. Having made the point about shows like *Popstars*, let me note here that many Generation Yers crave the limelight. Knowing this might affect the way you show your appreciation for work well done. Do it loudly and do it publicly.

One thing you will hear me say time and time again is that Generation Y have separated effort from reward. The issue is a subheading in the chapter titled Impatient. They think they are entitled to wealth and success just for showing up. It is not as easy as they think. They do not understand the concept of cause and effect or short-term sacrifice for long-term gain. Growing up, they often just got what they wanted, when they wanted it, because Mum and Dad were too busy to explain why they couldn't or shouldn't have it. This even applies to those from welfare-dependent backgrounds. The whole concept of welfare is to receive without first adding value. Hugh Mackay describes this tendency of the Baby Boomers to give in so easily as a way of making themselves feel less guilty about the lack of time they spent with their kids while they were growing up.

Hugh Mackay also states, in his book *Generations*, that it has been a Baby Boom tendency to judge their own success by the feats of their children, and that this tendency has led, in many ways, to a sort of over-parenting. Over-parenting in terms of expectations and standards set for the performance of their kids. Boomers have felt the competition and have learnt that not everyone succeeds, and as such, are determined to give their kids every opportunity to get the edge on the competition. This has driven these Generation Y kids to succeed at younger ages than ever before. Just take a look at professional sport, particularly tennis and swimming, if you want to know what I am talking about.

There is plenty of evidence to show that Generation Y want success and they want it badly. There are currently 50,000 Generation Yers who run their own businesses in Australia. Their desire for success is manifesting itself in entrepreneurial ways. The Australian Bureau of Statistics estimates that a third of students who leave school in 2005 will at some stage start their own business. There is a proliferation of awards programs and grants promoting entrepreneurialism among Australia's youth. Try Nescafé Big Break, and the Australian Youth Foundation grants to name a couple. My 16-year-old brother is a great example. He has a successful little business called Common Sense Computers. He builds computers for people who don't know enough about computers to make an educated choice themselves when they buy retail. To enable people to understand what they are getting, he uses metaphors to describe what each component of a computer does, and he uses this to help the customer determine just what sort of computer they will need. He noticed that the descriptions major retailers give to describe a computer made little or no sense to the non-computer-orientated consumer, and decided to start his own computer shop (his bedroom) to meet this need. To give you a little more insight into Generation Y, I should also mention that he describes his uneducated customers as 'idiots'. When he ran his business idea past me I asked him who his target market was, and his immediate reply was 'idiots'. There are plenty of talented young people out there in the marketplace like my little brother. Your job is to capture some of this talent and put it to good use in your organisation.

Your job is to capture some of this talent and put it to good use in your organisation.

Despite often being guilty of separating effort from reward, Generation Y certainly value education and training, and can see it as being a significant tool in helping them to become more successful. Valuable training is an excellent motivational tool for managers to not only improve performance, but to also improve retention. As you will discover, the types of training Generation Y desire will not be simple computer software courses, however. They will want personal development, professional skills development and other such education.

Image Conscious

I was tempted to leave this topic out because, firstly, it is obvious. Most teenagers, and in fact most people, are driven by their need to look good. We are very conscious about the way we look, and what people think about us. Generation Y are, of course, no different. In fact, they are probably worse. They have been brought up on brands, and on the marketing machine. You simply *have* to be seen in the right style and the right labels. Not only that, but it has been argued that Generation Y are the most influential customers in fashion, because the Baby Boomers are so attracted to being youthful that they attempt to dress like their Generation Y kids.

The second reason I was going to leave it out is because it could be perceived as having very little to do with employment-related issues. But the opposite is true. It has everything to do with employment. I often ask students in my seminars where they work, and some of them are ashamed to name the places and say they can barely wait to get a job elsewhere. It is as though their image is 'at risk' because of where they work. What are we talking about? Employment Branding. Buzz words, sure, but this is big news and seriously important. Your Employment Brand is the way people perceive you as an employer. In other words, are you an employer of choice? It will be crucial if you are to attract the best new talent. You don't want to be perceived as a place that people are 'ashamed' to have worked.

For Generation Y, your image could hinge solely on your uniform. A focus group was conducted by the United States Marines to try to find out how to make the armed forces more attractive to school leavers. They asked Generation Y what the armed forces could do differently in order to achieve this aim. Was it to further subsidise study costs, offer more money in the first year, give even cheaper home loans? No, no and no. The overwhelming feedback was that

Generation Y wanted to be able to wear black berets like the SWAT soldiers got to wear. The real lesson here is that the Marines listened and recruitment shot through the roof, through a simple change in uniform. For other Generation Yers, the problem may be what you sell, or where your store is located.

Start thinking of ways that you can make your image to potential employees more favourable. I, as a consumer, noticed a few years ago that Target had changed their uniform. Not the colours, just the style of the shirts their staff could wear. Specifically, the girls wore a more fitted, tapered shirt. I know as a Generation Y'er myself, it was a much cooler uniform. Oh, and if you didn't already know, the word 'cool' is now so not cool! Why not do what the Marines did and actually ask Generation Y themselves what you could do. Ask both those that already work for you and those that don't.

Executive Summary

Generation Y are a lifestyle-centred generation. This has resulted in them being:

- In search of meaningful experiences
- Motivated by deeper things than just money
- Potentially willing to treat work as no more than a means to an end
- Materialistic
- Success driven
- Image conscious

Generation Y's lifestyle centredness provides the following opportunities to business:

- Companies who can be flexible and have a genuine appreciation for the importance of work–life balance will be very attractive to Generation Y. So too will those that can offer positions that are fun and social, and the opportunity to travel and work on exciting new projects.
- If Australian Generation Yers are so keen to do things like travel and work overseas, the same is likely to be true in other countries. You may be able to access valuable international human capital.
- Managers who can show individuals in more menial roles not only the value in what they do, but make them feel more valued doing it, will see marked improvements in staff loyalty and retention rates.
- Those companies who invest resources into being an 'employer of choice' will not only generate a better performance from their current staff, but will also strengthen their employment brand, giving them a unique advantage in the fight for Generation Y talent.
- Education and training will be lucrative selling points for employers in the talent war. Especially training that looks at the personal and professional development needs of their Generation Yers, not just basic skills training.

- Companies willing to ask and really listen to Generation Y through focus groups and other such forums stand to learn powerful things about how they can improve their image as an employer.

Lifestyle centredness also poses the following challenges:

- Companies are going to have to work harder than ever at making their workplace more attractive.
- Managers will need to create variety in the more mundane areas of the workplace if they are going to get better productivity from their staff and improve retention.
- Managers will need to be very creative and diligent in creating accountability in the new, more flexible, work environment. Managers will also need to obtain some kind of consistency for their teams and clients in an environment that is becoming more and more flexible.
- HR departments and those responsible for employment negotiations will have to stay on their guard and be able to gently, but effectively, communicate both sides of the debate. Generation Y have a tendency to feel they are entitled to things that the rest of the world has to earn.
- Poor retention of Generation Y employees will be a major drain on company funds and intellectual property if companies do not work hard on the 'soft' people side of business.

Independently Dependent

<Definition: Driven by the desire to be self-reliant while clinging to the security of having your needs met by other people>

'I want my independence, and the freedom to make my own choices, but still need my parents to help me with necessities like new shoes and stuff.' **– Generation Yer**

Despite being intensely driven by the need to be independent, and to carve their own path in life, Generation Y are the most over-parented, over-indulged, over-educated, welfare-dependent generation ever. Generation Y stay at home longer and are in education longer than any other generation. Yet if you were to ask them what they value most, independence would rank near the top every time.

'They are individuals. They do not want to be packaged as just another graduate or just another employee.'

Linda Botter,
Lion Nathan Australia

Here are some stats you may find interesting. Just under 30% of 25 year olds, the eldest of Generation Y, are still not employed full time. According to the ABS, 28% of Generation Y aged between 20–24 leave home each year, however, another 14% return home. So half those who leave come back. In the same age group, 74% live with family members and only 19% live alone. These figures are more indicative when you know that only 35% of 20–24 year olds are participating in education. So even though only 35% are participating in education at this time, 75% still live with their family. I find this very strange for a generation that preaches its independence.

Generation Y want independence with strings. They

want to be free to have their own thoughts and views, to do their own things and make their own rules, but they want their parents to pay for their rent, their food, their education, and help them financially while they are doing it. Baby Boomer parents have no-one to blame for this than themselves, mind you. The Boomers obsession with 'being yourself', which permeated the education system almost as strongly as parental styles, has meant Generation Y have been encouraged from day one to be independent thinkers. A wonderful thing to do. But on the other hand, the Baby Boomer parents have also been obsessed with their kids always having the best. The best school, the best coaches, the best academic tutors, the best environment to grow up in, including their own room, computer and television. In fact, in some families the kids get their own floor. Generation Yers are so used to having access to the best quality of everything, that as they grow older, they realise they cannot afford such a lifestyle and so they stay home and let Mum and Dad keep providing it. Quite simply, many Generation Yers have had it too good.

'They want to be seen as individuals. They want to be seen as important and special. They dislike the herd mentality.'

Deborah Stonley,
Henry Davis York

Add to this the fact that usually both Mum and Dad work, so often the Generation Y teenager is, or was, left unsupervised. To counter this challenge, Boomer parents set up more and more structured forms of entertainment – sport being the most obvious choice. Even beyond high school, Generation Y continue to engage in structured entertainment, with 73.5% aged between 18–24 still engaged in organised sport. There also seems to be a growing commitment to certain organised religions among Generation Y, and a mass exodus from others. Interestingly, it appears as though the shift is in favour of some more fundamental belief structures. Religion, of course, provides some form of emotional security.

I guess it is not a paradox when you really think about. Generation Y love the security of being looked after, and they enjoy the freedom that comes with not having to be totally responsible for their life, particularly the financial needs. But like anyone, they also value being independent thinkers, with their own views and ideas and the freedom to choose their activities. The question becomes, however, how long can Generation Y have their cake and eat it, too? And more importantly, perhaps, how will this independent dependence play out in the workplace?

Open to mentoring

One of the best things about Generation Y is that they are so keen to learn. They want to be able to put their own ideas forward and have a say in how things are done, but they genuinely want your support as they do it. They will respond very well to mentoring, because they have been engaged in it for years. Notice I said 'mentoring', not just 'telling and directing'. Generation Y will reject any kind of dictatorial approach in the workplace. They will be gone faster than you can say 'Listen to me, young man!' If you want appalling retention rates just put in a supervisor or manager who thinks they are a commander in the SAS. The number one reason Generation Yers leave a job is because they do not like their supervisor. Generation Y will fight back harder than you care to imagine. After all, their whole life they have been taught to be themselves and not let anyone else push them around. Even their favourite music is teaching them to 'take no crap'.

A new, more emotionally intelligent approach is required by managers. Well let's be honest here. This new approach is required whether Generation Y enter the workforce or not. Retention at all levels in organisations is falling, and the big contributor to this poor retention is often the direct supervisor or manager. I once heard it said that people come to work for companies but they leave managers. People will not work for someone they do not like or respect. I am not talking about being weak and setting low standards. Mentoring does not mean being a pushover. If you make a rule, you had better enforce it. If you ask for something to be done, you had better hold that person accountable for doing it. There is no faster way to lose the respect of Generation Y than to ask them to do something that you weren't bothered enough to check was even done, or perhaps did not need to be done in the first place. You will only need to be inconsistent once and Generation Y will stop sticking to that policy.

I have heard that Generation Y have no respect for elders. I don't agree. I would say, however, that they don't respect you just because you are an elder. A Melbourne marketing agency surveyed what we define as Generation Y, and found that a whopping 94% identified their parents as their most admired role models, saying they appreciated their support during 'troubled and difficult times'. It is this kind of 'support' that will bring out the best of Generation Y in the workforce.

'They need stroking and nurturing. The sit down, shut up and do what you are told approach does not work with Generation Y.'

Trish Rodley
(Team Leader),
Marc Edward Agency

Generation Y value personal power. By personal power I mean the confidence to stand up for what you believe in and to not allow yourself to be pushed around or 'bullied'. Coaching allows for this personal power to be exercised. Generation Y like having a mentor, a 'big brother', to help them with decisions and their career. Organisations, thankfully, have already seen the huge potential of both mentoring and other more formal approaches to personal development and are embracing such programs in the workplace.

Will want to be empowered

Because their goal is to be seen to be independent, Generation Y will not want a supervisor looking over their shoulder all day and scrutinising their every move. Nor will they like to have to ask for approval for everything. They will want to be empowered. You know, have the decision-making power and the resources to do their job properly without having to run to the manager every time something slightly different needs to be done, or a customer has a slightly challenging problem.

Any sort of empowerment, especially decision-making power, given to someone with relatively little experience is a daunting and risky prospect. However, it can work if it is done properly. Firstly, ensure that clear boundaries and expectations are laid out, and that each Generation Y employee knows where their scope to make decisions lies. Secondly, ensure your 'empowerment' is real and is not window-dressing, which Generation Y will see straight through. And thirdly, be sure to check in regularly, review decisions from time to time to ensure all expectations are being met and customer satisfaction or profitability are not being undermined.

Executive Summary

Generation Y are independent in thought, and confident enough to express it, but at the same time enjoy the security, both emotional and financial, that comes with living with Mum and/or Dad, or that comes from belonging to an organisation such as a sporting or religious group. This independent dependence means that in the workplace they are:

- Coachable
- Desire empowerment

There are major opportunities for business today, knowing that Generation Y are independently dependent:

- Emotionally intelligent managers will find Generation Y are tremendous assets to their teams and workplaces, being willing to develop and improve.
- Managers with the confidence to empower their Generation Y staff will find them, if managed properly, willing and able to meet the challenge.

These challenges will also present themselves:

- Companies with entrenched cultures of treating staff like numbers, or managers that treat staff 'the way they were treated when they were that age' will find themselves losing significant numbers of their staff, and suffering further reductions in profitability.
- Generation Y need to be coached and nurtured for the best results, and this is a management style still relatively new to some workplaces and foreign to some organisational cultures.

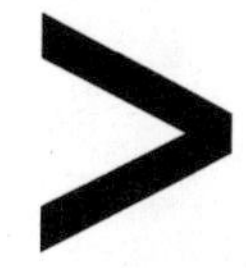

Informal

<Definition: To act without formality.
To be more relaxed in approach and regulation>

'I hate how my teachers always tell me to take my hat off inside. What is the big deal?' **– Generation Yer**

You may think that Generation Y have taken the term 'youthful arrogance' to a whole new level, but this means you are misinterpreting them. Sure, Generation Y are arrogant, and they do think they know everything, but often they are just being a little informal in the way they communicate, or in the way they approach things. Generation Y have been raised to go their own way, to express themselves and speak their mind. The problem is they are not always aware of the appropriate time and place to do these things.

When surveyed, Generation Y claim to have a healthy respect for tradition. However, their definition of tradition is fairly narrow, and they would not be including the pointless formalities that surround so much of what we do. Names and titles would fit this description. I recall a university lecturer who presented at one of my programs for Generation Y school students. He requested that I introduce him as Dr So and So, and that the students refer to him as Dr So and So. Not only did it seem pretentious to me, but I knew it would give the students the entirely wrong impression. Sure, it was appropriate for him to build credibility and allow me to introduce him as having done a PhD in a specific discipline, but he then needed to be personable and more open to his audience. Standing when a teacher enters the room is another example. We have already stated that Generation Y are a pragmatic bunch and if they see no point, they will refrain from doing it or, at best, resent it as they do it. I heard a student say, 'I would like to see the teachers stand when we enter the staff room.' If you told a Generation Yer to respect their elders they might reply by saying, 'What is an elder?' Generation Y respect practicality and relevance. If something does not have some relevance to their current situation, or has no practical value, then they will discard it. There are just too many other things to worry about without wasting valuable time and energy on things of no real consequence.

'I would like to see the teachers stand when we enter the staff room.'

Generation Y student

By 'healthy respect for tradition' I think Generation Y mean the historic significance of Anzac Day, or the tradition of fireworks on Sydney Harbour on New Year's Eve and so on. They certainly are not referring to the fact that workers in your factory have always worn blue overalls, or that just because things have always been done that way they should continue to be done that way. It is not being disrespectful of tradition, it is an in-built need to look more closely at alternatives, and to question the rationale behind everything.

It is no secret that the key to communication is to communicate with someone from within their frame of reference. Or more simply put, to speak to them the way they like to be spoken to. And you don't need to be a genius to figure out that being very formal and proper (stiff) is not going to work with Generation Y. For this reason, marketing campaigns that use Generation Y to sell to Generation Y have been extremely effective. Generation Y recruiters could do the same. In fact, you could start by using your current staff to help you find other suitable staff members. Maybe even involve them in the selection process and certainly in the orientation process. Lots more on these sorts of ideas later.

So what does Generation Y informality mean for business?

Innovative, creative and enterprising

Generation Y's blatant disregard for 'the way we have always done things' massively contributes to their innovative and creative nature. It is no secret that some of the major breakthroughs in industries have come from completely unrelated industries. Why? Because a fresh set of eyes gives a fresh perspective, and a fresh perspective illuminates opportunities that were previously overlooked.

Don't try to beat this informality out of your Generation Y staff. Use it. Embrace it. After all, employers have said that the number one character trait they are looking for in graduates is creativity. Sometimes creativity has side effects, informality being one of them. US Consultant and expert on Leadership Patricia Pitcher, author of *The Drama of Leadership*, puts it beautifully: 'You say you don't want emotional, volatile, and unpredictable, just imaginative? Sorry, they only come in a package'.

This does not mean you compromise on the essential things in your business. Like the consistency of dress, the consistency of how we treat and greet our clients. Your very survival will depend on staying true to some of these things. Just don't overdo the consistency thing to a point that it drowns out any individuality and creativity.

Communication Skills

Communication skills is probably the number one requested training topic for Generation Y. They may be passionate, they may even be well educated, but their ability to say it in the right way and to do so smoothly is sometimes lacking. In some of the more technical positions Generation Y are beginning to fill, it is sometimes a case of not being able to say it at all. You see, even though Generation Y are a well-connected generation, and value relationships, their communication is often online and on the telephone, and sometimes even in languages so abbreviated and unique that the average Baby Boomer or Generation Xer would struggle to understand it.

The challenge is that, even though businesses use many

of the same means of communication, they also rely heavily on more traditional forms such as verbal presentations and written reports and proposals. Put a Generation Yer in front of an audience, even if it is only three or four people, and see what happens. They will either mesmerise them with their ideas and passion, or struggle to put a coherent sentence together, leaving the 'gs' off the end of most words, and then tell you it would be 'fully sick' to work on that project or in that department. Writing is no different. The style of this book is about as formal as I get, and it was a struggle even to be this formal. That said, I understand structure and the importance of getting my ideas across clearly and simply. An academic might be appalled by my colloquial style (although by the time you read this, my text has probably been edited into a form that resembles correct English).

Depending on who your customer base is, it is going to be essential that Generation Y learn to communicate both in Gen'Y'nese and in English.

Generation Y are blunt and to the point. They certainly don't mind telling you what they think, whether that be informed by opinion, fact, or anything else. Of course, they were brought up to be expressive and to reveal their thoughts and emotions. I wonder if the Baby Boomers knew just how upfront their children would be. There is certainly just cause for Boomers thinking Generation Y are rude, and I suppose by traditional standards they are. However, I don't believe they are intending to be rude. Rather, I think it is just what they have learnt to be. Think about it from a customer service point of view. When was the last time you saw a Generation Yer receive (not give) outstanding customer service? Rarely I'd say, if my personal life is anything to go by. Not only that, but if you listen to commercial radio or watch much television, you will notice that being completely rude and insulting is considered to be funny and entertaining, and therefore good for the ratings. Jerry Springer! Need I say more?

The problem is that the ego of most supervisors and managers will not be able to handle this kind of abruptness, and thus conflict is inevitable. Worse still is the fact that Generation Y won't hold their tongue just because someone is a customer. If a customer is rude to them, they will outright give it back to the customer, then be completely bewildered that you think they have done something wrong.

Two things must happen here. Firstly, managers and supervisors will need to model outstanding customer service. Not just tell Generation Y to do it, but show them first. Secondly, management need to provide a safe place for Generation Y to air any grievances or express any thoughts they might have. That may be in regular staff meetings, or even in informal chats before a shift starts or as one ends. Not only that, but taking the time to listen to the views of your Generation Y employees will go a long way to earning their respect. Outline and live yourself what you consider to be model behaviour, explain it and then keep them accountable.

Etiquette

Generation Y don't have it, probably were not taught it, and are yet to use it. Tact is not something Generation Y were born with, that's for sure. They will say what they want and when they want. This is something that has gotten me into trouble in the business world already. I was in a meeting with a high-powered executive at a huge retail group (huge!). Obviously an excellent company and a good fit for my expertise. In the meeting, when asked to give an example of what Generation Y like and don't like, I proceeded to criticise a current recruitment program the firm had in place, specifically the wording of their ads, only to find that the executive responsible for this campaign was at the meeting. Oops!

Generation Y need to learn the art of being tactful. They will also need to know that you start from the outermost set of cutlery and work inwards from there, and that you put butter on your side plate before spreading it onto your bread. The list could go on. Even the more basic forms of etiquette like saying 'please', 'thank you', and 'hello' are foreign to many Generation Yers. Just go to your local supermarket or discount variety store and see for yourself. This is your staff and this is your brand. With brand and customer experience, the little things are often the big things. It is the job of the manager and supervisor to emphasise the importance of such things to Generation Y and then to keep them accountable for doing them.

Non-conforming

Surprise, surprise! Generation Y are unlikely to conform to all of your rules and regulations. This is not as bad as you might first think. Despite their in-built desire for freedom and independence (Generation Y style), they still have a healthy respect for rules that make sense. Generation Y will not abide by silly rules that have no practical value in the workplace. They will question every rule you put forth, and will only follow the ones for which you are able to give an intelligent and genuine explanation. This is not such bad thing, because it will allow you to free yourself and your team of some of the unnecessary burden years of operation and manager changes have left behind.

The key here is relevance. If your organisation has a uniform, great. If you expect Generation Y to wear it, you had better explain the importance of giving your customers a consistent experience when they come into contact with your brand. You had also better allow some individuality in regards to the uniform. If you don't, Generation Y will find it. They will look for any way they can to put their stamp on your uniform. If you say black pants, they will assume you mean black cargo pants, or black hipsters, or black tight pants with safety pins down the side, or maybe black shorts. This leads me to my next point.

Dress and Uniform

In operational roles, Generation Y are not renowned for their willingness to wear their uniform and adhere to a strict dress code. Those in white-collar professions start a little all over the place, but eventually get the picture. It is not that Generation Y don't know how to dress well, it is just their definition of 'well' differs from that of the rest of the world.

Your approach to dress code depends entirely on your organisation and what it does. Of course, Generation Yers who work in the major supermarkets and other retail organisations will have to wear a uniform. As will those young graduates and clerks working in accounting, finance and the legal fields. However, for everyone in between, you have options. Which option you take depends on what you do, what role different people need to fill, and what your customers expect. If you are a marketing group, day-to-day you may allow your staff to dress casually, and on the days that you report into your clients you might demand they wear smart business attire. You may also notice that Generation Y might think casual attire means Saturday afternoon at the pub. No matter what dress code you apply, be sure to give an accurate description of what that code actually means and then explain to Generation Y the logic behind the code. Then most importantly, enforce the code. If you have a dress code, it should not be negotiable. If it is negotiable, my advice is to scrap the code because every time you say one thing, but fail to enforce it, you lose a little more respect from your Generation Y employees.

You may also notice that Generation Y might think casual attire means Saturday afternoon at the pub.

In one of my Leadership programs, participants spend a day with an image consultant and learn what to wear and what not to wear. They are asked to choose clothes they would expect to wear to an interview or to the job. The students in the audience are usually from relatively wealthy homes and are, in the majority, sons and daughters of professional people. Year in year out they come dressed looking more like they are going to the movies than to a job interview. It astounds me. They are dead serious. They just don't get it. Pants that are too long, shirts untucked, no ties, unpolished shoes. The list is endless.

To sum up, you need to ensure guidelines and regulations are relevant and practical. Then once you have culled those that are not, you will need to be extremely diligent in enforcing those regulations that are.

Blatantly Breaking Rules

It is nothing new that a new generation will break the rules of the generation that has come before them. It is just part of human nature. The difference with Generation Y is that having been brought up on television and the 'marketing machine', they have seen many people break the rules and still become successful. In fact, some of the most publicly successful people are the ones who are the least cooperative and the most adversarial. Take Denis Rodman, Eminem and Anthony Mundine for example.

Not only that, but Generation Y have seen their Mum and Dad, who are extremely conscientious and extremely hard working, not achieve anywhere near the financial success or public fame of these other people. Some of the most moral people Generation Y know are the least financially successful.

Breaking the rules is not always that bad. There are some rules that truly should be broken. By rules, I am including a whole host of socially conditioned behaviour. Take, for example, the traditional linear career path. You know the one. Go to school, get good grades, go on to university, get a job and stay with the company for life. What a load of hogwash. But parents and teachers and other influential people are still feeding this to Generation Y. I was recently in a meeting with the director of marketing for an international training organisation. She was recounting to me a conversation she had just had with a very senior official from one of Sydney's most prestigious universities. She was explaining how her organisation was working closely with business to develop curriculums for their students so that graduates would be better equipped to deal with the workforce, and how it was being very well received by the business sector. The university official retorted that he thought it was not the place of businesses to be designing curriculums, and that it should be left primarily to the academics. Hmmmm.

There is more than one way to do anything, and Generation Y will continue to question everything and anything to find those other ways. But this is what makes them so innovative.

Executive Summary

Generation Y are very informal:

> In their disregard for the 'we have always done it this way' policy, instead looking for new, more efficient ways of doing things
> In their communication, be it verbal, written or other
> In the bluntness with which they speak
> In their business etiquette
> In their dress
> In their unwillingness to follow rules for the sake of following rules

This informality brings major opportunities to business:

> Generation Y are both innovative and creative because of their tendency to not settle for the way things have always been. It is their informality and lack of respect for many longstanding procedures and processes that will give them the ability to see new, more efficient ways of doing things.
> Most of Generation Y are the same, so you know they are informal and you should use that to your advantage in your recruiting and marketing campaigns. That is, market to them in less formal ways and do things a little differently.

On the other hand this informality poses a series of real challenges:

> One of the major focuses managers will need to have when it comes to training their Generation Y employees is communication skills. Businesses cannot afford to have inconsistent and unacceptable communication taking place at the front end of their business.
> Etiquette and tact and appropriate dress will be something you will need to teach. You only get one chance to make a good first impression, and while many people may not notice a lack of etiquette, the very people with whom you want to do business just might.

- Many organisations are dripping with tradition and history, some of which are crucial to the organisation's success. You will need to convince Generation Y of the validity of staying true to such traditions, and to demonstrate the value they add to the business.
- HR departments may have to look outside the traditional guidelines for what makes a good employee and start looking at less formal and less traditional forms of education and experience. Sure, more Generation Yers are going to university but this certainly does not imply that only the best go there.

Tech Savvy

<Definition: Advanced knowledge of the practical applications of technology>

'You are missing the point, Peter. Computers have a spirit.'
– Generation Yer

Generation Y are tech savvy like nothing or no-one you have ever seen before. It would not have taken Einstein to discover this. They thrive on technology and its uses. In fact, they live for it. They are not interested in the technology of yesterday, which many of you are still using; they want the latest and the fastest money can buy. Even when they don't have the money to buy it, they will learn about it and know better how to use it than their parents, who have been talked into buying it. Is 00:00 still flashing on your VCR? Do you still own a VCR?

'What do you want for Christmas? A website!'

A conversation between Steven Paull of HB Training & Personnel and his Generation Y daughter

Did you know that the processor in a $3.95 greeting card that today sings 'Happy Birthday' is more powerful than the processor that was used in the 1976 Cray Super Computers and has a higher processor capacity than that which existed in the entire world in 1950? And to think people tell me that Generation Y are no different from when they were kids. Yeah right!

Generation Y see technology as the solution to many of the problems that face the world today. They see it as the way to eliminate terrorism, to cure diseases, improve food production, and end world hunger. For them, technology is not a thing to be considered. It is a way of life.

For them, technology is not a thing to be considered. It is a way of life.

According to a Knowledge Researcher survey of Generation Y, if they had to choose only one medium from the internet, the telephone, television or radio, the most popular selection was for the internet, followed by television, then the telephone and lastly the radio.

Early Adopters

Generation Y will adopt and learn how to use technology faster than anyone else in your organisation. They want to learn about it and use it. Check this out. The time it took the following communications technologies to get a critical mass of 50 million users was:

- > **Radio 34 years**
- > **Television 13 years**
- > **Internet 4 years**
- > **Instant messaging 4 months**

Take advantage of this in your business. Trial new technology on a small scale in Generation Y teams and see what operational efficiency improvements are achieved.

Resourceful

While the rest of the world complains about the overflow of information, Generation Y are using technology to filter the information provided by technology. They use blogs and other such things to ensure they only get the best of what they need. Not only are they not drowning in information from the net, but they have honed their search skills so they can find exactly what they want. They store favourite sites for information they regularly access, and they can source anything. We have spoken already about their resourcefulness; their technology skills further enhance this resourcefulness.

A survey by Mercer Human Resource Consulting confirmed this. It showed that 83% of Generation Y surveyed found it quick and easy to find things on their company's intranet, where only 60% of Generation X and Baby Boomers said it was quick and easy.

I have already used my little brother Paul, who is quintessential Generation Y, as an example of what they are like. Let me use him once more. I paid a professional computer technician to network my office computers. He did, but the network never worked properly. I got so frustrated waiting for him to return my calls, and sick of him telling me it worked fine when he left, that I called my little bro to fix it. Fix it he did. He redid the whole thing in less than an hour. The other guy took almost a whole day and cost me hundreds. To get my brother to do it cost me a miniscule $30. No doubt about these Generation Yers.

As Sales People

Generation Y are the best people to sell technology, at a retail level anyway. They know better than anyone how things work, what the capabilities are, and whether you need one. Well, maybe not whether you need one because we have all bought the latest gadget and never could figure out how to make it work to its full capacity, even though at the time of sale the messy-haired 16 year old had convinced us that it was exactly what we needed. Seriously though, Generation Y have credibility when it comes to technology. It is their domain. They don't just understand it, they feel it in the gut. Customers of all ages recognise that. The chances are, they have already asked their son or daughter or niece or nephew what things to look for just so they won't sound like a complete fool.

They don't just understand it, they feel it in the gut.

As a Generation Yer myself, and a reasonably tech savvy one, nothing frustrates me more than sales people who know nothing about the product they are selling. I would prefer to be served by a snotty-nosed 15 year old who can at least tell me what a product can do, than a professional twice that age who is just smooth and well presented. Companies who are willing to teach these unpolished, tech-savvy teenagers how to properly sell and how to deliver memorable customer service, will reap a windfall.

Executive Summary

Generation Y are as tech savvy as it is possible to be. They will thrive in these chaotic times of change, which, by the way, are going to speed up rather than slow down in the coming decade. Being tech savvy makes Generation Y:

- Early adopters of new technology
- Fast learners
- Resourceful
- Excellent sales people of technological products, providing they are given sufficient sales and customer service training

The tech-savvy nature of Generation Y offers the following opportunities to business:

- You can test new technology in small trials using Generation Y teams, and evaluate major technologies before investing massively in fully developing them. In fact, you should be looking to trial anything new in Generation Y environments because they are open to and looking for change.
- With the appropriate training, Generation Y will be extremely valuable in the sales arena, particularly sales of technology, because they truly understand the power of technology and what it can do.

As always, some challenges will arise:

- Businesses will need to manage Generation Y's thirst for the latest technology. Generation Y may resort to blaming slightly out-of-date technology for their poor performance rather than taking into consideration their own attitude and application.
- Generation Y will be hard to keep up with, and it will be essential that all staff, not just Generation Y, work and communicate using the same technology.

Stimulus Junkies

<Definition: Addicted to excitement>

'We are the "busy doing" generation. Busy doing, busy doing, busy doing. What? STUFF! We are always busy doing stuff.'
– Generation Yer

Generation Y are addicted to stimulation in the same way a drug addict is addicted to drugs. It becomes a part of them. They have to have it, and they go AWOL if they don't get it. The opposite of stimulation is boredom, which is up there with 'not liking your supervisor' as a reason Generation Y retention is so low.

If you can't keep Generation Y entertained, you can't keep them.

If you think about the positions that the vast majority of Generation Y currently fill in the workforce, whether they be in retail, business or any other field, they are predominantly repetitive, well-systemised jobs. In other words, BORING! If you can't keep Generation Y entertained, you can't keep them.

'Variety is the spice of life' is what they used to say. 'Variety *is* life' is what they now say. When we talk about Generation Y, we are talking about a generation that knows no other world than one filled with *Big Brother*, the internet, mobile phones, Sony Playstation, Apple iPods and DVDs. So what is the common element of all of these? INTERACTIVITY. It is high tech, high visual-interactive entertainment.

I have often read that Generation Y are disengaged. Really! Like you can't tell. Of course they are disengaged. They are disengaged from the political system, the school system, the workforce. Why? They're BORED!

Research has shown that a normal Generation Yer spends an average of five hours each day in front of a screen. And a screen over which they are becoming more and more in control. Your jobs have to compete with this level of stimulation. Can you keep up? Can you keep them interested? And now that they are in control of what happens, can you manage them and their need to determine what they are going to do and when they are going to do it?

I know my tone here is a little in your face. It is meant to be. This is already costing businesses millions in attrition and failed attempts to improve it.

A New Paradigm

The challenge with keeping Generation Y entertained is that they have a different paradigm of what is interesting, interactive and entertaining. What you think is interesting, interactive and entertaining is not the same. Compare Pac-Man to Counter Strike if you don't believe me. You know what Pac-Man involves, but let me give you a brief description of what Counter Strike involves. As described by a 17-year-old professional gamer it is a 'multi player, online terrorist/counterterrorist simulation'. These games are played online and in international competitions with prize money. That is why I referred to my source as a 'professional' gamer. There is another game called EverQuest, which is based on an online world called Norrath. Inspired by the role-playing game Dungeons and Dragons, Norrath was developed by a group of software engineers in San Diego. In short, Norrath represents an entire world, with its own economic systems, politics, races and classes and is large enough to accommodate nearly 500,000 people each year. You basically become a citizen, on whichever continent you choose, as a member of your selected race and class, and begin your 'quest'. More than half a million people have subscribed to this online world, and at any one time, there will be 60,000 people playing simultaneously from their computers from all over the real world (you know, planet Earth). According to Professor Edward Castronova, of the University of California, revenue from online gaming (not gambling, gaming) will amount to over $US1.5 billion in 2004 alone. Do I mean sales of computer games will amount to that? No. It is altogether something different. This game is so real for the players that it has broken beyond its virtual walls. The game itself has a currency called the 'platinum piece', which is traded in online auction houses for real world currency. In fact, there is an official exchange rate between the platinum piece and the US dollar. And I mean official. People buy digital supplies, such as lasers, with real money, and characters themselves sell for up to $US2000. That is real money. Dr Castronova's research places Norrath as the 77th wealthiest country in the world, with a per capita gross national product of $2266, which is higher than China's. There are more than five million virtual world game players subscribed to EverQuest and other games like it. There are professional gamers who play for a living. Get this: the average player can earn $US3.42 an hour playing the game, and according to Dr Castronova, the average Norrath citizen spends 36 hours a week inside the virtual world. Thirty-six HOURS! Norrath has also developed its own language similar to those abbreviations you find in online chat rooms and on SMS messages.

'I command an army in my spare time and you want me to photocopy.'

Generation Yer

And you thought your orientation program was interesting. Think again. I am obviously not just talking about training. Imagine how boring working the checkout in a supermarket or manning the phones in the customer inquiry centre will be compared to a virtual world where you can be and do whatever you like. And it is not just games.

Don't assume that all Generation Yers are computer-game freaks. We are not. But we have an extremely high expectation of what is entertaining. You only need to look at the quality, from a Generation Y viewpoint, of the films that are coming out of Hollywood. Movies that have websites and merchandise along with the film. Advertisers know. Look at some of Nike's campaigns. They are designed purely to drive traffic to some of their product sites, where potential customers can engage in a fully interactive web experience.

The Entertainment Age

This is not the information age, it is the entertainment age. And the entertainment is interactive. Generation Y don't just watch television, they show up and cheer on their favourite characters at the live sets. Think *Australian Idol* concerts and *Big Brother* evictions. If they don't like a character, they just SMS them out. *Big Brother* again. They don't just go to the movies anymore, they go to the movies, download the screensaver, and play the computer game as well. Entertainment is no longer a passive activity.

If they don't like a character, they just SMS them out.

What is entertaining about working for your organisation?

With the entertainment age comes a new kind of education. It is called Edutainment. It is when you mix both education and entertainment. You can still have skills transfer in the training room when the audience is entertained. Research indicates that the more 'entertained' an audience is, the greater their retention and, therefore, the greater the level of skill transfer. A great story with a potent metaphor has always gone a lot further in the training room than the most eloquently presented serve of content. I know that real-life training and seminars will be as popular in the future as they are now because as interactive as the net or other computer-based learning systems can be, unless you are spending millions the systems will not have the same electric atmosphere and level of entertainment of a real-life program that fully engages its participants. Generation Y want it interactive, entertaining, and relevant to them and their circumstances.

How will you inject more edutainment into your training programs? I want you to give this some thought, and then read the chapters on Orientation and Training where I will share with you some effective ideas, and also explain that entertaining does not necessarily mean high tech.

Intense

Generation Y are either intensely interested and involved, or intensely bored. They are either intensely motivated or intensely disengaged. They are either intensely for or intensely against. There appears to be very little in the way of grey areas when it comes to Generation Y. They have been brought up in such extreme times that they do things full throttle. Hugh Mackay referred to the environment that Generation Y has grown up in as the 'pressure cooker'.

I have the privilege of working with more than 40,000 Generation Yers each year, often in the school environment. Talk about a generation of stress puppies. Some of them take school so seriously. It is like a micro example of the income inequality emerging in our egalitarian society. The richer are getting richer, and the poorer are getting poorer. The smart are getting smarter, and the dumb, dumber. The conscientious are getting more conscientious and the rebellious more rebellious. Just look at how serious sport is. Lleyton Hewitt was world number one at the age of 21. Imagine the pressure a young girl like Jelena Dokic was under with a father that driven. We have already discussed how serious computer games have become. Scary stuff. The key is to get their genuine commitment.

I suppose it was inevitable that Generation Y would be more intense than those who went before them. It seems that every generation is more intense than the one before. They take current trends to an extreme. Every teenager that has ever lived has been rebellious in some way. However, Generation Y are rebelling at a more extreme level now. Generation Xers, for example, are renowned for not wanting to commit their life to the corporation, and are beginning to bail out and start their own practices, consultancies or even coffee shops. But it has taken many of them ten years to make the shift. Generation Xers at least stay in a job for a few years, and then stay at least a few more months after they decide they want to leave. Generation Y leave the day they decide they don't like it anymore. Or the afternoon they do not get recognised for doing good work, and so just don't return after lunch.

Bored

Generation X have been described as the bored generation. Well, Generation Y will do that to a more extreme level and more quickly. Dr Colin McCowan, Careers Adviser at the Queensland University of Technology, said it used to take Generation X a few weeks to decide they did not like a particular subject or course, but with Generation Y it happens in days. He recalls the fastest was seven minutes. That is, it only took the Generation Y student seven minutes to get so bored in a lecture that they felt compelled to drop the subject completely, leave the room, walk to the careers office on the other side of campus and state their request. Seven minutes from the start of the lecture. Maybe now you know what I am talking about. An example from business. One of Australia's largest Generation Y employers has a 100% turnover of their teenage Generation Y staff in one store. None even last a full year. Why? Because they get bored. I was the same. I started a job with Royal and Sun Alliance in their call centre at 18 and only lasted a day. Way too slow for me. Then the following week I did a day's labouring with a builder. Yeah right! All I did was rip up the waterproof material from the ceiling of a large office block in North Sydney. I resigned that afternoon. I hated every minute of it. On the other hand, as a younger teenager I used to travel to outback New South Wales to chip cotton, which, by definition, is the most boring job on the planet. However, I got to do it with my friends and we chatted and laughed as we worked. It was just enough to make it bearable. Just.

Herein lies the greatest challenge managers of Generation Y will face. How do we stop them getting bored? Why will this be so hard, you ask? A number of reasons:

> Limited resources. There is only so much money you can spend on this. You can't compete with Hollywood.

> Some jobs have to get done, regardless of how tedious they are, and they are not worth paying someone older to do. Generation Y are the cheapest source of labour.

> Keeping it under control. If you do begin to add more fun to the work environment, things can get harder to 'manage'.

- There are limits to what you can allow the less experienced and skilled Generation Yers in your employment to do. Many projects will require different and more advanced skills that some Generation Yers may not yet possess.
- Logistics. How can you make serving on a cash register more fun? There is not a whole lot you can do, so you will have to use your imagination. Or better still, just ask those people working on the register what they think. More on this in Part Two.

Multi-Taskers

The whole stimulus junkie thing is not all bad. In fact, there are some major advantages. Generation Y can tell you in ten seconds flat what would make their job or your training program more interesting. You may also find that they will inject enthusiasm into the way they carry out their tasks to make them more interesting. But the most practical of all is that Generation Y are multi-taskers. There is no doubt they can do more than one thing at a time. They are carrying on an Instant Messaging conversation on their computer while they play Doom, having a conversation on the telephone while telling Mum they need $100 for something at school tomorrow, and all while catching the last few minutes of *The Simpsons.*

Give them more than one thing to do and they won't tell you that they already have too much to do. They will just add it to their list and probably be grateful for the variety. While probably incrementally small, there will be improvements in productivity as they begin to work out the most practical ways to do more than one thing at a time.

Executive Summary

Generation Y are the most over-stimulated group of people you will ever meet. They are all ADD compared to those many years older than them. They have been conditioned to be this way. Their addiction to stimulation has meant:

> The meaning of entertainment has been taken to a whole new level, and most of all that it has become a very interactive process
> They get bored easily
> They are intense
> They are multi-taskers

Generation Y's addiction to stimulation offers businesses opportunities:

> Generation Y aren't just addicted to entertainment unknowingly. They know what they like and what interests them, and can easily tell you how you could make a specific job or training program more interesting.
> If you can get Generation Y to 'buy-in' on your goals and projects, they will approach their tasks with the same level of intensity and enthusiasm that they attack the other things they are interested in.
> They have learnt to multi-task and will thrive in a high pressure, always on the go, kind of position. They will not be flustered easily because they can handle more than one thing at a time.

The challenges are very large in this regard for organisations:

> The workforce cannot compete with television, cinema, and computer games when it comes to entertainment. However, Generation Y aren't completely naïve, and they know that this is not possible. They will, however, still demand that their position be interesting, and managers will need to rethink many current job descriptions to make Generation Y jobs and tasks more appealing.

- Retention will suffer. Generation Y will not stay bored for long. They simply will not put up with it. If companies cannot spice up the positions they offer, they will have to accept the fact that people will not stay long in one place.
- Training and orientation programs need to be as entertaining and interactive as possible. This is likely to require an investment of time and energy, as well as possibly engaging more professional trainers with a proven ability to engage this audience.
- Managing a workforce that demands so much variety will be challenging just to keep their minds on the jobs they are doing.
- Attracting Generation Y to positions that are known to be boring will also be a difficult task. Even if you have done things to make it more interesting, how are you going to let your Generation Y prospects know this?

Sceptical

<Definition: Inclined to doubt accepted opinions>

***'I don't believe much of what I see and read. I used to get really excited by some ads, but was always disappointed when I actually bought it for real.'* – Generation Yer**

Generation Y, with their natural inclination to question everything and their informality and disrespect for pointless pomp and ceremony, are sceptical. They have a built-in bull-shit meter on their forehead, which rings loudly at any insincerity, ulterior motive or dishonesty.

According to the Brand Child study conducted by Martin Lindstrom, by age 12, a Generation Y Australian child is seeing 22,000 advertisements per year directed at selling to them. That is insane. The same research has shown that a third of Australian parents report that their youngest Generation Y kids said a brand name as one of their first words. Generation Y have literally been brought up with television, and have been a prime target of the 'marketing machine' the whole time. They have been sold to their whole life and have no doubt been taken advantage of somewhere along the way themselves. The obvious response would be to become sceptical. They barely had a choice; they were conditioned to be this way.

However, sceptical does not mean outright cynicism or pessimism, rather it is just a healthy amount of doubt applied to everything, at least initially. Once they have verified your sincerity, or a product's effectiveness, Generation Y will be committed, loyal and positive.

Generation Y are actually an extremely optimistic generation; and why wouldn't they be? They have so many options to choose from as consumers, in their lifestyles, and in careers. They are living in times of unprecedented prosperity and opportunity. In fact, they have so many options, they are in many ways confused.

Organisations that are upfront, tell the truth, and deliver quality will excel in the Generation Y market, both from an employer and sales point of view. If you can deliver what you promise, and let people know about it in a non-sleazy way, you stand a chance. It does, however, mean that some of the traditional 'one day all this could be yours' kind of motivation and pep speeches will not work. Generation Y don't believe you, and they know the likelihood is that it won't happen.

'They value honesty and integrity above all else.'

Deborah Stonley,
Henry Davis York

Exposed

Generation Y have seen so much, and have access to so much more information, that it should come as no surprise to you that they won't accept everything at face value, and won't believe everything you say.

If you are a Baby Boomer reading this, then it is likely you were brought up believing hard work pays off and that the good guy always wins. This is simply not true. People break the law, do the wrong thing, and will sometimes not just get off free, but may also be extremely successful as a result of it. Eminem pulls a gun on his ex-wife's boyfriend and then sings a song about it and how horrible his mother is, and his sales skyrocket. A group of youths gang-rape a girl they abducted from a suburban train station and get less than 18 months for it. Some Generation Yers have seen their parents down-sized and right-sized by the very businesses they dedicated their lives to. They know people who have lost their life savings because they invested in dodgy phone or insurance companies, and they have seen very little being done to the directors of those companies in comparison to the damage they caused to other people's wellbeing. They did not have an age of innocence and they certainly do not have rose-coloured glasses on.

They have been sold to and sold to and sold to. The commercial landscape today is filled with people trying to sell you something, whether you need it or not. Sure, this is the same for everyone. However, no-one experienced it from such a young age like Generation Y. It is estimated that the average Australian Generation Yer has five hours of screen time each day. That includes television, games, cinema and the net. Five hours per day. All of these mediums are filled with advertising. Even DVD and computer games are beginning to be filled with product placement. Did you see the recent remake of the movie *The Italian Job*? I could have sworn I was watching a three-hour advertisement. The net is no different with its myriad of spam, especially considering most of Generation Y have a hotmail, or similar, free email account, filled with spam and banner ads. It should come as no surprise to you that traditional interruption-based advertising does not work for Generation Y. That includes the way you advertise your jobs. The problem is that so often the advertising does not really match up with the product. Next time you go to a fast-food chain, see if what you order reflects in any way, shape, or form the picture advertising that selection on the menu board.

They have seen con artist after con artist exposed on television current affairs programs, though never successfully prosecuted. The good guy does not always win. Often the bad guy does, and Generation Y know it. It does not seem to matter if you do the wrong thing, just as long as you have enough money to win the matter in court. In my first two years of driving, I lost all but one point from my licence. As you can imagine, I was a lot more careful after that. One day, however, I thought I had been caught speeding and totally freaked out. My mate Jacob, also a Generation Yer, told me to chill out. 'Just take it to court and say you need your car for work and they will give your licence back.' Need I even add to this the examples of movies like *Gone in 60 Seconds*, which makes stealing cars look like a fun and noble profession.

Don't underestimate the effect film and television have on the formation of values and habits in young people.

A recent YouthSCAN survey by Australian company Qantum Market Research showed that 70% of Generation Yers thought that Australia was becoming a society of haves and have nots. The rich are getting richer and the poor, poorer, and Generation Y know it. They know that somewhere, someone is making a buck out of 'this' and they will be tentative before committing to anything they feel may not be kosher.

What about Generation Y watching their heroes be completely hammered and taken to pieces by the media, warranted or not? How would a 15-year-old boy feel as he watches his hero, say Shane Warne, crucified by the media as they expose his personal life on every television channel and in every newspaper in the country because a woman in England says Shane was stalking her with perverted text messages? What about the Princess of Wales, killed as she tries to flee the constant barrage of the media and their invasion of her personal life? What about David and Victoria Beckham and the claims made about them? What is an impressionable teenager supposed to think?

And what of our politicians' 'core promises'? Isn't a promise supposed to be a promise? Well, not according to our politicians. It is all right to break some promises, if they are not core promises? Although, from the United States, no Australian Generation Yer missed the debacle of then President Bill Clinton and his 'sexual relations'. And to think people complain that Generation Y are a little disengaged from the political leadership in this country. Of course they are. I hear, and so would many members of Generation Y, that Australia is going to spend $50 billion on tanks and missiles and unmanned planes for the military over the next ten years. Generation Y would have probably heard it on the radio on the way to school. That is to a school with old and out-of-date textbooks, no toilet seats and horrible toilet paper, no money for a decent gymnasium or sporting equipment, where they can no longer go on a school camp because the school can't afford the insurance. A school where they will have to sit in a cockroach-ridden, ageing classroom with as many as 30 other students who are either focused and paying attention, or doing their utmost to destroy the learning for everyone else. The teacher would love to do something about all of this, but has no resources to do it with, has too many kids in the classroom in the first place, and has no rights to discipline those who play up anyway, so why bother. Maybe the government should use their missiles to flatten some of these schools and rebuild ones that will instill a sense of pride in those who work there and attend school there. (I am seriously pissed off about this. Can you tell?)

And while we are at it, why not mention the quality of customer service the average teenager gets when he or she walks into a café or a shop. NONE! You wonder why the Generation Yers on your front line have no customer service skill? It is because they don't know the meaning of good customer service. Why? They have never experienced it. A huge mistake, by the way. Generation Y are considered to be a very powerful consumer group, not just because of their own money but because of the influence they exert on their parents' purchasing choices.

Basically Generation Y have an issue with trust. They don't believe much of what they hear or read. And that includes what you tell them about your company in the interview, and what your mission statement says you stand for. They want to see for themselves, first hand, what you are like. They are well aware that companies have PR departments who are excellent at creating spin for the world to see and hear, and they would much rather experience for real what the culture inside your business is like before they decide to believe anything you say about what a wonderful place it is to work. The implications for HR and marketing are obvious.

Generation Y have an issue with trust.

Optimistic

Despite all of this, Generation Y are very optimistic. A YouthSCAN survey showed that 86% rated themselves as very happy or pretty happy, up from 39% a decade earlier when Generation X were surveyed. Only 5% were unhappy. Sure, 40% were worried about getting a job, but that is down from 60% when the latter years of Generation X were surveyed. Despite the horror events of Bali and September 11, only 1% of Generation Y thought the future would be terrible, according to the same YouthSCAN survey. The same survey indicated that governments give Generation Y very little confidence.

The exposure that Generation Y have had through the media and online is not all bad. They have seen many a young star made on shows like *Australian Idol*, and occasionally, the current affairs shows profile a young success story. Dreams do come true! There are ever-increasing numbers of speakers going into schools, motivating and inspiring Generation Yers to follow their hearts and live their dreams and, being mainly the children of Baby Boomers, it is little surprise that they understand the power of positive thinking. After all, it was the Boomers, more than any other generation, who fuelled the growth of the personal development industry. A topic, by the way, that Generation Y are open to and enthusiastic about. And one that could be profitably applied by business. Personally developed people produce professional results.

Confused then focused

Generation Y are actually quite confused. It may seem like an odd juxtaposition to be optimistic about the future and still not know what you are going to do. When my Mum finished high school she had two choices: she could either become a teacher or a nurse. She and her best friend decided they would be teachers. That was until her best friend was given a scholarship to do nursing and took it. Women could also marry and have children. So few choices usually makes the decision easier. Today, however, just pick up the latest university course guide and see how many courses are now available. And that is just university. There are so many options, Generation Y just do not know what to choose. Add to that the pressure they feel to be successful and you have a confused and, at times, very stressed generation. The juxtaposition of 'confused' with 'optimistic' exists because Generation Y demand choice. Variety. Just because they are stressed and confused does not mean they want fewer options.

Generation Y demand choice.

Let me add to this. By the time the best Generation Y talent are applying to work in your organisation, they are much more focused and know what they want. In fact, they probably have a five-year plan and want to know how you will help them achieve it. This, I think, is one of the most powerful opportunities for organisations. If, by working for you, Generation Y are not limiting their options, they will be attracted to your organisation. If you can genuinely offer career advancement, as well as benefits such as travel, you will be very popular among Generation Y. I was in a meeting recently with the founding director of a successful recruiting company, who claimed that some of the big corporations are fairing much better than the small to medium enterprises in the war for Generation Y talent because the former have so many options to offer potential candidates.

It is deeper than just providing answers to career options. Generation Y are looking for something to believe in. If you can give them a cause to work for, and some meaning to their work, they will be attracted to your company. With Generation Y's commitment, you will see the best of their creativity and enthusiasm.

Generation Y are looking for something to believe in.

Executive Summary

Generation Y are a sceptical bunch, although this has not made them cynical or pessimistic. Generation Y and their scepticism means:

- They demand the rationale behind any request or instruction.
- They do not believe everything they see and hear.
- They are optimistic.
- They are confused at the school leaver age and very focused by the time they exit tertiary education.

Generation Y's scepticism presents corporations with opportunities:

- Companies who can be authentic and genuinely offer career opportunities for Generation Y will win the war for talent.
- Companies who can be a little more creative in the way they advertise their jobs will attract a better quality of candidate than those who advertise in more traditional ways.
- Managers who manage from a place of sincerity will be able to earn the respect and trust of their Generation Y employees and therefore get better performance from them.

Of course, Generation Y and their scepticism will pose some massive challenges for all businesses:

- Traditional advertising is much less effective with Generation Y than it has been for other generations, and a new, less cut and dried, but more authentic form of advertising is required. This includes employment advertising as well. The advertising will hinge on word of mouth endorsement, which is not vested in corporate interest. Strength of the brand and quality of the product will be powerful factors.

- The 'one day all this can be yours' speech will not work for Generation Y in the way it has motivated Baby Boomers in the past. Again, a more practical and genuine approach needs to be taken.
- Generation Y will be indecisive and 'jumpy'. Retention, job satisfaction and productivity will suffer as a result. Managers must take a coaching role and help map out a clear and mutually beneficial career path for their Generation Y staff. Generation Y are used to being nurtured and will respond positively to this kind of approach, providing it is genuine.

Impatient

<Definition: Lacking tolerance and patience. Restlessly eager>

'We want it all. We have a lot to aspire to, but a lot of the time we want it the easy way. Technology has allowed us to become increasingly lazier at times ... not to say we are lazy. At the same time we have become preoccupied with the materialistic and what's "in". It is not enough to get into uni, we want it to be a city uni. It is not enough to get a job, it has to offer perks ... The list goes on.' – **Generation Yer**

Patience is a virtue. Good things come to those who wait. YEAH RIGHT! Those who spend their life waiting get run over by the people who are doing. You can't tell me you believe either of these statements to be true. We all live in a world obsessed by speed. Just think elevators, bank-teller lines, fast food, and your need to constantly upgrade your computers. Doctors and sociologists have even invented a new disorder called 'hurry sickness'. Sociologists have also shown that, as a society increases its wealth and education, there is a corresponding increase in tension regarding time within that society. Australia has increased in both wealth and levels of education as Generation Y have grown up, so it is little wonder they are a little tense about time. They aren't just a little tense. They have no concept of time. It should be instant, and if it is not, then it is not good enough. Gone are the days when something of quality was represented by the time it took to create and get access to. For Generation Y, the faster the better.

They have no concept of time. It should be instant, and if it is not, then it is not good enough.

'They are just so demanding, and can be aggressive. Particularly if they know they are good. They just won't wait for anything. Compared to Generation Y, the Xers were not at all assertive about money.'

Deborah Stonley,
Henry Davis York

They got this trait from their parents, and the society they grew up in. The average time the door of an elevator stays open before it automatically closes is between two and four seconds according to Otis. You would scarcely believe this when you look at the buttons on the console and find the only one that no longer has the writing on it is the 'door close' button. Some of our greatest dilemmas take place in elevators. You know the door is starting to close but you see someone running for the elevator, asking you to hold the door, and you look at them as if you are going to do it but then don't, or you pretend you did not even see them. Why? Because you are in such a rush to do whatever it is you need to do.

Let's not get off track. I think you get the point. Generation Y have been raised in a world where speed is king! As such, they are an extremely impatient generation. Impatient about everything. They want to be rich now. They want to be the manager now. They want their food now. Generation Y are like Type A personalities cubed. Their intensity, success-driven attitude, and their tendency to separate effort from reward can be translated to mean 'we want what we want NOW!'. Part of what the information age and advances in technology have done to society is to make us even more impatient. Now you get any product you want, at any time of the day or night, by simply logging onto the net and buying it. The chances are, it will be shipped the next day, quite possibly with no human hand even touching it. Plus, we have our multimillionaire, 20-year-old internet start-up entrepreneurs. Success truly does come young, and you can generally have what you want fairly quickly, providing you can pay for it, thanks mainly to the internet. The problem is that not everything works that way. Least of all success and career development.

'They are just so thirsty. They want everything today. They want to be the managing director tomorrow.'

Linda Botter,
Lion Nathan Australia

Ambitious, verging on an obsession with progression

The competitive nature with which Generation Y have grown up has made them very ambitious. As we said in the chapter titled Lifestyle Centred, Generation Y are success centred. Much of Generation Y's entertainment has consisted of organised sport and computer games, both of which are competitive. Plus, the sheer pressure to perform well at school, and then to find the best job, has made them well accustomed to competition. Put simply, Generation Y want to be successful and they want to be successful now. If this involves changing jobs 50 times to keep climbing, then so be it. Long-term employment in the one organisation will be seen by Generation Y as a sign of weakness rather than as a sign of good character.

Their blatant ambition is great for business because they present as an enthusiastic, keen-to-learn new workforce coming your way. The challenge will be keeping them happy when they are not on the fast track, and explaining to them that they are yet to prove they deserve to be on the fast track. As opposed to genuinely working their way through the ranks, Generation Y will rely on their charm and interview ability to apply for a better job at another company as opposed to sticking it out with you. They will apply for jobs above their experience and skill level, and demand such opportunities from you.

Like you didn't already know that retention is, or is going to be, a problem when it comes to Generation Y. They want to climb the proverbial ladder fast. They will not wait around for you. If they feel they have the ability and you are not giving them an opportunity, they will go and find it elsewhere. In fact, you might as well just resign yourself to the fact that Generation Y will be on the lookout for a new job all the time. Even if they do not genuinely want to leave your business they will look anyway. They will look just in case there is an even better position out there. They are optimistic, after all. They will look in order to stay abreast of the job market and to be sure they are getting fairly compensated for their work.

Combine this with Generation Xers beginning to look for a better life and more balance, an ageing population, and a business environment that exists more and more on the intellectual capital of people, and it is no wonder the experts are calling it a War for Talent.

Some of the keys to better retention we have already discovered, such as a good supervisor/manager, variety, fun, purpose, and genuine support. There is a whole chapter devoted to this later. Open, honest and regular communication are essential. If you promised quarterly performance reviews, then you had better deliver quarterly performance reviews. There will also be an education process required. You will need to make sure Generation Y understand that pay rises and promotions are linked to productivity and performance, not just to how confident they are. Generation Y will want training, and expect that you will give it to them. They want you to give them the education they need to climb the ladder. Just like their parents did for them. They will want the best training, the best resources and the best facilities in order to get the job done. And from time to time you will need to explain the dynamics of the two-way street that is known as work!

The great divide (between desire and competency)

Sure, Generation Y are ambitious, and they are keen to learn, but do they have the ability to deliver the goods at the higher positions they demand? Herein lies a massive problem for all organisations, and for Generation Y themselves. I call it the great divide. And I am not talking about the gap between generations. I am talking about the competency of a Generation Y employee and the level of responsibility and compensation he or she thinks they deserve. More simply put, Generation Y think they are better than they are. Sure they offer some wonderful things, and truly are an exceptional asset to any organisation, however, at times their expectations and demands exceed their proven skill and competency level. How do you manage this? How do you keep Generation Y focused and motivated to progress, but also have them acknowledge their real level of skill? You, of course, don't come straight out and tell them they are not yet good enough so bad luck. You will need to provide all the usual support. Perhaps the best way is to have Generation Y partially involved in new, more sophisticated projects. Maybe let them do a different job under your supervision. The only way they will develop the skills and competence is if you give them the opportunity to try to learn.

Training and development are the key. The way to help Generation Y mature and enhance their competency will hinge largely on training. Training will give them the opportunity to learn what they need to, and your job as the manager will be to allow them to use it, as soon as possible, in a well-supported environment.

One of my current sales staff, a Generation Yer to whom I have already referred in this book, told me three months into her job that she thought entering surveys was beneath her. One of her responsibilities was to enter all the email addresses we receive from our seminar participants' surveys. There are usually 1000 plus a week, but 'beneath her' was a little pretentious I thought. Needless to say, I had to again make it clear that this is a crucial task, and that even though it is not very exciting, there is a very good reason for it. As soon as I gave a pragmatic justification for the task, she had no problem doing it.

'Burger flipping is not beneath your dignity. Your grandparents had a different name for it; they called it opportunity.'
– Bill Gates (allegedly)

Great line. Whether he truly delivered that speech or not, I don't know, but I love that line. Generation Y do not want to start at the bottom. They despise the very thought of it. They want to start at least in the middle. And if they do start at the bottom they do not intend to be there for very long.

Control

I mentioned in the introduction to the chapter Stimulus Junkies that Generation Y are becoming more and more in control of what they see on their screens. This applies not only to their entertainment. They are a latchkey generation. In other words, they have their own key to the house, come and go as they please (to a certain extent), and are left to take charge of their own life from a very young age (but are given ample support and finances to do this). Dual-income families and single-parent families, and chequebook parenting are clearly the contributing factors. Generation Y are in control of what they do and when they do it most of the time. Even at school, teachers don't have the authority to stop them or discipline them. Of course, this will affect the attitude they take into the workforce. The problem is that the workforce is hardly going to embrace the 'I am in charge, and this is how I want things to be' attitude, especially from a 22 year old.

People-orientated managers are the solution. Managers who know how to communicate and influence people, and are willing to acknowledge the other party's point of view and then gently explain some other alternatives and the rationale behind those alternatives, will be able to disarm the inherent assertiveness of these confident Generation Yers. More on how to do this later.

Separating Effort from Reward

As we have seen, all of this has resulted in a generation that separates effort from reward. They expect high salaries just for showing up, discounting any need to make a contribution. I call it their appearance fee. Generation Y just don't get that they are expected to give the business a return on their investment – the investment being the weekly wage. Managers will need to educate Generation Y employees that they are not superstar athletes and that the term 'appearance fee' does not apply to them. But they will need to do it in a way that inspires the employee to learn more and develop more so they truly can add value to the business.

Eric Chester, author of *Generation WHY*, a book written about this generation for the United States business market, has a great metaphor for describing this characteristic of

Generation Y. He says Generation Yers think DVD, not VCR. If you think about a VCR, no matter what part of a film you want to watch you need to start at the beginning and move your way through to the end. You may be able to fast forward the process or rewind, but you still need to pass through all the sequences of events that occur between the beginning and the end. However, DVD is different. You can instantly click to the scene you want to view. And this is how most Generation Y toys work. Click a button and what you want is there at your fingertips.

Generation Y's obsession to get what they want without investing the effort is rampant even in computer games. There are codes you can enter into games that allow you to skip to whatever level you wish, or give you unlimited lives or whatever. They are called cracks or cheats. Even the game EverQuest has these cracks. When players began trading weapons and cracks online, Sony Corporation, who own the software company that developed EverQuest, tried to ban it because they thought it violated the integrity of the game when so many other people were trying to succeed in Norrath playing by the rules. And it is not just computer games. The increased popularity of fast food and snack foods is simply an extension of our society's impatience and busyness. Generation Y are products of such a society.

A further result of Generation Y's tendency to separate effort from reward is the emergence of a 'you owe me' attitude. Generation Y rarely appreciate the things you do for them. It is as if they are entitled to the best training, the day off for their friend's 21st or whatever else you give them out of the ordinary obligation you have as their employer. Yet when they do something, even if it is just a part of their job description, they expect praise and they want it to be public. Managers may need to remember who is the older of the two parties, and to swallow their ego and not expect Generation Y to understand just how much is done for them or how good they have it, and to continue to offer appreciation for what they do. I am not saying you have to fold to the demands of Generation Y, but genuine appreciation for work they do will be an excellent way to get them to buy-in. A simple start would be with the words 'Thank you'.

Quite disturbing, as discovered in earlier chapters, is the amount of debt that Generation Y are already in. In the CPA Australia study previously quoted, 62% of Generation Y respondents see debt as an acceptable method to get now what they want and to do more of what they want to do. The point being, borrowing allows them to get what they want now without having to engage in the discipline of saving first. Or as I like to say, it allows them to separate effort from reward.

Demanding

I recently came across an insightful report from Mercer Human Resource Consulting in the United States, which highlights the demanding nature of Generation Y. It was done in 2002 when the eldest Generation Yer was 24. Although it is a US survey, it illustrates perfectly the point that Generation Y are very demanding in terms of work–life balance, workplace training and opportunities, and management feedback and mentoring.

Despite rating their employment experience more positively than any other age group in areas such as work–life balance, quality of training and their companies reputation for good customer service, the Generation Yers were the least satisfied overall in terms of job satisfaction.

Put simply, Generation Y have higher standards for how they should be treated in the workplace. It takes much more to keep them satisfied than the workers that have gone before them.

Interactivity (again)

One of the keys to understanding Generation Y is to understand 'interactivity'. Generation Y want some say in what they do and how they do it. They want to be involved, and to feel like they are important. Given their resourcefulness and creativity, it could be well worth your while to do just this. Invite them to share ideas about how you could make their job more interesting. You will be surprised. I could almost guarantee they will come up with a way that is more fun for them, and quite possibly, even more efficient for you, not to mention the improvements in retention you would see.

Instant Communication

Generation Y, as we already know, are a connected generation. They like to be contactable and expect you to be the same. I drive many of my Generation Y friends insane because I rarely have my mobile phone on. As a speaker and consultant, it is a little hard to have it on all the time. It is not good enough that I have someone manning the phones in my business five days a week and who can take messages and pass them on to me. No, my friends need to talk to me when they want to talk to me, not a few hours later. Look at the proliferation of SMS messages from mobile phones and instant messaging over the net. For Generation Y, snail mail actually means email, not traditional post. The thought of sending anything by traditional post is beyond comprehension for a Generation Yer. The problem is, their messages are hard to understand if you are not familiar with Gen'y'ese.

So what does this mean for you the manager? Be accessible. If your Generation Yer has to stew about something which happened in their shift, particularly if it is a problem they are having at work, and you have not given them the opportunity to talk it over with you, there is a distinct possibility that they may have already decided to move on, will have applied online to ten different places, and accepted a position down the road doing the same thing. All before their next shift. You might also want to keep your inter-office and down-the-line communication short and to the point, because no-one, particularly Generation Y, wants to read copious amounts of information.

From a recruiting point of view, if your selection process is long and arduous, you will lose many potential Generation Yers because they will not wait around for your decision. The degree of impatience here depends very much on the level of position you are talking about. The more entry level the position is, the faster you will need to respond.

Executive Summary

Generation Y are impatient. Their impatience manifests itself as:

- Ambition
- Always being on the lookout for something better
- A certain delusion about personal ability and competence
- A desire to be involved in the process of designing their workplace activities and how they do them
- A tendency to separate effort from reward and a desire for instant gratification
- A 'you owe me' attitude
- A need for instantaneous communication and speedy feedback

The impatience of Generation Y offers business major opportunities:

- They are ambitious and eager to learn and do more. A motivated person in need of skills is more valuable to your company than an unmotivated employee with all the skills
- Impatience + Resourcefulness = Efficiency and Increased Productivity

As always, there are some serious challenges:

- Overeager Generation Yers have an easily bruised ego and will jump ship at any sign of potential advancement.
- Generation Y will not want to start at the bottom; as with any other DVD they will expect to be able to flick to whatever stage they want.
- You can train and train and train your Generation Y employees, but unless you give them the opportunity to use their new skills, your investment will be wasted. Window-dressing this 'Development of People' stuff is not going to work with Generation Y.
- There will be a clear skills gap between what Generation Y profess to be capable of and what they will realistically be able to produce. Your job is to fill the gaps.

- Managers will need to be more mature in the way they deal with Generation Y and, hardest of all, will need to release their need to be acknowledged and give that gift to their Generation Y employees instead.
- Recruiting and selection processes in some instances will need to be sped up. More on that in Part 2.

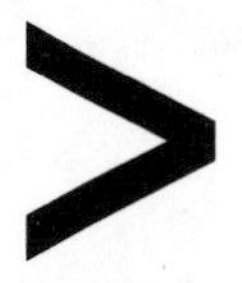

What Generation Y Want

This chapter is designed to give you a short-cut view of what Generation Y want from a workplace, a boss and a job. Although we go into detail regarding many Best Practices for managing Generation Y later, if you at least understand these principles you will be able to take a constructive view of all of your practices and know which will be effective and which will not. And that is my challenge to you. Don't just read the seven things Generation Y want from a boss and move on, take a look at how you, your supervisors and managers 'manage', and decide where you may be able to make significant improvement. Then take a look at what they want from a workplace and evaluate whether you are offering this. Your recruiting challenges may simply lie in changing the language or focus of what you offer youthful candidates. As you will discover, some suggestions simply won't suit you and your organisation, and ultimately, you will need to take from this book what is relevant for you and devise the most effective practices to meet the needs of your team, division or business. This chapter could easily have been a summation after I introduced all the techniques, but I think it is more valuable for you to look at these desires now, to start your brain thinking about better ways to do things; these will be reinforced and added to as you read the rest of the book.

I strongly believe that these desires of Generation Y are actually those of all workers, at some level. Recently, in a conversation with a HR consultant, I was discussing how most challenges that Generation Y are presenting to employers are actually beginning to apply across the board. Many Baby Boomers are opting out of the workforce to pursue a better quality of life, and just as many Generation Xers are turning their back on the promises of 'one day all this will be yours' and getting out and starting their own businesses. If you, as an organisation, were to become more Generation Y friendly, you would by default become more employee friendly. You would clearly be an employer of choice. This is because Generation Y want the same things we all want from a job, the only difference being that they expect it. Or, more powerfully, they demand it.

Due to supply and demand, for Generation Y the power truly lies in the hands of the individual, not the company. An employee of yours knows that he or she can get what they want somewhere else, and that if you aren't prepared to give it to them they will happily look elsewhere. And in my head I can hear the Baby Boomers screaming, 'Where is the loyalty?' Well, I ask you the same question. Where is the loyalty? Why are so many talented young lawyers and architects and IT professionals being forced to work on a contract basis? Why are there so many casual opportunities but very little permanent part-time work? Why? Because no-one wants to make a commitment to employees. There is no such thing anymore as a job for life, or in some cases a job for a few years. Yet you expect undying and unwavering loyalty to your company or firm. Not going to happen!

From a Job

Purpose and meaning> It sounds obvious, but Generation Y want their job to have a purpose. They need to feel as though it actually makes a difference and contributes in some way. Now, that does not necessarily mean in a truly philanthropic way, it may simply mean that they contribute to the goals of the company. Let me give you an example. A Generation Y friend of mine is on the graduate program at a very prestigious law firm. He hates one thing about his job

'Generation Y want REAL work.'

David Cvetkovski,
Ford Australia

'Generation Y don't want little graduate jobs. They want big meaty projects that give them a chance to prove themselves.'

Linda Botter,
Lion Nathan Australia

with a passion (his words not mine). He hates it when he gets what he calls everyone else's 'shit work'. By that, he is referring to the instances when he gets handed a brief from an already settled case, and his job is to make duplicates for the interested parties and file the firm's documentation. He says it is like being a glorified file boy. Remember, he has spent more than $30,000 and six years of his life studying, and he is now a fully-fledged solicitor. He says he doesn't mind doing some of the menial tasks, but he would at least expect to have been involved in the case when it was still active. He acknowledges that you must have the bad with the good, but he doesn't appreciate everyone else's bad. He knows that the case is settled and his work makes no noticeable contribution to the client's condition.

'Generation Y want to do work that actually makes a contribution.'

Edward Kaleel,
Marc Edward Agency

If your organisation does make a noticeable contribution to society, be sure to point that out to your Generation Y staff. Ensure they know what they do impacts that contribution, and that what the company does makes a difference. This new breed of talent does not work for the sake of working. It has to have meaning or a result.

Responsibility> Generation Y value and will respond positively to increased responsibility. In fact, they will expect to get some responsibility. Responsibility makes them feel important, like they are significant and valued in the business. To continue to use my solicitor friend as an example, this is what he said to me over lunch a little while ago: 'Fuck acknowledgment. I want challenge, good work and responsibility.' We already know what he means by good work, and we will discuss shortly the desire for a challenge, but let's focus on responsibility. I said, 'You are charged out at over $100 an hour, you deal with real clients and real cases, surely that is responsibility enough?' He went on to explain there are two types of responsibility. There is the 'figure it out' kind of responsibility and the 'do this' kind of responsibility.

'Figure it out' responsibility is the good stuff. It is when you are given a brief of a real-life situation and asked to do some research and come back with your findings. He said it requires you to use your brain, make mistakes and seek guidance, and ultimately places you under genuine pressure to produce a good result for your boss and client.

The 'do this' responsibility, he says, is not really responsibility at all. It is when you are given a hypothetical case, usually from the past, and asked to read it, learn the facts of the case and make suggestions from your research. My friend likens it to a 'mock trial' at high school. (Mock trial is a hypothetical court simulation game played by students in a make-believe courtroom.)

The message here is that they want REAL responsibility.

Promotional opportunity> It comes as no surprise that an ambitious group of people like Generation Y desperately want promotional opportunity. They are dying to make their mark in the world, and to climb the proverbial ladder. My friend, after all his hard work and his highly sought-after job in a prestigious law firm, is considering trying to get a job in finance. Why? I asked. Because there is scope to move up the ladder more quickly.

Another colleague works in marketing in Sydney. She said the most important thing for her in her current position was 'the opportunity to develop and progress in my career'.

'Generation Y are very attracted to the clear and achievable career path at HDY. We focus on promoting partners from within the firm and Generation Y like that.'

Deborah Stonley,
Henry Davis York

New challenges and experiences> Generation Y, being stimulus junkies, want authentic participatory experiences. And these had better be challenging. They want to work on the cool projects that count. They want to travel to interesting locations that challenge them physically and intellectually. A recent *Business Review Weekly* article mentioned that this is becoming relevant for all employees, not just at work, but on holidays as well. The article indicated that white-collar workers wanted a vacation that tested them, after which they felt they had accomplished something, rather than a vacation where they sat by the pool drinking pina coladas.

As you will discover a little further into the book, Generation Y will be attracted to jobs and companies that offer this. One of the keys to turning a job, a project, or a task into an experience is to make it interactive. Generation Y have a deep desire to be involved in crafting their activities. Just remember they think DVD (interactive and digital), not VHS (linear).

Fair compensation>You have really got to keep up with the 'Joneses' when it comes to salaries and wages for Generation Y even though it has been shown time and time again that money by itself is a short-term and ultimately ineffective motivator. Not having fair compensation will be an instant demotivator. Generation Y will disengage if they feel as though they are being taken advantage of in any way. You may even like to pay just a little bit more; that way you will be seen as being more than fair.

Increased employability> Generation Y take jobs to build their resume. Let me give you an example – not from Australia, but an excellent example nonetheless. A well-established firm in the United States, the Southwestern Company, employs approximately 3000 college students over their summer break, and has been doing so for over a century. The firm offers no guarantee of salary, requiring an average 80 hours per six-day week during the holidays. Oh, and the work sucks! Door-to-door sales of books. Rejection after rejection. Not only that, but recruits have to pay for their own travel, accommodation, and other expenses, and are required to do a one-week training course for which they do not get paid. Over 30,000 people applied. Why so many, despite everything against it? Employability (and the opportunity to make plenty of money). There is courage in accepting a commission-only job, and many US employers know just how hard

'What Generation Y want to know are the intangibles. How are you going to develop me?'

Linda Botter,
Lion Nathan Australia

the Southwestern experience is. Hence, working for Southwestern looks good on the resume.

Other activities such as training, and unique projects, can increase the employability of your young staff and as such, are attractive elements of a company or job. It almost seems paradoxical, and perhaps it is, that you should be trying to enhance the resume of your Generation Y staff, because they might just take all that training and experience somewhere else. Sure they might, but not before at least using some of it with you. And if you continue to provide 'what they want' they will continue to use that extra skill in your organisation, giving you a more productive workforce. Plus, you do it to other companies. If we all trained and developed our young people we would all benefit. More importantly though, if you are an organisation that greatly enhances the resume of your staff, you will be viewed as an employer of choice and will attract the best talent. You can't be an attractive option for young talent if you do not increase their employability.

'The number one attraction of Ford to graduates is that we have an intensive and well-structured development program. It is by far and away the most important thing the best Generation Y talent are looking for. To be developed. They even ask questions as specific as "Where will I be in three years as a result of joining your company?".'

David Cvetkovski,
Ford Australia

Individuality and creativity> Abraham Maslow, the popular psychologist in the 1950s, believed that humans have a hierarchy of needs. In his original work, at the pinnacle of his pyramid-based hierarchy, was self-actualisation. He said the highest need as a human develops consciousness is self-expression. It seems that Generation Y are an extremely 'conscious' and 'aware' generation. They are not just aware of social issues and the environment, but of their own needs and desires. They want to express their individuality. They want a vehicle for their creativity and knowledge, and they expect a job to give them that. Allowing individuality will be key in retaining and engaging your young talent.

'The key to engaging Generation Y is to be clear and upfront about expectations and limitations, and to set boundaries that still allow them to explore their individuality and creativity.'

Edward Kaleel,
Marc Edward Agency

From a workplace

'One of the keys to our excellent retention of Generation Y is that we are willing to be flexible. We even have two lawyers who telecommute which is almost unheard of in this industry.'

Deborah Stonley,
Henry Davis York

Flexibility> Being as lifestyle centred as they are, Generation Y will expect a degree of flexibility in their workplace. Whether that be flexibility in regards to dress, or scheduling or flexibility in a work program will depend on where and for whom they work. I think this is something that businesses are beginning to attempt experimenting with: working from home, beanbag rooms, in-house coffee shops and the like. That does not mean they are doing it well, but at least some are trying. Technology is making telecommuting and flexible working hours more possible every day, and they will continue to emerge as a key aspects of an employer of choice.

To again quote some great research by Mercer, one of their surveys showed that 82% of Generation Y cited flexible working arrangements as a factor that influenced their motivation and commitment, compared to the average of other age groups (Generation X and Baby Boomers) where between 58% and 69% said it was a factor influencing their motivation and commitment.

Ethical> The increased 'consciousness' and 'awareness' we spoke about is also going to have a serious effect on the way organisations are perceived in the talent marketplace. If you have questionable business practices, do serious damage to the environment, and create negative social consequences through the operation of your business, you will be black-marked by talented young people. They will not only boycott the products of such companies, but they won't want to work for them either. I recall a leadership program I presented for a prominent Australian retailer in which more than 70% of the people in the program named their current CEO when asked who they looked up to in the world, dead or alive. Answers included Gandhi and Nelson Mandela among others. I almost fell off my chair. Not that it was totally outrageous, because the CEO was one of my business heroes, but to hear so many internal staff share that opinion was very impressive. Further investigation revealed that it was his 'integrity' that made him so admirable. Integrity! That should be a part of every business's STRATEGY, not just their PR-produced Mission Statement.

Fun> I don't care how serious the work is, there is no excuse for not making the workplace fun. We don't need a massive Gallup poll to prove (though there probably is one) that workers who have fun at work are more productive than those who don't. What are you doing in your organisation to make it more fun? Generation Y will be attracted to workplaces that are fun. A great Australian example of someone who has done this well is Janine Allis and her Boost Juice stores. Those places are electric. Full of weird and wacky young customer service stars who make great smoothies while they dance and hum their favourite tune as it pumps through the speakers in the store. And they are seriously busy stores. It is not just an experience for the staff, but for the customer as well.

There is a great lesson to be learnt from our youth that we could remind ourselves of every now and then. No matter how serious the situation is, it is still possible to have fun. I think one of the most powerful things about having a more youthful mindset is that it generates a more playful attitude, and this makes the workplace more enjoyable, stimulating and, importantly, more productive.

'Something that has made the Marc Edward Agency attractive to Generation Y is the variety of the roles. Our account executives and promotional staff are working on new projects and brands every week. They love this variety and the fun environment within which they get the opportunity to work.'

Edward Kaleel,
Marc Edward Agency

Belong and be engaged> Generation Y NEED to feel as though they belong. It is part of human nature really, the need to feel part of something. If you merely give uninteresting tasks to your young talent, the chances of them feeling as though they belong are very slim. If you want to truly engage them, then you are going to need to keep them in the loop. Communication is the key here, and specifically, communication about the business as a whole and how their role contributes to that business.

Part of making people feel they belong is creating a social atmosphere in the workplace. Do your teams have anything to do with each other outside work? Do you have regular gatherings for staff that are not specifically related to 'work'? If there is one saying I hate in the business world it is this: 'It's business. It's not personal. It's business.' Business, and especially good business, is all personal. How can it not be? Business is conducted by people and relies almost entirely on trust and relationships to work. Of course business is personal, and the sooner we realise this and make it part of our cultures and the way we manage our people, then the better off companies will be. I cannot emphasise this point strongly enough. Generation Y want to be treated with respect, they want to be engaged in the affairs of the company and they want to form relationships with their workmates.

Modern and edgy> Are you hip? Don't worry, I'm actually talking about being on the cutting edge. I am not sure that going and creating open-plan offices, beanbag rooms, and letting everyone work from home a couple of days a week is going to be enough. In fact, in some organisations, not only will it not work, it is just not possible. By saying Generation Y expect a workplace to be modern and edgy refers to how 'up to date' your workspace and operations are. What is your décor like? What condition is your office equipment in? Is your technology (hardware and software) up to date, or are you doing things the old way because that is how you have always done things in your department? You can be sure that if there is a funky new device or piece of technology that can do what you currently do faster and better, then Generation Y will already know about it and are just waiting for you to start using it.

'We have a young staff, and positioning ourselves as being more modern than other firms has meant we've been able to attract a better quality of candidate.'

Deborah Stonley,
Henry Davis York

Stay current, and embrace technology where possible (and profitable). You will never stay ahead of Generation Y with your tech savvy but you will at least be able to keep within range of them.

Passion and optimism> I was at dinner recently with the Manager of Knowledge and Communication for a large division of an established Australian insurance company. He was relaying a story to me about his Generation Y son's friends, and how optimistic they are (his word not mine). He said they were just so confident about their ability and about their future. He was impressed to say the least. I call it 'self-esteem on steroids'.

Generation Y are truly optimistic and are motivated by what the future holds. If you want to attract and make profitable the best young talent in your organisation, then you better be giving them fuel for their optimistic outlook on life. Your culture better evoke passion in your people, and you should be portraying an optimistic, but realistic, vision of the future. If you are a pessimistic manager, get a new job. Management's key roles are inspiring people to excel, and developing talent.

Everyone wants permission to dream big dreams. Everyone wants to be inspired. This applies even to those more marginal and less than optimistic people. Generate some passion and inspiration in your workplace.

'The big thing at Ford is passion. It is all about passion for the business and the products. We want people who are driven and have a passion for our business and the "car" business.'

David Cvetkovski, Ford Australia

From a boss

Empowerment> Empowerment is such a fad word. However, the concept is here to stay. Generation Y expect their boss to give them the resources required to do their job well. And in essence, I think this is what being empowered is about: having the resources to do your job properly. Resources include the proper training, the equipment, the decision-making ability, and anything else that may be required to perform a set task.

Young team members will appreciate a boss who gives them a chance to do things on their own, the sort of 'figure it out' responsibility my Generation Y solicitor friend talked about. This is no different. Standing over the shoulder of your young staff and watching their every move is a sure-fire way to create resentment and a lack of respect from them. Empower your managers to empower their staff.

Mentored not directed> Thankfully, as we will discuss in more detail later, Generation Y are very coachable. They respond favourably to the 'manager as mentor', and negatively to the director manager. Generation Y do not like a boss who is 'bossy' in the way he or she gives orders. Common courtesy is not enough, though. Being a mentor is about giving regular, open and honest feedback. And not just at the quarterly performance review.

Young talent will want to be given the space to try new things, make a few mistakes and learn from them. They would much prefer this than to be told step by step how to do everything. It takes a great deal of confidence for a manager to manage this way, because it requires trust in your less-experienced team members. However, if you have properly empowered your staff, and they respect you, then this will not be a problem. If you create a culture in your team that says it is all right to make mistakes and it is all right to ask for guidance, then this kind of managing will be extremely effective.

Young talent will want to be given the space to try new things, make a few mistakes and learn from them.

Fairness> Generation Y value fairness. They will work well with a manager who treats everyone fairly. They don't mind high standards and accountability, as long as these are consistent across the board. It will be a tough line to walk for managers though, because Generation Y also want to be treated as individuals, though still expecting 'rule for one, rule for all'. If allowances are made for one member of the team, then similar allowances will need to be made for other members.

This fairness ethic spreads to the way a manager communicates with Generation Y. They will see it as hypocritical to be expected to treat their boss with 'respect' if none is shown to them. Why? Because it is just not fair. The golden rule has turned platinum. Treat your Generation Y staff as you would like to be treated.

Treat your Generation Y staff as you would like to be treated.

Recognition> I received one of the worst pieces of advice ever from one of my first bosses. He is an extremely successful entrepreneur and a man I like and respect deeply, but this advice was just plain wrong. He said to me to, 'Always find something wrong. Give them something to improve upon.' And I found he did the same to me. He always picked something I could have done better. After meetings, I could barely remember the positive things he had said, because I would be focusing on the thing he had said I did wrong. For example, I would work my heart out promoting an event that would see a measurable increase in profitability for the business, and he would suggest that next time I try to get an extra editorial article instead of paying for advertising space, or that I could have charged at the door to get in and we would have made even more money. It drove me nuts. Sure, there is a time and a place for constructive criticism, but 'always'? I don't think so. A better piece of advice would have been to always find something I did right.

Generation Y like a boss who recognises their contribution and accomplishments. At times this might be best done publicly or through a private 'thank you' as you pass by. Just some recognition. Might I add here though that recognition will not be enough on its own. Remember my solicitor friend and his outburst: 'Fuck acknowledgment – I want challenge, good work and responsibility'? However, remember also the saying that 'people come to work for companies but they leave bosses'. The little things are the big things.

Personal connection> This may sound like I am contradicting myself, having made the comment that the boss who taught me to always find something wrong was in fact wrong, when I say he also had one of the best retention rates of casual staff in the hospitality industry. Despite bugging me, and other staff, by always finding something wrong, I know the staff, prior to me taking over the reins, looked up to him and respected him. When researching the company, before accepting a position there, I chatted to staff over the bar, and asked what made him such a great boss. The answer was always the same: 'He treats us all like individuals. He understands that sometimes we need to take a night or two off for family things. He gives us presents on our birthdays that he must have really thought about.' When I asked him personally why he thought he was so effective at getting such high level buy-in from his staff, and why he had such great retention rates, he replied with two answers: 'Firstly, I recruit the right people and secondly, it is all about personal connection. People don't work for companies, they work for people. And if they don't like the person they work for, they either won't work or they just leave.' Great advice.

'The key to engaging talent of all ages is the leader. If the relationship with the leader is good, then achievement will follow.'

Linda Botter,
Lion Nathan Australia

If you have survived so far by employing technicians to be managers, you have been lucky, but I doubt you will continue to survive by doing this. The Generation Y attitude will make it impossible to retain key talent if your managers and supervisors are not exceptional people persons. They must make a personal connection with their staff because if they don't, Generation Y will hardly be inspired to invest their time and energy into making your company great. Key Lesson: Employ managers to manage, not technicians.

A good manager will get to know his or her staff individually. They will be genuinely interested in how each individual's life is going at, and outside of, work. All good managers know that the most significant barrier to good performance is far more often a personal challenge than genuine incompetence. The manager will then use this personal connection to get more from his or her staff, and to reward their team in more appropriate ways. For example, instead of giving a cash bonus you might organise a paid holiday to a resort or some other place a team member wanted desperately to go.

Involved and Valued> Your best young talent will want a boss who engages them in decision-making processes, seeks their thoughts and ideas on key projects, and generally values their input. In essence, we are talking about a manager who involves his or her staff and makes them feel valued. It may be as simple as having regular team meetings where you go around the table and get everyone's input, or just keeping the team informed of where things are going in the company, and suggesting they come and see you if they have any comments to make or value to add. Perhaps a suggestions box that you actually look at and respond to. What could you do as a boss, or what could your managers do, to involve younger staff at a deeper level?

Competency> While I stand by my statement that you need to promote a manager, not technicians, to management positions, I will also state that Generation Y will not tolerate incompetence. It sounds so arrogant to say that. 'Generation Y won't tolerate …' But it is true. As I have said previously, Generation Y take youthful arrogance to a new level. The thing is, now they will talk with their feet rather than put up with an incompetent, uninteresting and uninspiring work environment. Competence, in this sense, is not referring to the technical aspects of the job, but rather to the organising of the office and team to get the job done. A manager who forgets key meetings, who is not open to new ideas, who is on a power trip and so on is what I mean when I say incompetence. Call it Managerial Incompetence.

'Often the real challenge is not with Generation Y themselves, but with those that have to manage them. It is essential that they have the tools to deal with Generation Y.'

Deborah Stonley, Henry Davis York

Part Two >

Attracting Generation Y

Recruiting

Become a talent scout! Go after young talent. ACTIVELY recruit them. 'Active' being the operative word. Traditional recruiting practices won't cut it with this new generation. Let me rephrase that. If you want to win the War for Talent with the new generation, traditional recruiting practices won't work. And you can scarcely afford not to win in this new business environment. With the majority of the workforce now in service positions, and the microchip creating even further efficiency in both blue-collar and clerical procedures, the success of your organisation depends solely on the talent of your people, and how well you use that talent. It is no longer okay to polish yesterday's apples. You can't do what you have always done and get what you always got. If you do what you've always done, you will get nothing! Squat! Naught! Business needs to be innovative, fresh and on the cutting edge, and in order to be that, you need innovative, fresh people who live on the cutting edge.

The tough part about recruiting Generation Y is that they have been played up to, nurtured and made to feel important their whole life. The jobs that you would have thought were a great opportunity at their age, they believe are below their dignity. They will not grovel and come looking for you. They will stay in their Baby Boomer funded home waiting for you to come and find them. And as recruiters, we have contributed to this. Just go to your next industry or university careers fair and see what happens. See all the little gifts and gadgets we offer and the sign-on bonuses. Everything says we NEED and we WANT you. Generation Y know this. For the first time in our lives the power lies with the candidate. Generation Y have options. They know there is more than just your firm, or your company wanting to recruit. There are many, and Generation Y will use their bargaining power to get what they want. So what implications does this have for recruitment? Big! Lets start with: SEND YOUR HIRING MANAGERS ON A MARKETING COURSE!

Peter Sheahan's Seven Tips for Marketing to Generation Y

1> **It should always be about outcomes**
Concern yourself only with the benefits associated with your 'product' for the end user, be that status, money, image. Whatever! Just make sure your main marketing message is built on these outcomes and not on the fact that you have been in business for 100 years. Who cares?

2> **Use Generation Y to understand Generation Y**
Sometimes the best way to find out what your customers, or potential employees, want is to ask them. Get out and about – not a bloody focus group – and ask them. Then use this for number 1.

3> **Use Generation Y to communicate with Generation Y**
There are few more powerful endorsements than peer recommendation. Use Generation Y to attract Generation Y. They understand things about their peers that no textbook or focus group could ever help you to understand.

4> **Market to Generation Y where they hang out**
If you want to catch a crook, you need to go undercover and hang out with the crooks. If you want to appeal to

Generation Y I suggest you go and market where Generation Y is.

5> **Integrate everything online**
Nothing beats the internet and its power to build buzz for your product. Via chatrooms and instant messaging, a Generation Yer can communicate with thousands of people across the globe almost instantly. Use this powerful tool to help market and create a positive message about your brand that spreads through your target market like a virus.

6> **Use the power of association and the non-sell**
Stop selling. Generation Y have bullshit detectors on their foreheads, and marketing that seems like a hard sell will cause a Generation Yer to switch off instantly. Stop being sleazy and find a way to be authentic.

7> **Be authentic**
If you have to say it's cool, it's not. Stop trying to be something you are not. If you have to make stuff up about your product, or get some celebrity to endorse it, then the chances are the product probably sucks. Get to work on the product.

In order to find and attract the best talent, you will need to understand the power and importance of your brand. You will need to know what messages Generation Y respond to and in what mediums they look for them. You will have to do a SWOT (Strengths, Weaknesses, Opportunities, Threats) analysis; make sure you have a unique value proposition that appeals to the self-interest of Generation Y and that it is at the right price point. If none of that made sense, go and do a marketing course. NOW!

Many of the principles and ideas presented in this chapter on Recruiting come from marketing. Take, for example, the concept of a product having a Unique Value

Proposition; we should be talking about creating Employee Value Propositions. These would simply be: Why would a talented young person want to work for you? What do you offer that others can't? What is unique and valuable about your product – meaning the job you are trying to fill? These might seem like strange questions, but marketers have been asking them for years. They have also been asking where they might find people interested in their product, and what is the best way to communicate with them.

Where to start? Create a Talent Mindset in your organisation. Your managers should eat, drink and breathe talent. Your company should behave like a professional sports team, because like a professional sports team, its success hinges on the talent in its ranks. And it should start at the top. Talent should be a strategy thing, not something we give lip service too. I am forever reading about companies who claim to take this 'people thing' seriously, but who do very little in reality to make their organisations attractive to talented people. Ask yourself, is this a place where talented people would want to work? If not, what could you do differently that would make it so? Then put your people on 24/7 talent detail. Make every manager, every supervisor, and every project leader a certified 'talent scout'. Recruit talent at all levels of the organisation. Start with getting kick-ass call-centre staff, then develop them and unleash them into other areas, such as the marketing department. IT IS ALL ABOUT TALENT!

Criteria

Again, I don't aim to tell you what you already know about recruiting, and I know it goes without saying. Before you think about where to source candidates and how to attract them to your organisation, you had better first be very clear on exactly what you are looking for. That includes a precise job description, an understanding of the culture of the teams and environment in which this job will take place, and of course, primarily what character traits will create the best fit for that culture. Secondly, you must be clear about what skills will be required to perform that job.

What you are looking for in a candidate will determine where you look and how you will attempt to woo them. You certainly won't find all the various young talent available in all of the same places. As such, a clear understanding of the job and culture is important *before* you begin recruiting. Here are a few thoughts, starting with the usual stuff:

- **Write a precise job description.**
- **What skills will be required to perform this job?**
- **Which of these skills can be learnt on the job and which are absolute prerequisites?**
- **Where would you be most likely to find someone with these skills?**

Now let's consider the culture:

- **Who will this person be reporting to? What is that person like and what is their management style?**
- **What are the values and what is the culture of the prospective team and work environment where this person will be required to work?**
- **What character traits and attitudes will be required for someone to thrive working for such a manager, in such a team, and in such an environment?**
- **Where will you be most likely to find such people?**

Even as I reread these they seem like such basic concepts, yet so few people follow them. I know, for example, that in more than one national law firm, a lot of emphasis is placed on finding a well-rounded employee who has interests out of work, but within the organisation it is expected that people will work obscene hours (80+) to get ahead. Why employ someone with many outside interests if you are not going to make it possible for them to pursue them?

As a business professional, you will already be aware of the growing 'Hollywoodisation' of the workforce. By that I mean a movement away from heavy, overpopulated workforces to a core group of key talent (people) who team up with outside professionals and contractors to work on a project, only to disperse and return to where they started from at its completion. Just like Hollywood. The producer selects the movie (project), finds an appropriate director (team leader), recruits the best actors and camera people (talent) and shoots the movie (project). Upon completion, many involved go onto other movies, or even become unemployed, while the core group stay and begin work on a new project, using the same, or new, talent. This new kind of workplace means that we need to examine at an even deeper level what we are looking for. Do we want an addition to the core group of talent, or do we just need certain expertise for a certain project? It may turn out that you would be better looking for one of the more entrepreneurial types freelancing their expertise in such areas.

Source

In order to attract young talent, you will need to change the medium through which you communicate to your potential candidates. Then you will need to alter your message to attract them. Remember, new times require new ways. Don't just do what you have always done. For example, companies should place more emphasis on their own sourcing and attraction of talent as opposed to relying on recruitment companies. Generation Y do not appreciate the way the average recruitment consultant treats them in the recruiting process, and they may well be turned off your company from the experience.

Your Customers

An untapped resource. This is most relevant for fast food and retail outlets seeking entry-level Generation Y employees. Why not look for employees in your store? If they shop there or eat there they obviously like your product. McDonald's in the United States have cottoned on to this. Now when you order a burger at Macca's, the paper it is wrapped in also doubles as a job application. Seriously! When you go into Macca's you order not only a McChicken Burger but a McJob as well.

When you go into Macca's you order not only a McChicken Burger but a McJob as well.

Are you tapping into your customer base? This may be an issue for those with a more sophisticated client base, but hey, it is worth a thought. A close friend of mine, whose company I won't name, recruited two great people from the same client. He justifies it by saying if the original client organisation were great employers then the two people would never have left. Hmmm? Poaching. I don't know if this is always a great idea, but it is at least worth a thought.

Your Current Workforce

Generation Y are a connected bunch. They love working together, especially with their friends. If you have an excellent Generation Y employee, the chances are he or she will be friends with people of similar calibre and with similar interests. Ask your own staff if they know anyone who may like to apply for a position you have available. This technique offers several potential benefits:

> **Reduced recruiting costs**
> **A personal reference for the candidate (ie your current member of staff)**
> **A built-in friend in the workplace for your new worker**
> **Improved variety and job enjoyment for your referring, and new, staff member**
> **A sense of importance and an opportunity to contribute in a different way than normal for your existing employee**

Find your champions and have them refer you to some of their champion friends.

Obviously, there are some risks with 'refer-a-friend' style programs, however, I am suggesting a more targeted approach. Seek your best talent and ask them. I would not necessarily make it a formal thing. Like-minded people usually hang out together. We are talking here about real talent. People with flair, creativity and skill. Find your champions and have them refer you to some of their champion friends.

Strategic Alliances

I recently asked a group of HR professionals at a conference in Melbourne if they could name the three high schools closest to their top-performing stores or to their head office. None of them could tell me. None! These were people who came to the conference because they were having trouble attracting young workers into their apprenticeships and traineeship programs. Get your store managers to team up with local high schools. Start with the careers adviser. Teachers know that school is not for everyone, and as such, will welcome any opportunities you can offer their students to enter the workforce, where many of these potentially good kids will flourish. Better still for you, though, is that the teachers know first-hand who are the best candidates, and who are truly most interested and most capable of doing the job. They have taught these kids and interacted with them in some cases for as many as six years. Who better to help you select the best candidate?

It is not about quantity, it is about quality. Think about it. A careers adviser at the local high school will not send you someone who may embarrass them because the advisers need you as a resource. Schools are always looking for workplaces where students can do work experience and for people in business who might be willing to share some of their ideas and expertise with their students. You represent that for them and they will do whatever it takes to nurture that relationship, even for simple part-time jobs, Christmas casual positions and the like.

It was my careers adviser who encouraged me to pursue cadetship opportunities straight out of school with some of the big accounting firms.

For those of you looking for more mature candidates, do a similar thing with the careers department at local and interstate universities. You can advertise on university intranets for a very reasonable fee. Not only that, but universities often have expos on campus where you can actively recruit and showcase your organisation. Make the relationship personal, offer value where you can, because like everything in life, what goes around comes around.

Don't stop at the universities. Do the same with the private colleges and TAFE colleges. I am a big fan of private providers because they are working in a very competitive marketplace. They have to keep abreast of their fields, offer exceptional learning opportunities to students, and ensure their candidates are the most suitable for work because if they don't, students will simply go elsewhere. Competitive forces at their best. These providers are also more agile than the bureaucratic universities and can adjust to the needs of the employment landscape much faster. Most private courses require students to be doing real work experience for the entirety of their course. And often this is free for the employer. Could your business offer such opportunities to students? If so, embrace it because you will get to road test some great talent, and it costs you nothing. Plus, if they turn out to be someone you want they will already know your business processes and understand your culture, and thus will hit the ground running.

Recruit Where They Are

An infamous United States criminal was asked why he robbed banks. His reply? 'Because that is where the money is.' If you want talent, you need to recruit where talented people are. Different strokes for different folks. If you are a professional service firm looking for the best graduates then you will obviously go on campus as well as attending employment expos. Sponsor events such as SIFE (Students in Free Enterprise) and YAA (Young Achievement Australia) too.

On the other hand, if you are looking for the most basic candidates for your franchise operations, such as fast food, then you could simply hand out flyers at the local skate park or video arcade, or even send a batch to the local school to be distributed and advertised.

United States consultant Eric Chester, in his book *Generation Why*, cites a funny example of this, where IKEA in the United States advertised positions on toilet doors in public bathrooms. A spokesperson for the company reported a fivefold increase in the number of applications compared with the usual method of advertising in the newspaper.

It is impossible to give all the likely places to do this, but perhaps you could ask some of your current Generation Y employees who match the criteria you are looking for to brainstorm some unique but targeted places to source young talent just like them. Some other ideas might be:

- **Networking events**
- **On-campus productions (including theatrical)**
- **Pubs and clubs (think IKEA and the toilet doors)**
- **THE NET!**

If you are recruiting Generation Y and are not yet online then put this book down and go and get started. Get with the program. The net not only offers supreme cost savings, but you are talking about an online generation. Generation Y are the biggest users of the internet of all generations, and they will expect that you have a site. If you don't, then trust me you are 'sooooo yesterday'. And I am not talking about placing an ad on www.seek.com. Definitely advertise on these traditional job-seeker sites, but what about your own site? Do you have a careers page and an online application process there? Do you collect details of people who are interested in careers in your organisation in an online database, who you can notify if an opportunity arises?

The Talent Zone (now known as Pinpoint HRM) Australasian Graduate Recruitment Benchmarking survey showed that 94% of companies used their own website to recruit Generation Y talent, and overall rated it as the most useful advertising medium. Well above more traditional mediums such as newspapers and brochures. It also showed that 88% of all Generation Y applications were received online.

Are you on the university, TAFE and private colleges intranets? What about youth sites like <www.thesource.gov.au>? Give someone the unique project this month of researching all the potential places you could have a presence online that would be powerful exposure for any employment opportunities you have. Many of these sites will welcome your input because the value they offer their youth audience depends on companies like you having jobs and other information of relevance to them.

Check out <www.marcedwardagency.com.au> if you want to know what the future of websites is looking like, and what is appealing to Generation Y. This technology is only in its infancy. For another cool youth site check out <www.pepsi.com.au>. While the Pepsi site is not a recruitment site, the MEA site is and both are a good place to start if you want to get a little more Generation Y friendly in your online experiences.

If you are serious about online recruiting, consider the following products in your decision:

> **Nga.net**
> **PageUp**
> **Recruit Manager**
> **Recruit ASP**
> **CVMail**

Other

Here is a list of the most common places to advertise and source Generation Y talent:

> **Individual university websites**
> **Traditional job seeker sites (AKA Job Boards)**
  – Seek
  – Gradlink
  – My Career
  – Unimail
  – Career One
> **Expos**
  – On-campus university careers fairs
  – EOC Asia Pacific <www.eoc.com.au>
> **Career magazines**
  – Unimail
  – Graduate Opportunities
  – Job Focus
  – Graduate Outlook
  – *Burst* <www.eoc.com.au>

- **On-campus activities**
  - **– Sponsor events**
  - **– Internal presentation to students**
  - **– Subject awards and scholarships**

Attract

So your message is out there, but no-one is interested. So you have interviewed a few but none seem overwhelmingly positive about the prospects of working for your company. What is missing? A solid, attraction strategy. You can't hire people who don't apply! And you can't hire those who want to work, but just not for you.

So what would be attractive to Generation Y? Well, it certainly won't be your typical four-line newspaper ad that is mass produced and very general. You probably know by this stage what Generation Y are looking for in the workplace and from a job. If you are still wondering, review the chapter What Generation Y Want. You should also have a unique insight into their behaviour and how they came to be that way. If not, review Part One. Use that information to craft your message. And by craft your message, I mean to write your job advertisement and your script for describing the position to a potential candidate in an interview. This is no different from creating the advertising message and sales process from a marketing and sales point of view. The issues are: what is good about this job, your company and the future for young talent in both? And how are they better, and different, from your competitors? In essence, what is your Employee Value Proposition?

Here are a few things to think about.

Be Creative

Being creative starts with the advertisement. The wording must be funky and attractive. Does it excite you to read the description of the job? Does it excite you to look at the ad? What could you do to make it a little more appealing? Are you rehashing an old ad or have you genuinely put some thought into this one? Read the chapter on communicating with Generation Y for more ideas on how to best get the message across.

Who says the ad has to be only what they see? Direct applicants to a website. Have them request an application pack, keeping in mind that the ad itself will have to be interesting enough to make them take that action. Harness the power of the website to attract a candidate.

Create an Experience

Generation Y crave intense, new experiences. Is your recruiting process stimulating? Do you engage your candidate pool at expos and give them a taste of who your company is and what it does? Do they get to meet your people and see the contribution you make to your clients? Are you just a newspaper ad, or are your actual real employees out and about, in schools, on campus, talking and interacting with Generation Y? The more inventive ways of recruiting are far more effective at attracting the right talent to your organisation because they provide a different experience and a more appealing one compared to the usual application from the newspaper or by submitting a resume online. And remember, first impressions count.

The key to Generation Y experience is interactivity. DVD style. Let them be involved. Get them onto your website to learn more about your company. Use them in internships over the Christmas break. Let them see a demonstration of a day in the life at your company. Whatever is appropriate for you. You know that glossy brochure you have had made up? Keep it, sure, but just understand that Generation Y may not even read it. At least not in its entirety. Boring! Generation Y are stimulus junkies.

Obsessions!

Employers miss out on such wonderful talent ALL THE TIME because of their obsession with experience and qualifications. I will talk more about this later, but ask yourself this. Does your list of requirements automatically disqualify a massive portion of potential applicants for your job? Of the different people I have enjoyed working with in my company, some of the most impressive did not have degrees. I had a 19 year old who out-marketed, out-impressed, and outclassed a 25 year old in the same position with a marketing degree and three years' experience. By getting too specific in the advertising, you could lose the possibility of finding someone a little left of field who may be perfect for that job, regardless of the fact that they might not have a degree or perhaps have not worked in your industry. Some of the greatest breakthroughs and innovations come from people who have never worked in a given industry.

The above can seem like a bit of a contradiction, having said you must get very specific about what you want before devising your recruiting strategy. Of course, you need to know exactly the job you are trying to fill and the culture of the team and workplace, and yes you should have a good idea of what sort of person will successfully fill that position and fit into that culture. However, at the same time you need to keep an open mind and be careful not to eliminate potential talent from your applications. Remember, you can't hire people who don't apply.

Youth 2 Youth

It is a marketing technique, practised for years, to use the market to penetrate the market. The same applies for recruiters. Use Generation Y wherever possible to attract Generation Y. It is more about making a connection and finding some common ground than about being the same age, however, you may find in your organisation that your younger employees are better at doing this with other young people. Here are some ideas:

> **Involve them in the process of brainstorming where to source applicants.**

> **Get their feedback on your newspaper and online ads.**

> **Get them to brainstorm ideas on how to be more creative in how and where you advertise.**

> **Have them man your stands at expos and on campus. Generation Y have credibility with Generation Y**

because they know they will get the real story from them. It is like a mutual respect.

- **Let them respond to the applications immediately to get a feel for the applicants. Have them phone applicants for a chat, to tell the person a bit about the job, to ask them a few questions and to get them to fill out a comments sheet and attach it to the resume (this is very appealing to a Generation Y applicant, that you cared enough to have someone call them and that you were fast about doing it).**

One idea I did not mention above, because it requires a little more explanation, is to involve Generation Y in the interview process. Not as the decision maker, but just to have them involved. This is for a number of reasons:

- **They can help you to translate Gen'y'nese (just kidding!)**
- **They will know if the person will fit into your company culture.**
- **It makes your current Generation Y employee feel important and adds some variety to his or her job.**
- **It will make the applicant feel more comfortable in the interview and as such, you will get a more realistic view of who they are and what they are like.**
- **It gives the applicant a friend and potential mentor in the workplace, who has been there a little longer than them, but is easy to relate to. This will also help the new employee settle in faster and therefore be more productive earlier.**

Do not base your strategy or the decision-making process entirely on this because such a 'market to market' approach creates the risk of things like the 'Halo Effect', where employees recommend people who might be like them in a certain way, though may not have the same competence or other skills. Just use the involvement strategy as a support.

Let me give you a product-based example of how powerful Youth 2 Youth (or more accurately 'viral') marketing can be. McDonald's in late 2003 were preparing to launch their new Salads Plus menu, and wanted specifically to target females between the ages of 14–25 (all Generation Y). The company then ran an email collection drive in their stores, which yielded 100,000 email addresses of which 45,000 did not work. Using their remaining 55,000 email addresses, and staying well within privacy regulations, Macca's devised a brilliant and cost-effective campaign to increase their subscriber base. They offered a prize draw of a trip to the Gold Coast with friends, and for every friend that signed up to the mailing list, that person and a friend both went into the draw to win. McDonald's went from 55,000 email addresses to 650,000 targeted and legitimate subscribers in less than three months. That is certainly one of those 'things that make you go hmmm ...'

Speed

He who hesitates is lost. Move fast. Ensure your application process is not slow and arduous. As soon as someone applies you should be in touch with them. Even if it is only a short email or a quick phone call from a member of your staff. This is the generation that thinks two-minute noodles take too long and complain when they have to wait even 30 seconds for their burger to be ready at McDonald's. Speed freaks! Get back in touch. FAST! This is not that hard to do. If you receive applications online, using the information you collected, you could automatically generate a personalised email message thanking people for their application and outlining what the procedure will be from here. If applications are coming in by mail, have your other Generation Y staff give applicants a call the same or following day during a quiet period, and have them actually conduct a mini preliminary interview. Generation Y will love doing this, and after all, they are the people the applicant will have to work with. Doing this makes your current employees feel important and makes you more efficient, freeing you up to do more leveraged activities.

It bewilders me to hear about companies that wait

sometimes as long as three weeks to get back to applicants. My sister, also a Generation Yer, applied for a job and simply never heard back. Really good for the organisation's employment brand. It was not like she applied weeks before the applications closed. It was just two days before. This established private educational provider made a mistake by not getting back to applicants because these are people who work with its target market every day, and are responsible for recommending such institutions (remember this is a private provider not a public university) to their students. DUMB!

For the most basic entry-level positions, it is likely that applicants have dropped their resume into many stores just like yours. And will take the first job they are offered. So if you are taking applications, and want to find the best talent available, move.

Remove the obstacles that make applying difficult, take out the unnecessary steps, especially for the more entry-level positions. Remember the McJob. How simple is that. Just buy a burger, fill out the wrapper and give it back to the cashier. And as for those of you looking for more sophisticated Generation Y staff, if your application stinks of red tape and bureaucracy, Generation Y will be instantly turned off regardless of the job. If your company claims to be fresh and innovative then your recruitment process should reflect that. Does it?

Remove the obstacles that make applying difficult.

Keep Them Engaged

Finding the right people does not happen overnight, and it does need contact with applicants. What do you do to keep in touch with people who have applied for work in your organisation? Even if you are only a small franchise operation. I have a friend who won't let his Mum shop at a particular food outlet because of how he was treated when he applied for a job in that store. They say customers who have a bad experience tell everyone. The same applies here. If you want to keep an applicant interested, you need to be in touch with them, making sure they know what is the next step, and when decisions will be made. Then you must keep as close as possible to those dates. I cannot emphasise enough how important this will be when trying to attract young talent. They just won't wait around for you to get back to them; remember, they are used to instant gratification and control over what is happening.

You could even do something like sending applicants a password to enter a restricted part of your website, which gives them more information about your company, the career opportunities available, travel opportunities and the like. Anything to keep them engaged.

Exclusivity

Yes, you want to be fast. And yes, you want to keep in touch. But that does not mean being desperate. Psychologists are well aware of the effect scarcity has on motivation. If Generation Y think there are not many openings with your company, and you have an excellent employer brand, then they will be extra keen to work for your organisation. I know, personally, and among my friends, companies like Macquarie Bank and Mallesons fit that description. These are companies who are 'exclusive'. This is no excuse for not staying in touch, however. Just be sure people know how 'competitive' it is to get into your company. You cannot artificially create this. Generation Y will know if you are a great company to work for, or will at least have formed an opinion about this (accurate or inaccurate), so making things up won't suffice.

If you seem desperate and appear to be grovelling, you will not appeal to Generation Y. It is similar to a product being considered 'cheap'. If it is cheap, everyone can afford it, but if it is Tommy Hilfiger, everyone knows it is valuable (and usually expensive).

Remember Who You Are Recruiting

You must always keep in mind the characteristics of Generation Y when you are devising your entire recruiting process. What you say in your advertisements, where you advertise, how the interview process will look, and what you say in that interview process should all be coloured with the Generation Y brush. When you sell to someone, it should be within their frame of reference. For example, when I purchased a new car, about three months before the birth of my first daughter (I started young), I was concerned with a couple of specific things. Number one was safety for me and for my soon-to-be family. I do over 30,000 kilometres per year, travelling from conference to conference and speech to speech. So I needed a safe vehicle. It also had to be very comfortable, and have cruise control. Sporty and fast was not my priority in this case. It was safety and comfort. Oh, and good sound. I went to a number of car yards and they began showing me convertibles, sports cars, and everything I had told them I did not want. Finally, a dealer showed me a car that was the epitome of what I was looking for. Big and comfortable. Lots of room for the baby, and an impeccable safety-testing record. The salesman showed me stats on every car tested, proving how this model was one of the safest cars on the road. Then he got out some serious techno music and cranked it up on the Harmon Kardon sound system. Needless to say, I bought it. He was speaking my language. Unlike the other sales people who thought I needed an ego stroke (my ego is already big enough) and thought a sports car would be the answer. And were busy asking me 'yes' questions that they had been taught in their sales training about what colour would I like. I was not really interested in colour; that could come later.

Sell (your jobs) from within their frame of reference. And if you still have no clue what it is about your company that is of interest to Generation Y, ask the Generation Yers already in your employ and review the chapter on What Generation Y Want.

Recruiting and attracting Generation Y is no different. We have talked about being creative in the way you communicate and where you communicate your message. But we have not talked specifically about what should be said in that message. There is no point touting your unique value proposition if it does not resonate with Generation Y. You need to focus on what Generation Y like, and push that in every step of your recruiting process.

For example, we have discovered that Generation Y are big on training and education, and will clearly be attracted to companies that offer such training and support further education. Australian Bureau of Statistics research indicates that a worker spends on average a mere 16.5 hours per year in employer-supported training. That sucks. So if you are proactive in this regard and you offer big education and training opportunities, then you could make this a major selling point for your job and your company. What other things appeal to Generation Y?

- **Opportunity to travel**
- **Potential career advancement**
- **Excellent company reputation**
- **Lateral opportunities**
- **Flexible work schedule**
- **Significant responsibility**
- **Autonomy**
- **A fun team culture**

Be careful, though, not to create unrealistic expectations. The breakdown of all relationships is due to missed expectations. Employer–employee relationships are no different. Don't gloss over the tough stuff because you think it may scare off Generation Y. Recall Southwestern and the door-to-door selling. If parts of the job are boring and repetitive, then say so. Mention the parts that are great first, but just don't try to make things sound better than they are. It will only come back and bite you down the track.

In a recent conversation with a leading consultant in the legal profession, we decided this was one of the mistakes, if not the biggest, law firms make when recruiting young talent. Some of the most prestigious Australian firms are having huge problems with attrition. It does not surprise me when you juxtapose the fun and playful persona these firms communicate at careers fairs with the reality of 80+ hour weeks and drudgery that many of their graduates are subjected to when they start with the firm. You must paint a real and honest picture of what it is like to work with your company. Generation Y will figure it out quickly enough, and unlike those that have gone before they will not put up with it. Tell them upfront and they will respect your honesty.

Consider the fact that Generation Y have been the target of more than 22,000 ads per year for most of their life, and it is fair to say that they won't fall for any hype or exaggerated opportunity. They will smell a lie a long way off. Saying things like 'you will be involved in marketing', instead of telling the truth that they will be sitting in a cubicle making cold calls all day, is not going to get you through with Generation Y. The lesson here is to tell the truth, because they value the truth.

I mentioned earlier that in a speech at his high school, Bill Gates allegedly told the Generation Y kids that the jobs they think are below their dignity their parents would have called opportunity. So what? That won't change. If your job sucks, Generation Y will simply think it sucks. You would be better to look at ways to make it a little more interesting than to try to make it sound better than it is. And to be truthful, many of you may not be looking for the innovative and fresh Generation Y talent to which I keep referring and are just looking for a cubicle slave or a cog in the system to do the jobs in your business that you, and others, don't want to do. If this is the case, then get used to the fact that most applicants are thinking 'car', not 'career'.

So yes, selling this is going to be tough, but as you will find in the chapter on management, there are ways to make these jobs more appealing to Generation Y. By doing this you will be able to attract better people to your organisation.

I think it is very important to be optimistic with Generation Y. Don't even try to make them think this is the only job they will get and that they will be treated worse anywhere else because that is simply not true. There is abundance out there, and Generation Y knows it.

Do a market analysis. Find out exactly what your

product (the job and your company) offers. Find out what the customer (your Generation Y candidates) will value most about that. Do the same for your competitors and their products, and then exploit and sing from creative rooftops the unique value that you offer.

One more point on the creativity thing and who you are recruiting. A great campaign by the I Group, who are specialists in recruiting young talent for organisations, involved a video clip of an employee doing a most disgusting, though very funny, thing to the office water cooler. Then up came the words: 'We know where a job is going'. The I Group lost one of their blue chip clients, who had come to them in the first place because they could not attract good young talent. Well, if they still don't know how to attract them, they never will. For Generation Y, it is not about what is attractive to you and other people your age, but what is attractive to them.

Exploit Your Employer Brand (Being an Employer of Choice)

Employment Brand. Employer of Choice. Buzz words, I know. But they are not a fad. They are the new reality. You *must* be an Employer of Choice. It is the law of supply and demand. Sure there are plenty of people available to work. The question is, do they have the talent? This book is not about winning the war for young labour. It is about winning the war for young talent. The truth is there is a war for good young talent out there, and those on the demand side (employer) have had to improve their offering to be more attractive to the suppliers (employees). It is those employers who offer the best of what the talent wants that we call Employers of Choice. Some factors that impact on your status as an Employer of Choice include:

- **Recruitment process**
- **Performance evaluation process**
- **Reward and recognition systems**
- **Culture**
- **Work environment**
- **Training and development**
- **Promotional opportunities**

And much more. These factors, coupled with the following, go to form your Employer Brand:

> **Vision and leadership**
> **Public reputation**
> **PR and publicity**
> **Product offering**
> **Market share**

Let me give you a real example of how important the brand is. A good friend of mine, and a contributor to this book, recently left an important post at a well-respected Australian retailer to work for Australia's leading airline. She left for a position that initially was a step down in terms of responsibility, which intrigued me. When I questioned her on why, her answer was twofold: the quality of the airline's brand (and she was passionate about the business) and the challenge it posed for her.

If branding is an entirely new concept for you, here is a quick introduction. The following model describes what constitutes your Employer Brand. Importantly, the model is the metaphor. Meaning the foundation of the brand is positioning, and the name is the tip. Think of the iceberg metaphor. The name is what everyone sees, yet 95% of the iceberg is invisible. The name is the label for all of the assumptions and associations that lie below the surface.

The Employer Brand

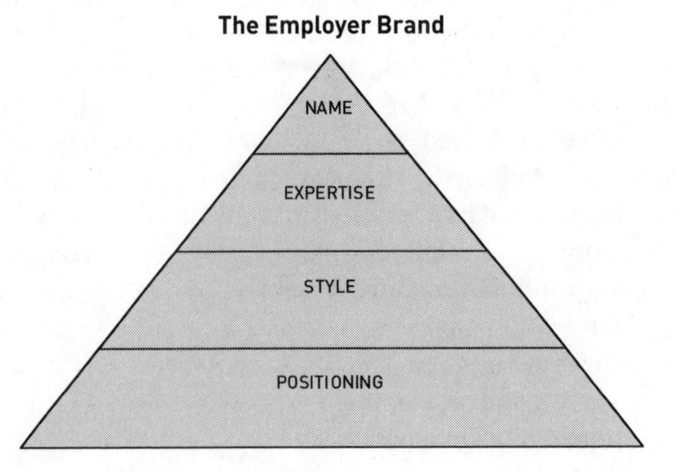

Name> This is your company name. It is your logo. Both being the label that people refer to when talking and thinking about your company. I know of companies that use the individual product names to attract people to their company. Lion Nathan, who is profiled in this book, does this very effectively. Its Employment Brand is the same as its Consumer Brand. Lion Nathan is little known compared with say Tooheys, one of its products.

Expertise> This is what you do. The products you offer, the services you provide and the industries and markets you work in. Consider the recent ban on tobacco companies from marketing their graduate positions on the campuses of Australian universities. This is an example of how a company's 'expertise' is destroying their Employer Brand. Three of the four companies profiled in this book cite their products and the industry they work in as one of the most powerful ways they attract young talent.

Style> Style is the collection of all the things that go into defining what your company is like to work for. It includes your office location, the culture within the company, the salaries and other benefits you offer, the attitude and personality of your leaders and so on.

Positioning> Positioning is concerned with how you are different. Specifically, it is what is different about you that would be considered a competitive advantage in attracting the best young talent. Is it the fact that you have a very powerful Consumer Brand, or is it because you offer wonderful promotional opportunities and the chance to travel? Is it because you have a charismatic CEO? Positioning refers to where that point of difference places you in the mind of the potential candidate. For example: Virgin Blue may be an attractive place to work because of the edginess of its product and the fact that it was started by Richard Branson. Qantas, on the other hand, is attractive perhaps because of its status as an Australian icon. The question is, which of these points of difference are the most attractive to hot young talent?

It is essential that branding becomes a cornerstone of HR. Like I said, send HR on a marketing course. Marketing your Employer Brand is just as important as marketing your products, because the quality of your products, or distribution of products that your company sells, hinges on the quality of the talent within your organisation.

Brands that appeal to Generation Y are authentic, unique, integral and show a commitment to the common good. In other words, Generation Y like companies that are a little creative and original, do what they say without ripping people off in the process, including their employees, and share their success in ways that benefit the community.

Given that Generation Y are a connected generation, be sure to communicate the value of your brand in many different channels, and in many different ways. Keep the essence the same because that is what branding is about, but at the same time, be diverse and creative in letting people know about you and what you offer as an Employer of Choice. Here are some ideas you may like to think about:

- **Careers expos, on and off educational campuses**
- **Sponsored events**
- **A value-packed website, which has a look and feel consistent with the value you are trying to convey with your brand**
- **Consistent messages in the interview process**
- **Awards programs**
- **Publicity for awards and recognition**
- **Visible environmental and other socially motivated projects**
- **Having staff involved in things like mentoring kids off the street**
- **Donating**
- **Being seen to be a transparent organisation**

Peter Sheahan's Seven Trade Show and Expo Tips

1> **Create a multi-sensory experience**
Use all mediums of communication to stimulate as many senses as possible. Focus on being highly visual and kinesthetic. Add food and drink and 'things' people can play with or interact with to find out more about what you are offering.

2> **It is all about the show**
Put on a show. Entice and entertain people. Employ actors if you have to. Do whatever it takes to not be ordinary. If fishmongers at the markets can get up and make a show out of buying fish, then you should be able to do it about your product.

3> **Bold, outcome-based statements**
An outcome-based statement does not talk about how long you have been in business or even how to use your product. It simply talks about what benefit the user gets when they use your product (even if that product is the opportunity to work for your company). Find the most relevant two or three statements and make big banners that scream this message.

4> **Use a combination of Generation Y and older exhibitors**
Use Generation Y in your stand, but also use people who may be a little older but genuinely know what they are talking about. Make sure there is someone on the stand who can answer virtually any question you might be asked. 'We'll find out and get back to you' is not good enough.

5> **Have an objective**
Have a clear objective of what you want to achieve from being at the expo. Don't just say 'brand awareness' because it is a cop out. It may be part of the objective, but you had better have some way of

measuring that. If you are looking to build your 'talent pool' then you had better be collecting names.

6> **Get out and about**
Don't sit in your stand behind some big and intimidating table. Get out and mix with the crowd. Use the aisle, not just your stand. Instigate the conversation instead of waiting for people to come to you. They won't!

7> **Be well resourced**
First and foremost have enough people so you can have one-on-one conversations. Otherwise you may as well stick to mass marketing (which doesn't work anyway). You must connect with people through one-on-one conversations, and there is no excuse for running out of brochures and giveaways. Stock up.

It may seem obvious at this point, but in order to communicate the value of your brand, you first need to know what value you offer. Go through the pyramid model above and make notes on what you have in each of these areas that is valuable.

I will speak in more detail in a later chapter on how essential effective exit strategies are for protecting your brand. And for those of you who think branding does not apply, think again. Branding is local and global, it is for entry-level positions and qualified professionals, it affects young and old, it affects everything. Consider too that Generation Y have been brought up on brands and use them as a shortcut to make decisions. So powerful have they become, that Martin Lindstrom's Brand Child research showed that for one fifth of Australian children their first word was a brand name. Think Hi 5! The better your Employer Brand the better candidates you will attract. It is as simple as that!

Use the workspace as an attraction tool

If you have a Generation Y–friendly workspace that is funky and fun to work in, then you should be using this as an attraction tool. There is increasing evidence that not only is a great workspace very important to talented people but that it significantly increases their productivity, the likelihood of collaboration between people and teams, and improved retention levels.

If you are running a Dilbert version of corporate slavery, then be aware that this will be a negative force in your recruiting efforts, and you should be doing something about changing it, and fast. Generation Y talent, and in fact talented people across all ages, want to work in an environment that supports and inspires them.

As part of the research for this book I interviewed Rosemary Kirkby who with architect James Grose and their team built Campus MLC at North Sydney and National at Docklands in Melbourne. Campus MLC is arguably Australia's most celebrated workspace, and has delivered extremely good return on investment for MLC's parent company the National Australia Bank. In the interviews, we discussed the example of a division of an advertising agency in Los Angeles who were forced to set up in a warehouse while their new offices were being finished. When it came time to move into the new offices the team did not want to leave the warehouse environment. I am not suggesting you all move to warehouses, but I am saying that workspace is important, and should certainly be used as a way to attract the best young talent to your organisation. There will be more on this idea of workspace later, with some specifics tips from Rosemary Kirkby herself.

What Australia's best have to say about attracting Generation Y

MEA's secrets to attracting Generation Y are:

- A powerful consumer brand and experience to match
- Variety of the role with clear objectives
- Edgy website that sells our culture online
- Having an open door policy; we do not discriminate in the application process

Edward Kaleel, Marc Edward Agency

HDY's strategy and secret to attracting Generation Y is:

- Promoting that we are a vibrant firm with a relatively young team
- Marketing our philosophy of promoting to partnership from within the firm
- Showing a clear and achievable career pathway
- Actively promoting and supporting activity and a life outside of work

Deborah Stonley, Henry Davis York

What makes LNA attractive to Generation Y is:

- Great consumer brands
- Freedom, autonomy and challenge
- Putting young people in serious jobs and giving them opportunities for personal growth and development
- Having a core purpose to make the world a more sociable place

Linda Botter, Lion Nathan Australia

We attract Generation Y to Ford because:

- We are a powerful consumer brand
- We have a proactive and realistic work–life balance approach
- We offer great financial and non-financial benefits
- All staff can contribute to a charity of their choice and we facilitate that through their salary
- We have built in rotation programs
- By far the most important thing is that we DEVELOP them

David Cvetkovski, Ford Australia

Henry Davis York in focus

Six years ago, Henry Davis York was little known to graduating lawyers in Sydney, despite being a firm of significant size and despite being around for over 100 years. It had become clear they were not getting the quality of candidates they desired applying to work at their firm. A recruiting strategy was devised which included:

> **A new and more youthful website**
> **Establishing of alliances with the law faculties at multiple Sydney-based university campuses**
> **Sponsoring of on-campus events to build credibility**
> **Ramping up their summer clerkship program and using it as a means to spread the word about Henry Davis York on campus; those who were on the program would return to their respective campuses and share with their classmates their positive experiences**
> **Repositioning themselves as a different employment option to the large national firms – a more dynamic, personable firm without the career blocks that can often exist**

The result was marked and almost immediate. In the year before the new strategy was implemented, HDY only recruited three graduates and struggled to attract the top-calibre candidates. In the first year after the new strategy was implemented, they recruited first-rate graduates due to a vastly improved talent pool to choose from.

The real power of their strategy was in their positioning. Rather than go head to head with the national firms, they deliberately played up their uniqueness, and all of a sudden candidates had only two choices. A large national firm, or a medium-sized Sydney-based firm with a young and vibrant culture and a clearly mapped-out and achievable career path. The power of this brand is what underpinned their success. Candidates knew there were major blocks in the national firms that had already saturated their market, whereas a smaller, growing firm like HDY would have more opportunities for lawyers to move up the ranks and eventually to become partners. Of the eleven graduates that joined HDY in 1999, nine are still at the firm in 2005.

Your Quest!

Give some thought to these questions:

- Do your hiring managers understand that recruiting is just like marketing?
- Is talent on the strategy agenda at a board level in your company? If not, how can you get it there?
- How might you use your client base and customers to recruit great talent?
- How might you use your existing workforce to recruit great talent?
- Who could you align yourself with to help you source and even select better-quality candidates?
- Assuming you know the type of people you are looking for (if not, go back and find out) where would you be most likely to find them?
- Do you have an online presence? If not, GET ONE! If yes, is it attractive to Generation Y? Does it position you as an employer of choice?
- Are you a little 'on the edge' in the way you attract talent?
- How could you turn the recruiting process into an experience?
- Do you have any obsessions?
- How might you use Generation Y to help you recruit other top-quality Generation Yers?
- What can you do to speed up the recruitment and selection process?
- How do you intend to stay in touch with applicants?
- Do a SWOT (Strengths, Weaknesses, Opportunities, Threats) analysis.

And a little activity. Get all of your marketing collateral, including printouts from your website. Get photos of your banners and the displays you use at careers fairs. Everything. Then conduct the following word analyses. Place the major headings and points of your campaigns under one of the following headings:

Credibility	Process	Outcome

Credibility includes anything you say about your company that is designed to make you sound like the best company:

> We are the biggest ...
> We have been in business for ...
> Australia's first ...

Process includes anything you say about how you go about employing and selecting:

> Apply online
> Come and see us for a chat

Outcome includes anything you say that represents what someone will get for joining your organisation:

> Start on a minimum of $47,000
> We will develop you and your skills to make you even more employable
> Work on the biggest consumer brands in the world

Ideally, you want most of your headings and key points in all of your marketing to be in the outcome column because they represent what is in it for Generation Y.

Selecting

Well surely we don't need any more literature on selection. Maybe not, but I have a few ideas you may be interested in. Ones that will allow you to be a little more open when considering Generation Y talent for your organisation. In fact, the more you think about selection the better because if you were to seriously analyse the challenges experienced in the workplace, many would not exist if the right people had been selected in the first place. I will not go over too much old ground here, just some new and interesting ways to look at recruiting Generation Y.

Select outside the Square

Recruit for talent and train for skill

I have always believed that talents are more important than skills. Marcus Buckingham, who authored the book *First Break All the Rules,* will agree. Buckingham reports on the findings of the biggest management and staff survey ever conducted by Gallup organisation, which found that the best managers look for talent not skills. There is a difference between a talent and a skill. A talent is something for which you have a natural flair. For instance, you may have been born with the ability to sculpt, or draw, or speak in public. You can of course train people in such skills, but they will never be as great as those who have a genetic disposition towards them. Teaching someone to file is transferring a skill, and is not that hard to do. However, you can't train someone to be a natural sales person.

Don't get too obsessed with the specific skills your staff may have learnt in a previous job, or at university. It is said now that in engineering alone the skills gained at university will have a half-life of only five years. If someone clearly has the talent, forget about whether they have the skills required to fully utilise their talent because you can train them. We are also talking about 'young' talent, which means they may not have much of the experience you require either. This is a big call considering how focused companies are on experience and tertiary qualifications. BIG CALL! All you need to do is read a few job descriptions on <www.seek.com> or in the newspaper and you will know what I am talking about. There are lots of talented people out there going to waste because of this obsession.

Recruit for attitude and train for skill

The reality of the workplace is that there are now four generations working together on teams, and while the eldest of those generations is gradually retiring from the workforce, the need for cultural, or should I say attitudinal, fit is more important than ever. And that goes for all generations. Recruit for attitude and train for skill. Again, if people are willing to learn, you can teach them. If they are willing to cooperate, you can help them develop team-building skills. But if they have a bad attitude you can do nothing with them. Commonsense I know, but is commonsense very common?

Even though you are looking for cultural fit, be careful not to recruit a team of clones because innovation and creativity come from diversity. Real synergy comes from a difference in opinion and perception.

In this new business environment, accounting is not the governing force. Imagination is. Recruit people with up and go. Risk takers. Guts!

'We are just as interested in what people like to do outside of work as in what university they went to. We certainly do not favour one university over another. We look at every individual.'

Deborah Stonley,
Henry Davis York

Old Paradigms

Look outside the normal qualifications sphere. This includes looking at candidates who have studied in very different fields. Most breakthroughs in a specific industry come from people who have never had anything to do with that particular industry. This is why consultants can be so valuable in the workplace. They see things you are too close to see, and they bring knowledge from many different industries.

A recent study of university leavers found that traditional disciplines such as accounting and commerce were still by far the most popular among business employers. I would love to see some people from a creative arts background recruited into marketing, or from technical backgrounds into sales, or vice versa. Get a fresh perspective. Add experience to the old paradigms.

You should be looking at different sorts of experience. Why would you want someone with the same experience as the last person in the job, or as the rest of the team? Get someone new. How else will you get new ideas and fresh perspectives?

For many years, the education system has been obsessed with mathematical and logical human intelligence. Finally, we are seeing the value in the less rigid, more creative human intelligences, including emotional intelligence.

If you are after risk takers, people prepared to do things differently, look for Generation Yers who have been overseas after school instead of to university. Look for those who have had, or been involved in, their own entrepreneurial ventures. Were they leaders at school? What have they started? Have they ever shown initiative and organised a dance party or something like it? Even if they failed miserably, you couldn't teach what they will have learnt from such an experience. Plus they have the give it a go attitude.

For those of you not looking for candidates with creativity and imagination, don't discard this information. Ask yourself if perhaps you should be. Customers demand experiences, not commodities. They buy experiences, not goods and services. Who is working your cash registers? Do these people leave a positive, memorable impression on your customers? What about the people in your call centre? Are they pleasant and fun? Get people with personality because they will help to make any job fun, and will be able to create memorable experiences for your customers.

Look at the fringe

If your job is really that bad and that boring, then face the fact that you will not have much talent to choose from and you may have to take what you get. You could, of course, do something proactive to add some spice and variety to the job. That might be as simple as taking that look off your face and smiling! (Just kidding ... Sort of.) In all seriousness though, there are some jobs that are simply boring, and not much can be done to change that. Here is what I would do if I were you. Look to the fringe and employ people many others won't give the opportunity to. You know, those applicants with the strange hairstyles and the interesting piercings. Perhaps you could have some faith in a kid no-one has ever put faith in. Occasionally you will get burnt, but no more than you would have otherwise. More often than not, they will be so grateful for the opportunity that they will show you a loyalty that scarcely exists in today's work environment. These are people often just waiting for someone like you to give them a go. Someone who will respect their individuality.

'Experience is out. Inexperience is in.'

Alan Webber, founding editor of *Fast Company* magazine in the United States

Recruiting from the fringe is much more than this, though. In their groundbreaking book *The Deviant's Advantage*, Watts Wacker and Ryan Matthews show how all mass-market ideas first started way out on the fringe before becoming what they called 'Social Convention'. We live in a world that values innovation and uniqueness. Doing more of the same, or enhancing current products, will simply not do it. We need to create new and extraordinary things, and the way to do this is to look at more unconventional approaches, which will require unconventional people.

'You say you don't want emotional, volatile and unpredictable, just imaginative. Sorry they only come in a package' – **Patricia Pitcher, *The Drama of Leadership***

'It is the cracked ones that let light into the world' – **Bumper sticker**

Offbeat = Innovative

Research into graduate programs revealed that companies recruited people from traditional disciplines. And we wonder why so many employer satisfaction surveys come back saying their graduates lack creativity. If you want creative employees, you need to look outside the traditional academic disciplines. Or perhaps even outside some academic institutions altogether.

Creative application and interview processes

'I've had lawyers working marketing. We even have someone in HR who studied criminology at university. We want both intellect and emotional intelligence. Just because you have an MBA from Harvard it does not mean you will automatically get a job with Lion Nathan.'

Linda Botter,
Lion Nathan Australia

A move away from the traditional interview and application process could be a good thing. Any attempt to get a better indication of what people are capable of before they start the job is a good thing. I brainstormed a few ideas ...

Have them do something creative. Instead of asking for a cover letter, get applicants to analyse a hypothetical problem and, in one page, suggest some potential solutions to the problem. Writing the one pager will give you a good indication of just how motivated they are to work for your company. You will also get a feel for their style of thinking, how creative they are, and their writing abilities.

In the last round of interviews, instead of bringing the candidates in for another interview, ask them to present to you, or even a panel, a fifteen-minute presentation about why they want to work in your company and why they think they would be an asset to your team. Let them be as creative as they want. You will see how they are under pressure, again see how creative they are, and just as importantly, how gutsy they are. Are they prepared to put themselves on the line and do something different?

Group Interviews

Absolutely essential for companies that put on large numbers of staff in over short periods. For example, supermarkets, Christmas casuals in retail and so on. But take the group interview to another level. At the Marc Edward Agency, applicants are required to speak in front of all the people at the group interview, to explain who they are, what they do and why they want to work for the Marc Edward Agency. They have permission to do whatever they wish in their 60 seconds or so, including sing and dance. Some people literally do sing and dance. Not only is this a fun and energetic environment, but it pushes the comfort zones of all those present, which they will need to do in their jobs.

In the Talent Zone Graduate Recruitment Benchmarking Study, only 46% of graduate recruiters had some kind of group interview in their selection process. Thankfully, this represented a jump from just 33% the year before, but it is still far too low. If you want to see how people perform in a group situation you need to put them in one as opposed to have them sit some test on a computer.

Questions and where to interview

Ask different questions. Get into a peer-to-peer conversation where possible to get a better feel for the applicant. Give Generation Y the space to be themselves in the interview room and you will make better choices in regards to cultural fit.

I like the idea of spending more time with those you are seriously considering for key positions. Take them out to lunch so you can observe their etiquette and, most importantly, see how they engage with the wait staff and other people. It usually relaxes your potential employee enough to get a better understanding of who they really are, as opposed to who they want you to think they are.

By doing something different and by being asked thoughtful questions, Generation Y will feel as though you are treating them as a person, not just a number. If they feel like they are the tenth interview of the day and you just want to clock off and go for a beer, it is highly unlikely they will be excited about the prospect of working for you.

GUT!

I say go with the gut. But I do so on the assumption that the rest of your selection process is in order. I am assuming you have checked out references, verified information, interviewed thoroughly. Ultimately, it comes down to gut anyway. I don't care who you are or what you say, we all make decisions with our emotions. We justify them intellectually, but we make them emotionally. Who feels right? Who has energy and pizzazz? Select them. Not the person who sounds like they have memorised their answer to every interview question you asked. It is, after all, essential to have some sort of cultural fit, even if it is a contrary character you are looking for.

'I always go with the gut. I give candidates an opportunity to sell themselves in whatever way they wish. Some even sing a song, and dance. I love it. These are the kind of people we need, to stay one step ahead of our competition. People who are thinking a little differently. One of my best performers in our marketing team is from an acting and communications background.'

Edward Kaleel,
Marc Edward Agency

In order to do this, you will really need to engage in authentic communication with the applicant. Ask them about real things and real situations. Get a feel for their values and what is important to them. What are their aspirations? What are their priorities? It is so easy to turn it on at the interview, that unless you engage in some genuine dialogue, how will you know what the applicant is really like? This is why I interview over lunch. Of course, being a small company, this is easy to do. All I am saying is make it as real as possible and then go with the person who feels right.

Involve people from the team or division where the applicant is are going to work in the interview process. They will, after all, be the people working day-to-day with the new hire.

While I understand this may not be feasible

when recruiting large numbers of people for say a graduate program, or a Christmas retail push, if you are filling a key position with someone from Generation Y, this is what it will ultimately come down to.

Your Quest!

> Do you look beyond skills and experience and look for raw talent?
> Are you stuck in old, ineffective paradigms? How are they tainting your selection processes?
> Are you taking risks with some of your employment choices? Are you willing to look outside the conventional square?
> How might you make your interview process more creative?
> What cool things could you have candidates do, that would give you insights into their attitude, talents and creativity?
> Are you willing to admit that you make decisions emotionally?

Part Three >
Managing Generation Y

>

Orientation

If your orientation program is dry and boring, you run the risk of already losing 'buy-in'. In fact, if it is really boring, then Generation Y will already begin to question whether they have made the right decision to work for you and may even begin considering their other options. It has long been known that 'first impressions count' and that they also last. Does your orientation program leave the impression on your new recruits that it is intended to? Does it inspire them to invest their time and energy in your company? Does it make them feel valued and important as an employee of your organisation, and does it make them feel a part of a bigger, more important purpose? Is it representative of the organisational culture you are trying to create or that Generation Y want?

It is essential for you to remember that most of the talented young people you employ will, at some stage, have had a job and will have already been involved in some sort of orientation program. The problem with this is that most of those orientations would have been boring and demotivating. As such, they will probably come into your orientation program expecting it to be the same. Expectations often create reality, so you had better jolt them out of this perception and 'knock their socks off'. The same will apply for training. You cannot rely on the initial excitement of orientation to pull your Generation Y participants through. You will need to continue it well throughout their employment. But for now, let's just concentrate on creating an orientation program that genuinely engages and inspires them.

Involve important people in the process

A good Generation Y orientation program will include upper management. By involving someone of significant power and importance in the organisation, you are demonstrating just how important these new recruits are to your company. For those in more operational roles, this would mean the store manager, the factory manager and the like. I was once involved in a program where the CEO of a multi-billion-dollar Australian company was present for the induction of 25 new recruits. A big call I know, and not really practical in most organisations, but you should have seen the awe on the faces of the new recruits when they finished. The CEO's presence had a serious impact, and those involved were visibly inspired.

At Ford, Jeff Polites, former President of Ford Australia prior to leaving recently to work for Global Operations, said this to a group of graduates in their orientation program: 'Well, you might not have one at the moment, but I expect each one of you to have the Ford logo tattooed to your ass before six months have passed.'

This is the president of one of Australia's most respected brands. It is little wonder they have been so successful in recent years. It is this non-pompous, to the point, and of course passionate leadership that draws out the absolute best in Generation Y. My hat is off to Jeff Polites.

Your orientation program should also include the people who interviewed them and then ultimately employed them. By including these people, your new recruits will feel as though they are not on their own and that at least they know someone there.

Make it reflective of your culture

If you are touting that you have a modern, innovative company that values its employees and their ideas and creativity, then your orientation program had better reflect this.

Nothing will turn Generation Y off faster than the smell of hypocrisy.

Nothing will turn Generation Y off faster than the smell of hypocrisy. If you lured them with promises of an empowered culture which thrived on teamwork, then this had better be true, and the orientation program their first experience of such a culture.

For example, if you have a fun and playful culture you may include cooking competitions and other such activities in your orientation program. You may like to include some sort of production or performance where new recruits really push through any 'new kid' jitters and go all out. If you are emphasising the importance of working together, you may offer hypothetical problems and have recruits work in groups to figure out the answer. Make it interactive and engaging. Don't just have someone come and teach them about how to dress and business etiquette. Do that, but intersperse it between activities that create a sense of how you want them to behave and feel on the job.

Offer some inspiration

Gen Y, Gen X Gen Z Gen ABC, whatever! EVERYONE on the face of the planet wants to be inspired. We are emotional creatures, and want to be emotionally engaged. Inspiration is the key to extraordinary performance. If you want to turn your Generation Y talent into profit, then be sure to show them the value in their new role, and show them how it makes a significant contribution to the organisation. Be sure they see how they are just one part of a much bigger picture. A bigger contribution that is making huge differences in the lives of people.

You may like to use a speech coach to help those involved in coordinating the orientation program to craft an inspiring speech. You may even consider using an outside speaker. If you use a professional speaker, be sure to look for some customisation of the message. You want your new employees to be inspired by your company and their potential in your company, not by the thought of climbing a mountain, or sailing the seven seas.

If your founder was an inspiring person, particularly if he or she is still alive, tell their story. Tell the story how only ten years ago your company was on the verge of bankruptcy, but your dedication to quality and to the customer turned it around, and now you are the market leaders. I think you get the drift. Just make sure the person delivering it can do it inspirationally.

Give them permission to dream of the possibilities that your organisation provides them, be they promotional, travel or any other kind of opportunity. Make sure you have real examples of how that is done and systems in place to allow them to engage in such things themselves, but be sure they know about it. Ground all of this in performance, not in just showing up. Ensure Generation Y know that providing they produce the goods they will be well rewarded for their efforts.

Inspire them about the future of your company. Where it is going, what exciting new developments lie on the immediate horizon? What new products will be launched? What innovations are just waiting to be unleashed into the workplace?

Educate them about your company

You must make Generation Y feel as though they are a part of something bigger. They need to know that what they do will make a difference. At the same time, they want to know that they have rights and will be valued for the roles they play. As such, it is essential to educate them about your company. Focus on these issues:

> **The ultimate value you deliver to the consumer**
> **The ways in which you support the community**
> **Your environmental policies**
> **Your stand on gender issues and bullying in the workplace**

You must also educate them about the impact their role and their performance has on the organisation. Now is certainly not the time to let them know they are not irreplaceable.

They must feel as though what they do counts. Focus on the net effect of what they do, who and what other departments rely on them and so on.

They must know that the company exists for a bigger reason than the mere production of goods and services. What was the passion behind starting this company? What is the mission behind it? By doing this, you will instill a sense of purpose into your Generation Y employees, something we have come to realise is essential if you want them truly engaged and committed.

Make it Fun!

It sounds trite, but it is true. I once heard it said that we are all kids dressed in adult clothes. Make the orientation program fun. Not corny. Fun! Add some excitement to it. Do something different. Add a competitive element. Build some team-based activities into the program.

My first position in the corporate world was at one of the then 'big six', now 'big four' accounting firms. I fell asleep in the orientation program. Stone cold asleep. I was woken up because I grunted or something, and the person next to me gave me a swift elbow to the ribs. I am the least likely person to do something like this. It was just so boring. I left after eight days, and apparently set the record for the swiftest exit from the cadetship program.

By adding a bit of excitement, not only will your new employees be stimulated, they will feel more comfortable. It will create an environment where people feel as though they are a part of the team. As though they belong.

Your Quest!

Your assignment, should you choose to accept it, is to answer and then act on the answers to these questions:

- Does your orientation program leave the impression on your new recruits that it is intended to?
- Does it inspire them to invest their time and energy into your company?
- Are the presenters inspiring?
- Does it make them feel valued and important as an employee of your organisation and does it make them feel a part of a bigger, more important purpose?
- Do you involve people who would by their mere presence indicate that these new recruits are important?
- Is it representative of the organisational culture you are trying to create?
- How might you add more fun to your orientation program?

>

Training

Rarely will you recruit Generation Y talent that does not need training. And the good news is you will rarely recruit Generation Y talent that does not want training. Generation Y will embrace training, providing it is relevant, interactive, personalised and entertaining. And most of all, providing it is effective and practical. No doubt you have a system of in-house and outsourced training. Generation Y will cause you to rethink this system, including both style and content. And especially the trainers. You will need to be very diligent in who you choose to do that training, and as always, will need to make sure the workplace is open and conducive to the application of the skills transferred in the training room.

If what you are doing is not working as well as it should, then you should do something about it. Be wary of taking the easy option, which would be to simply tweak your current program, because you may just end up getting more of what you don't want. There is an old analogy – if you use bad mud, it does not matter what shape you mould the brick into, it is still made of bad mud. Your training program may not need to be tweaked and adjusted, it may need to be destroyed and then rebuilt. Management guru Tom Peters says 'Destruction is cool!'

The training that Generation Y require will often be in areas you least expect. While they are innovative and tech savvy, they may lack basic written and verbal communication skills. The type of training required will vary greatly depending on whether they are frontline workers or whether they are part of the intellectual capital of your service organisation. As such, the old mass training programs may no longer be effective. You will need more specific, customised training. Training on demand. This is true for all businesses whether you be a fast food outlet, or a massive professional service firm. United States management consultants Bruce Tulgan and Carolyn Martin, in their book *Managing Generation Y*, said that 'organisations that can't – or won't – customise training need a wake-up call.'

Whatever you do, do not overlook training. One of the dilemmas many organisations face is that they train their new recruits and invest heavily in their development, only to have them leave. Well, what is the alternative? Not train them, and have them do a poor job and then leave anyway, costing you thousands to replace them? Or worse still, not train them and then have them stay.

There are four keys to Generation Y training. In fact, these are the four keys to communicating with Generation Y, PERIOD!

> **Relevant**
> **Interactive**
> **Personalised**
> **Entertaining**

'It takes faith to put your business success in the hands of Gen Y, and the key to surviving is in training and development. We recently increased the number of staff we include in our development programs and deliberately went after people we thought were good, with the intention of making them excellent. In the process, reliability went up by 100% and the performance on the job was also substantially improved. It was an excellent investment.'

Edward Kaleel,
Marc Edward Agency

1> Relevant

My advice to a group of Generation Y business mentors the other night was to prepare for the WHYne. Meaning prepare for the constant barrage of questioning and asking 'Why?': Why should I? Why do you do it this way? Why don't you do this? Why don't you do that? I think you know what I mean. That is, unless of course you have mastered the art of educating Generation Y, where you construct your delivery to pre-empt the 'why' behind everything you teach.

To keep your training relevant, you need to make sure it is practical, rational, mature, fresh and free from bullshit.

Practical> Make your training as hands-on and involved as possible. You may even like to counterpoise your training with structured, on-the-job use of the skills being taught in the classroom. You should facilitate the practical application of the skills being taught as quickly as possible. This may require a staggered approach to training as opposed to massive, week-long chunks. You may choose to do a series of workshops over a month or a couple of months.

Often this kind of staggered approach is not possible, so the trainer must endeavour to have as many role plays and real-life examples of how things are done as possible. Everyone, not just Generation Y, learns best using metaphor and practical simulation in the training room, but it is even more important to Generation Y because of their obsession with relevance.

You could even go as far as showing them for real. For example, if you were training a small group in customer service, you might take them to a retail store or department store renowned for customer service and let them go off for fifteen minutes, pretending they are buying something, and see how they are treated. Straight after, take them to a retail store known for the opposite (if they are still in business – and I know of one really big one that is) and let them see the difference themselves. Maybe you could let them sit on hold on the customer service line of some large telco and then straight after have them call a smaller provider who has real people answering the phone.

Don't train for training's sake. It is often the case that a simple job card or instructional poster would be more efficient and effective than a long and intensive training program. You may not need to cover everything that is in the manual; some points are better made by simple employee-to-employee instruction or using a job card or poster where the task will be performed.

Rationale> The trainer's job is both that of sales person and teacher. You must first sell the reasons for listening and learning a new skill or piece of information before you attempt to teach it. You need 'buy-in'. In order to be an effective salesperson; you will need to know very clearly why a particular thing is done and why it is so important. In other words, you need to know the rationale behind anything and everything.

This is not the drama you may think. By forcing you to truly analyse your procedures and systems, Generation Y will help you to reveal areas of red tape, allowing you to increase your productivity. If you don't have a reason, DUMP IT! For example, uniforms in call centres. It astounds me that some call centres still have a strict uniform code when the reps never have to see a customer face to face. Now I am not suggesting that they wear shorts and a singlet, because they will be seen entering the office and at times people will be touring the offices and see the staff. But keep things in perspective – a tie and jacket are probably not necessary.

If you don't have a reason, DUMP IT!

Mature> Don't treat me like an idiot is what Generation Y will think, and possibly say, if you take things too slowly in the training room, or if you tailor everything to the lowest common denominator. You will get what you expect from your Generation Y employees, so raise the bar and expect them to act and learn as adults. Sure it has been said that you need to make training fun and interesting, but this does not mean make it elementary or corny.

The more basic things may need to be simply mentioned, and then explain that a poster or a job card will be given to employees, which will outline what they need to know at the point of use. Do not spend 45 minutes explaining how the photocopier works. This is not training. Remember, Generation Y feel technology in their gut; they will figure it out. Just create a set of instructions, type them up, laminate them and stick them over the photocopier machines. You are far better off spending that time talking about the various opportunities for promotion and development that exist for Generation Y in your organisation.

Fresh> Spice it up a little. In some of my presentations I have used a phrase that is so overdone I need to apologise before using it. The phrase is 'Think outside the square'. Even with profuse apologies and playing on the fact that I acknowledge it is a cliché, I still get moans from my Generation Y audiences.

These guys hate clichés. Be individual. Think of something new. Stay away from cheesy team-building activities that serve little purpose and do nothing for team building. You had better be able to tie in and show the relevance of anything you do. I am not suggesting that in the middle of your training you do random things that have nothing to do with what needs to be learnt. Although, as I type this it strikes me as a reasonable idea, providing you explain that it is designed for a bit of fun and variety, and not as a serious learning opportunity.

Use current examples. A show that is huge on television right now is *American Idol*. I watched the first couple of episodes to pick up on some good analogies and references to use in my presentations. I continually update examples and one-liners to be more aligned with contemporary sources, which means this week for Generation Y.

Recently I gave a talk to a group of Year 12 students. Before my presentation, the principal decided he wanted to do his own motivational talk and proceeded to tell the students about some 'inspiring' documentary he had been watching on the ABC about the Sahara Desert. I was cringing as he went on, thinking how bad a note he was getting the program off to, but then I had a new thought – how good will I look after this rubbish. Keep it fresh! The Sahara Desert is not fresh.

Oh, and Generation Y do not have any friends named Bill and Joyce so be sure to get rid of them from your examples and role plays and manuals.

No Bullshit> Well this is pretty simple. Make sure you believe what you say and that it is true because Generation Y will smell a lie a mile away. The slightest embellishment or insincerity will set it off their bullshit meter. You shouldn't need to make it up. If you have analysed the rationale behind everything, and you are the expert in your topic, which you should be, then there will be no need to make anything up.

2> Interactive

Now that you have made sure everything is relevant, you have to make the delivery interactive. Before you think too far into this, there are many different ways to be interactive and they do not all require people on stage and group activities. You can be interactive with an audience and engage them by using potent examples they have had some experience with or can relate to. You can be interactive by asking simple questions, and getting your audience to truly think about what you are saying and what they are doing in relation to what you are saying. One of my favourite techniques is to ask 'Have you ever ...' or 'Do you ever ...' and to create a scenario I know my audience have experienced. This is interactive. Regardless of how, you must do it. Here are some ideas:

Group Activities> Breaking your audience up into groups to go and brainstorm a problem or deal with a hypothetical situation is priceless. People of all ages will become engaged in such a process, providing the problem or situation is relevant and in some way interesting.

You might actually get some brilliant insights and solutions to problems you had not been able to solve. Use these environments to perhaps deal with real company problems using the team-working, problem-solving or creative-thinking tools you have just been teaching them.

Group activities and assignments turn training into a work in progress. Say, for example, you were teaching a five-step problem-solving technique. Start with a problem and have the groups work on its solution using the technique you are teaching. But do it step by step. You might teach step 1 of the problem-solving technique and have the group work on that, and then teach step 2 and have them work on that and so on.

You could then have each group role-play and teach the rest of the participants what they did to solve the problem, or how they handled a customer complaint in front of the group. It will certainly make your trainings more interactive and even funny.

I am a big fan of using competition to create interaction. Competition is sometimes avoided because we are usually attempting to create a team culture, but I firmly believe it has a place within organisations. Companies should promote the competitive spirit. The true competitive spirit, that is. Competition, by root definition, actually means to conspire together. You want some healthy competition within your organisation because it promotes efficiency, creates motivation and at the end of the day, business is competitive. Use the same principles in the training room. Find the best solution. Have the participants judge. Have some fun with this. You could even make it lighthearted. For example, for every good idea someone has in a brainstorm, or for every 100% score on a skills test, the participant gets three shots at a mini basketball ring, or hoops on a stake. If they get three out of three they win lunch, or $10, or tickets to the movies. Be inventive.

Questions> Build questions into your presentations – thoughtful ones – both as a part of your dialogue as well as formal, preset questions. Use questions as a means to engage your audience. This creates the opportunity for your Generation Y participants to come up with their own conclusions and ideas on the training material. Allow them to share their views on this. You may be pleasantly surprised at just how well some of them grasp the material, and how some will have potent personal examples and experiences they can share with the group.

Role Plays and Simulation> It is not my intention to rattle off all the techniques good trainers already use, and apply them to Generation Y. But I am going to make particular mention of role play. Role plays can help to create a better understanding of how some theoretical piece of information applies in the real world. They also keep people involved and active, as opposed to passive, in their learning. Just as important, it makes the whole experience a little more humorous and fun.

I would like to make a comment here about the use of e-learning, CD ROMs, video and other technology-based forms of training. All have their place and all can be effective, but let me just say this. The computer is not a passive instrument. It is highly interactive and user controlled. And so is DVD. DVDs are interactive, allowing the user to instantly skip to where he or she wants to go. Oh, and if you are still using videos, THROW THEM OUT! It is not that expensive to have the footage put onto DVD, which gives you much more control and flexibility. You can break it up into short segments. I have seen CD ROMs that are just like reading a book on the computer screen. This does not work. People, especially not Generation Y, don't like to read copious amounts of words on the screen. Just ask Stephen King. The key to using any of these mediums is to make them as interactive as possible. Ensure that the user has control, and that the program is active, not passive.

3> Personalised

Ask any marketer how effective a mass-appeal campaign is with Generation Y. Not at all will be their answer. Generation Y do not respond to anything that is clearly not designed for them. If you don't care enough to personalise the message, then they don't care enough to listen to it. Personalising the message is both easy and difficult. It can be as simple as keeping the group size down so it becomes more personal, or using examples and case studies from the group itself. Or it can be as challenging and complicated as training on demand, and allowing people to work at their own pace.

Job Specific> Keep all training specific to people's jobs. Don't try to save on budget by putting together people in completely different positions to learn how to use some new piece of technology if they each will need to use it in different ways. Sure, if the application is the same then it is not a problem, but otherwise avoid things like this. By keeping people in groups where the application is similar, you can use more relevant examples, and the training will feel more personalised.

Don't train people in what they don't need. Don't just do it because you have always done it, or because everyone else who works here gets this training. Training will need to be personalised and customised as much as possible. Don't use the blanket approach because you will get blanket results. Look for the skill deficiencies and train there. In many cases, it will be things like communication skills, relationship-building skills and other softer skills where your Generation Y talent will need the most attention.

Training on Demand> The concept of training on demand is not new. At least not to industries that have been training Generation Y for a while. The idea is that people have access to the information they need when they need it, and not before. At first glance, it seems most appropriate to entry-level positions, but if you think about it carefully, it applies in more professional positions as well. Let me give an example of each. Having an easily accessible manual, job cards or even an online or computer-based learning program means that when a new employee needs to know how to make a purchase order, or transfer a phonecall, or ring off and count a cash register, they can access clear and easy to understand instructions on how to do that, when they need it. Or perhaps for the first three months a new graduate is with you, they don't see clients, and when they do, they will be required to observe as opposed to being in control. As such, an intense communications skills program can wait a couple of months. Allow your new staff to acclimatise themselves in the environment and to integrate their already learnt skills before lumbering them with more information that is not relevant yet.

Online learning tools are good for this, and so are DVDs. The problem is having them readily accessible and at the point of use. Think hard about what the best training schedule would be like, and how you can make the training you offer, and when it is offered, more flexible. This may prove a little difficult if you are not a massive corporation with regular training programs running on say, customer service skills, in which department managers can enroll their people at will.

One Australian company that is leading the way in this regard is Rebel Sport. They have more than 2300 staff, and all new staff must do an online induction course covering product knowledge, merchandising and excellence in customer service. It is called 'Rebeluni' and includes four inductions, fourteen product, and five skill-based online modules. They claim it is extremely effective.

Self-Controlled Learning> The age-old challenge of education is how do you educate a group when each person learns in different ways and at different speeds? Still a tough gig, but technology is making it all the more possible. Using technology, certain types of training can be controlled by the end user. For example, a CD ROM can give you the option of hearing an audio clip explaining a technique, allow you to see a flow chart and some general text about it, and can even give you a hypothetical scenario in which you can apply it. Powerful, huh! And the user can choose which they prefer, or all.

This kind of self-controlled learning can create serious leverage for your organisation. If you train large numbers of people, and the training lends itself to this kind of mass production, then there could be some huge savings to be made here. Is your company getting with the technology program? Are you using it to its full potential?

It is important that you factor into any type of self-controlled learning some sort of skill validation. Whether it be in the form of a question for each topic that must be answered correctly before your staff can move on, or managers making sure the skills are being sufficiently learnt.

For those of you who must stay in the 'pit' (the inside name for the training platform or floor), a small piece of advice: keep Generation Y on their toes. You would be better off pushing them and keeping things moving than going too slowly.

4> Entertaining

If you are yet to join the rest of the world in the new millennium, then here is a reality check. We are no longer in the information age. We are in the entertainment age. If you are not entertaining people, you are dead. But listen carefully! By entertaining I don't mean performance, with all the bells and whistles. I mean genuinely engaging people. Joseph Pine and James Gilmore, of the Harvard Business School, in their ground-breaking book *The Experience Economy*, say that an experience is an event that engages someone in a personal way. Are your trainings an experience? Are your participants engaged in a personal way? Do they leave eager to share their experience with someone else? If they don't, they need to be. Generation Y will not just sit around and absorb information like sponges. They want to be stimulated. And by stimulated I mean engaged in a personal way. They want to be Edutained!

We are no longer in the information age. We are in the entertainment age.

You are trying to educate a generation that has five hours of screen time a day. A day. Try competing with that! Is it possible? Absolutely! But I have news for you ... POWERPOINT IS NOT ENTERTAINING!

So many presenters and trainers make the mistake of going high tech to entertain. High tech is not going to guarantee that your audience is engaged. In fact, if it is not done right, it will do the opposite. If your trainers require PowerPoint to be entertaining then get new trainers! And realistically, how entertained do you think Generation Y will be by your high-tech devices? Have you seen just how advanced game technology has become? Have you seen how intense the special effects are in the latest Hollywood blockbusters? You did see *Lord of the Rings*, didn't you? And what about *The Matrix*? Think about it. Unless you have the budget of a Hollywood production to design your training experience, then you are just not going to compete. It costs $56 million dollars, on average (AVERAGE!), to make a Hollywood movie. The solution is not necessarily high tech. It can help, but it should be an enhancement, not the only thing. The chances of creating an entertaining DVD on your budget are pretty slim. Use it, sure, they work as an aid, but they are not the whole answer. Training takes people. Devices rarely engage people emotionally, people do. Even in movies and games and on the net it is the people factor, be they characters, be they your selected player on the game, be it your mate on the other side of the world that you are speaking to over the net. It is ALWAYS about people. The key to engaging and entertaining your staff in the training environment is a good trainer.

The key to engaging and entertaining your staff in the training environment is a good trainer.

Sack the trainer!> Is it time you did something different with your training department? Are they staying with the times? If you are a trainer, ask yourself this: Are you still inspired by what you do each day? If not, sack yourself! There is no place on our platforms and in our seminar rooms for people who are not inspired by the opportunity to make a positive difference in the lives of others.

WOW Factor> If your training is to become the experience you need it to be in order to engage Generation Y, then you need a WOW factor. People need to be seriously moved emotionally. Again, it is all about the presenter. Why not complement your programs with someone from the outside. Someone who gets paid to add WOW to conferences and training programs all the time. Hire a WOWer!

High Stimulation> After you have hired great trainers and secured the WOW factor, go looking for extra stimulation.

You will find it in visual aids. And yes, that could include PowerPoint. It could even include a whiteboard or flipchart. Use all of them if needs be and use them with colour.

Use music. In fact, appeal to as many senses as possible. Let them see, feel, touch, try, smell, taste and experience what it is that you are talking about. Give them an experience. This is engaging. If you want to learn more about how to appeal to the different senses and different learning styles, get in touch with Glenn Capelli at the True Learning Centre <www.glenncapelli.com>.

Humour is still the universal language. If you can be funny, that's great. If you can't, don't try. Of course, you don't have to be funny to be entertaining, a mistake I made in my first year or so as a speaker. I realised, quickly, that people are entertained if you are passionate and are delivering information of value. Whether it be funny or not. Just don't be BORING! Boring is the enemy of Generation Y. It repulses them. Generation Y would prefer physical pain to being bored. Isn't that insane?

As a trainer, we can get too caught up in using one aid, or delivering our material in the same way. Avoid this. The world-famous presenter and speech coach, Patricia Fripp, says that the enemy of the speaker is sameness. Variety is your source of life in a training room full of Generation Yers. Mix it up. Tell stories, do role plays and group activities, involve them in competition. You could even use a short film, or some music. Just don't use the same one ALL THE TIME!

Variety is your source of life in a training room full of Generation Yers.

Let me make a couple of quick points about manuals, workbooks and videos.

Manuals and Workbooks:

- **Avoid being repetitive**
- **Use colour**
- **Be visual**

Videos:

- **Throw them out and replace them with DVDs**
- **Make a series of short and sharp segments**
- **Avoid corny. If you can't, be so corny everyone knows it is a joke**
- **Invest the money in doing it right**

Youth 2 Youth

One of the best strategies I know for keeping your orientation and training programs Generation Y friendly is to use Generation Y in the creation and delivery of them. Consider these options:

- **Have current Generation Y employees share their insights and experiences with new recruits at orientation and training days.**
- **Consider having some of your top-performing Generation Yers teach the new ones in your office a particular aspect of the training. Let them share some of the insider secrets that have led to their success. The experience will be an excellent way to develop the communication skills of your existing Generation Y employees. Don't take this too far. Just because someone is excellent at a particular task, it does not automatically mean they will be excellent at training other people in that same task.**
- **Team new talent up with other young talent who have been in the job for a while, so they can buddy them through and help them get settled in their new job.**
- **Get feedback from all seminar participants to give you ideas on how training could be improved and made more entertaining.**
- **Set up a Generation Y taskforce to brainstorm and devise ways to improve your current training. The experience will be excellent for them, and they will enjoy the extra responsibility, the challenge, and the creativity the task requires.**
- **Where possible, invite Generation Y themselves to share their ideas and experiences in a particular area.**

Tips for Presenters and Trainers

You will already have gathered that training the trainer will be essential. The problem will be finding someone who can train the trainer to be effective with Generation Y. I have seen many speakers and trainers working with this generation, and very few are able to keep them interested and engaged. It is possible, and I have had to do it myself in some very difficult circumstances, with the worst material and with the toughest audiences you can imagine. It can be done.

When I first set up my speaking and consulting business, I went to see Doug Malouf, a world-renowned speaker and one of the pioneers in the industry in Australia. I wanted to learn from Doug. He made me do all sorts of strange activities, one of which was to do my talk to a brick wall. When I questioned Doug as to the effectiveness of such a technique, he replied, 'If you can't be passionate and inspiring in front of a brick wall, you will have no chance when you get in front of 200 sixteen year olds sitting with their arms folded thinking, "Just try and teach me something, mate".' Point taken!

As a presenter in the Ask the Experts session at the National Speakers Association of Australia 2003 Conference, I was asked to share with other professional speakers the secrets of communicating to Generation Y. Here are the secrets I shared at that conference and have since shared with a number of other groups, including teachers and business trainers:

Peter Sheahan's Seven Tips for Presenters and Trainers

1> **Come out blazing**

You don't need to warm up your Generation Y audience. You need to set them on fire. Don't start a presentation to Generation Y with 'Good morning, please bear with me as I get through some important points', or 'Can you hear me down the back?'. An ice-breaker is always good. It shows you are not overly serious and that you know how to have a bit of fun. It also gets your audience's attention and can help you set the tone for your workshop or seminar.

You have to prove from the first minute that you are no ordinary trainer or speaker, and that you are good at what you do. You also want to demonstrate early that you are passionate about what you do and not just there for the pay cheque. It is not always very easy when you are presenting, day in day out, the same material. I was asked by a careers adviser in a school last year, after one of my presentations, if I get bored, considering I do over 450 presentations per year. I explained that I almost never do, but that the key is to remind myself every time I go on stage why I do what I do and how important it is for the audience to hear what I say, and for the company or school that engages me to deliver it.

2> **Leave your ego at the door**

It was once said to me that to be a seminar presenter, you need to be both thick-skinned and thin-skinned at the same time. Thin-skinned enough to be passionate enough to do what you do and share your ideas and insights, but thick-skinned enough to handle the fact that not everyone is going to like you. And knowing just how blunt Generation Y can be, you had better be even more thick-skinned. I remember after about six months in business, I confided to a mentor of mine, a long-time speaker, that I was a little upset that about 5% of my audiences, no matter what I did or said, just did not seem to get what I was trying to convey, or worse, did not seem to like me. He said, 'Are you serious? About 30% don't like me.' Now when I speak to organisations, I aim for more like the 30% on the 'not like' scale because my job as a presenter is to provoke and challenge paradigms, not to keep the status quo. And when you challenge the status quo people will inevitably resist.

3> **Ramp it up!**

With Generation Y, everything is intensified. You really need to be outrageous to get their attention. You really need to put yourself on the line for them to respect you. It is a natural tendency when faced with a tough audience like Generation Y that we hold back a little to avoid looking stupid. This is all about ego. It is about your fear of not looking good. Training and speaking is not about you. It is about the audience. So dump any need you have to protect 'how good you look', and just get stuck into it. My advice, when your audience are getting tough and look like they are losing interest is to RAMP IT UP!

I assure you that there will be plenty of times when you need to do this. Talented young people have the 'youthful arrogance' to go with it, and will test you. They will push and push and push just to see if you can take it.

4> **Straight shoot**

Tell the truth. Get to the point. And keep it simple, stupid! Generation Y will not appreciate you dancing around the important issues. Or trying to soften things. They respect the truth, and they can handle the truth.

5> **Weave Your Magic**

Use every tool in your belt. Metaphors, stories, insightful questions, role plays, characters and dialogue. The lot. And at times, you may need to just dump the script and go with the heart, and get in the flow. Generation Y will be as unpredictable as any audience you have come across, so be prepared for that. I always keep a few activities or stories up my sleeve to use if things get a little dry and boring.

One of the most powerful techniques I have used with Generation Y is to play on the curiosity factor. For the first 20 minutes of one of my presentations aimed at a young audience at school or in entry-level positions in the workplace, I come across as a bum, because after school, I made what may at first seem like 'crazy choices'. They turned out to be excellent choices, but I don't let my audience know that for a while. You have to keep them guessing. By being passionate and a little outrageous, you will keep Generation Y's attention. You won't need any visuals or even group activities if you have them curious to know what you are going to do or say next.

As a trainer and a speaker, your content will often be fixed. If you notice that some of your material is not being well received by your Generation Y participants, this is not reason to change your message. Just change how you present it. Change your style. Maybe add or change a few stories. Consider using a role play or some sort of group activity. Don't avoid it or give it insufficient time because it is harder to present.

6> **Don't be something that you are not**

Don't try to get down on their level if you are not one of them. For example, don't wear SMP or Billabong if it just isn't your style. Don't use words like 'cool', 'grouse', 'sick' or other parts of Gen'y'nese if it just doesn't suit your image or style. They will see it as you trying to manipulate them. Trying to win them over. Trying to be cool is not cool! Or as a Generation Yer said to me the other day, 'If someone has to say they are cool then they are not.'

You do not need to be one of them. You just need to be personable. Likeable! I find building rapport with Generation Y very easy because I am one of them. So naturally, I have more rapport and therefore greater power to influence. However, it is essential that I remain just a little different. Not better, or higher, but I certainly need to demand a certain level of respect or else how will I create a shift in their thinking, behaviour and therefore performance? You must learn to keep the balance.

7> **Don't judge the book by its cover**
I have already said that you will get from Generation Y what you expect. I received an excellent piece of advice in one of my talks from a 16-year-old boy with a mohawk and more visible piercings than I have fingers. He told me, 'It's not about what I think looks good that matters. It's about what the people I want to do business with think looks good that matters.' Generation Y are smart, insightful, and in most cases, pretty switched on. Sure they may be more confident at times than they are competent, but they are a genuine asset to your company. If you think of them this way and approach them this way, you are guaranteed to get better results. We have all read about the studies where a teacher was told he or she had a gifted and talented class, even though the students actually had learning disabilities, and the teacher would not let them settle for a second-rate performance, but instead demanded more from them. After all, he or she thought they were gifted and talented. The teacher's expectations were met. The students excelled. They did the same in reverse. Give a teacher the gifted and talented class, but say the students have a learning disability, and the students will perform poorly. Thankfully, researchers don't interfere with people's lives and development in this way anymore in the name of science, but the principle still holds true. People will inevitably live up to your expectations of them. It is known as the self-fulfilling prophecy.

So think highly of your Generation Y audiences. They are not as scary as you think or as they might look.

Real training does not take place in the classroom

Real training is not the forcing of information into the minds of your employees, and it does not really take place in the training room. Real training takes place on the job, where Generation Y get to use some of what they were taught. It is one thing to 'get it' in the training room, it is another to 'do it' in the workplace. You and your managers and supervisors, and in fact your entire department, need to be the example. Your new staff are more likely to do what you do than do what you say they should do in the training room. No matter how independent and free-thinking Generation Y are, they, like everyone, have an intense need to belong and to fit in. They crave connection. As such, they will either morph to the culture of your organisation, or leave. What culture are they going into? Is this the culture you want and need?

You sure didn't learn how to drive a car in a classroom, or by sitting the driving test. You learnt to drive by doing it. Under supervision and instruction of course, but ultimately, you did it yourself.

Skills transfer (the role of training) does not necessarily create behavioural change (often management's delusion as to the role of training). It is the old adage: you can take a horse to water but you can't make it drink. You can teach a man, but you can't make him think. You can ask a man, but you can't make him do. Sure you might have the best training programs in the world, but if your managers are lousy and your reward and recognition system is not conducive to the desired behaviour, then behavioural change will not occur. Training, and ultimately behavioural change, must break past the boundaries of the training room, and the responsibility of training needs to be not just on the back of the trainer but on the back of the managers, supervisors and everyone in the workplace. It is the job of every good manager to ensure their staff know how to do their job. A manager or supervisor should have some sort of checks in place, allowing them to ensure their staff are performing as they should be, using the tools and techniques they 'learnt' in the training room.

Training and, more broadly, learning, should become part of our everyday lives. The world is changing so fast that we must learn constantly if we are to stay abreast. **Remember what Eric Hoffer said, 'in times of change, the learner will inherit the earth while the learned will find themselves well equipped to deal with a world that no longer exists.'**

Your Quest!

These ought to get you thinking:

> Are your training programs still relevant for the work? Do they need to be reinvented or destroyed?

> Have you looked at the rationale behind everything that you teach? If not, do it now and dump what no longer makes a difference, or no longer makes sense.

> Are you appealing to the lowest common denominator, or does your training challenge participants to step up to a higher level?

> Are your examples, stories and metaphors fresh? What about your training aids and workbooks?

> How interactive are your training programs?

> If you use CD ROMS, DVDs or computer-based training, ask yourself: How interactive are they?

> Do you offer training on demand? How might you, and your organisation, offer more personalised training solutions for your staff?

> Are your training programs built on an 'entertaining' foundation? Are your trainers entertaining? Do you need a fresh new team in your training department? Should you perhaps outsource more training?

> Are you using the existing knowledge of your Generation Y talent to tailor and improve your training programs to better suit people like them?

Managing

Managing comprises so many different elements it could be a book in itself. In order to make this chapter more readable, and more practical, we will break Managing into the following chapters:

- **Motivating**
- **Day-to-day Management**
- **Communicating**
- **Developing**

In many ways, the simple answer to managing Generation Y is to treat everyone like an individual, and more importantly, like a human being. Generation Y simply will not tolerate being treated like a number, or a cog in a wheel. They have a personality, a soul, needs and wants. The simple concept that we manage people (underline PEOPLE) might be enough. I, of course, will not leave it at that, rather I will share with you a few ideas and a few strategies for better managing your Generation Y talent. Strategies that, if applied, will improve the productivity of your workforce and better still, reduce the tension you feel just trying to stay in control on a day-to-day basis.

It is so tempting in a time like this to revert to more regulation and less flexibility in the workplace, but such a decision will kill an organisation, especially one that relies heavily on talent. We must embrace all talented individuals, their ambiguity, fleeting attention and seeming nonchalance, because by doing so, we will, as promised, see the fruits of their creativity and flair in the workplace. Don't, however, think I mean give them free reign. NO WAY! Accountability is a big part of managing Generation Y. Few others have taught them the need to be accountable, so as employers, we had better not make the same mistake.

One of the areas of resistance I have found in big Australian companies and firms comes from the fear that if they are to adapt to Generation Y they will be adopting this kind of free-reign management. It is just not true. But on the other hand, we will not be reverting to the autocratic style of management of years gone by. Imagine a pendulum similar to the one in the diagram below that sways between Directing on the left and Coaching on the right. And in the middle you have Mentoring.

Transformational Management

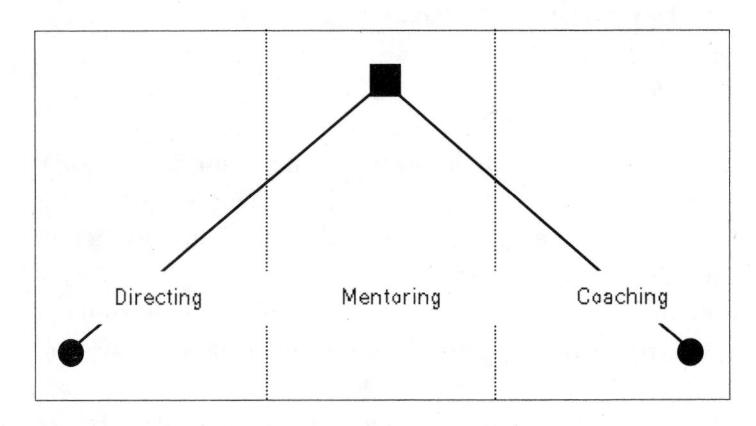

This is indicative of the three major management approaches.

1> Directing is to create very rigid systems and procedures and to ensure they are strictly adhered to. There is no leeway for creativity or personal input. The manager tells, never seeks input, and supervises not only results but methodology as well.

2> Mentoring is a combination of telling and asking. It is a process of setting clear objectives and results, but allowing for some creativity and input regarding methodology.

3> Coaching is to support and bring out of someone the results they desire. Coaching, in a management context, involves drawing out of, as opposed to forcing in. It is based on the premise that if you ask the right questions, people will come up with the right answers for themselves. By its very nature, it requires the manager to have no 'personal agenda' when entering a coaching session with a team member. Great idea in theory, impossible in practice.

Some managers fear the coaching style of management, and in some ways rightly so. I think the mentoring model is actually more effective. It is a two-way street and engages the needs and objectives of the organisation (through the manager) with the desire on the side of the employee to have some flexibility to use their knowledge and creativity in the way they choose in order to meet those objectives, while at the same time, ensuring that the collective knowledge of the manager and company is used in the formulation of that methodology. In simple terms, combine asking and allowing the individual to do things their way with telling and input based on many years of experience.

This kind of mentoring approach will produce the best results with Generation Y. You will notice, however, that I refer twice to the role of coaching in the management of Generation Y. This is true. They are open to coaching and it definitely needs to be a major part of how we manage Generation Y. It does, however, need to be combined with clear direction and expectations, and knowledge that the usually more experienced manager has.

It has also been my experience that when companies take a coaching approach to the way they lead and manage they do so only after setting clear performance expectations. Which by my definition is actually mentoring – a combination of directing and coaching. These companies actually mentor because they combine the skill of coaching with advice and clearly set objectives and deliverables. They have begun to see the need to add the skill of coaching to the already developed directing skills of managers, which in my language will result in a very powerful mentoring relationship between leader (manager) and team player (employee).

I will pay particular attention to the need for more coaching both in the chapter on motivating and again in developing. And I will pay fairly limited attention to directing because I see coaching as the major deficiency in the way most companies I work with manage their young staff.

I call it 'Transformational Management'. Mentoring as a management approach will transform the skills and qualities of those involved, making both the leader and the team player more powerful and effective people. It is 360-degree mentoring, where both players are mentor and mentee. And if you were to analyse what Generation Y say they want from a job, a boss and a workplace it is exactly that: to be transformed. To become smarter, stronger, wealthier and hopefully healthier than when they started. As you will discover in the chapter on Exiting, if you look at your role as one of transformer then you will go further in developing your people and in protecting your employer brand when people leave, because you will know this is what happens, and that this is what is best for the individual and the company. You will allow your people to move on and be further transformed elsewhere, hopefully one day to return to you and your organisation an even more powerful and effective person.

I won't lie; it will be a bumpy ride with Generation Y. I know. I work with more than 40,000 each year. But it is a very rewarding ride. I assure you hope is not lost. A few tweaks to your current management tactics, or possibly a complete reinvention of you as a manager may be required, but whichever it is, invest the time and energy because the rewards will be worth it. **Generation Y will not only force you to be better managers of them, but TO BE BETTER MANAGERS FULL STOP.**

This last point is perhaps the most important of the entire book. The strategies and approaches detailed throughout are more and more becoming the demands of the entire workforce. In fact, some business experts even argue that the problem is not really Generation Y but a combination of things: Generation Y's unwillingness to put up with old-directing-style bosses, Generation X's unwillingness to continue with the long hours and 'corporate slavery', and the Baby Boomers' move to pursue a better quality of life.

Motivating

Many of you will find that the Generation Yers entering your workforce are thinking 'car' not 'career'. However, the truly talented will not. And even those that are could start thinking 'career' if you show them what is possible. If you motivate them and engage them in what you do and how they can play an important role. A survey of 11,000 17–21 year olds who had recently enlisted in the United States Army is testament to this fact. Despite a bloody war raging in Iraq, and with the United States under more and more threat of terrorist activity each day, Generation Y are joining the army in record numbers. When asked why, it was not the signing bonus, nor was it the tuition reimbursement. It was the desperate desire to belong to something bigger than themselves.

Generation Y are on a passionate quest for experience. They want to live the life. They want to make a difference. But they want to be active in choosing and moulding that experience. They potentially seek some of that experience in the workforce, in which case they will become dedicated and loyal employees. If you are not providing it at work, they will seek it elsewhere and treat work as a means to achieving that end.

Even if Generation Y are treating work as a means to another end, and are thinking car instead of career, fine. Use this to motivate them. Set a standard of work that is acceptable and have them live up to it. You may be a means to an end, but to be honest, some jobs will never be any more than that. Let's get real. Convincing a Generation Yer that flipping burgers is making a significant, positive contribution to the world just won't work. These guys aren't stupid. However, this does not mean flipping burgers can't be fun. Motivation comes in many forms. Career, making a difference, buying a car, buying 'stuff'. Whatever! The key is to make your workplace as engaging for your Generation Y employees as possible. Whether that be through a burning desire to make a difference in the world, or just a straight out fun place to work is in some ways irrelevant. Both will produce profitable results for your business.

Diverse Rewards

Money

In order to motivate the new talent force in our businesses, we need to look at more than the traditional forms of monetary compensation. Not because they don't work, they clearly do. However, everyone uses them, so in many ways, it is a given. The golden rule with monetary compensation is that it needs to be fair and equitable. Salaries for Generation Y need to reflect the marketplace as well as be considered fair relative to the incomes of the people they work with. It is as simple as that. Generation Y, like everyone else, will only be motivated so much by money. Sure, initially it is certainly a powerful motivator, but once it becomes fair, it ceases to motivate. A satisfied need no longer motivates. Once you have met the desired compensation of an employee, throwing more and more money at them to improve performance simply will not work. You must begin then to look at more intrinsic elements. After all, lasting motivation is always intrinsic.

If I am as valuable to you as you say I am, PAY ME MORE!

Before moving on, though, I want to make a couple of final points about money. The fastest and easiest way for an employee to judge how much they are valued by the company they work for is to see how much they are paid. End of story. One of my own staff said, if I am as valuable to you as you say I am, PAY ME MORE! Generation Y are, after all, a very materialistic generation and will need good cashflow to maintain their lifestyles. Generation Y are more motivated by money than Generation X have been.

In some of the most basic, entry-level positions in Australia, employees are paid less, or only slightly more, money than if they were on welfare. A disgrace! Something for you to think about. If cash were all that mattered, no-one would work these jobs, they would simply take welfare. Clearly, employment is about much more than just cash. If cash were the only answer, then commission-based employees would all be superstars. This is not the case.

Non-Cash Benefits

One manager who gets it right is Edward Kaleel. I have mentioned Edward's company, the Marc Edward Agency, a couple of times. He knows that money is important, but he also knows that his staff are human beings with dreams and aspirations. Instead of giving a Christmas bonus to his best-performing staff, he helps them realise some of their dreams. For instance, one of his staff was constantly talking about how much she wanted to go to Paris. One day, Edward walked in with a plane ticket and said, 'Here. Take two weeks off next month and enjoy Paris.' Sounds expensive, but $2000 for tickets, for a key employee, is not that expensive. He did the same for a team member who wanted to go to London. Ed also buys all the female staff Tiffany's for their birthdays and Christmas. It truly is the effort and the thought that counts. These sorts of things will be infinitely more memorable than a cash bonus. Talk about creating employee loyalty. Brilliant, I say.

If you want to know what other benefits your Generation Y employees will be grateful for, why don't you ask them? What is a motivator and reward for you will not necessarily be a motivator and a reward for someone else. You are not a mind reader and no-one expects you to be, so why not just ask. A little tip I learnt in the hotel industry was to listen very carefully at Staffies. Staffies is where, after work, the staff who did the night shift stay back for a quiet drink. It was in these conversations that I learnt the most about my staff. Sure, the hotel industry has many transient employees who come and go. But are most other businesses any different? We all have businesses like that. It was the core group of talented managers and supervisors I was most concerned with. I remember hearing a conversation with one of the full-time waitresses and one of my female duty managers. They were both commenting on how they had never been to a tropical resort. Both key members of my team, so keeping them happy and engaged was clearly important. I called one of the major liquor companies we dealt with and requested a promotion. Not for patrons but for staff. I wanted one prize, and a bonus for running the promotion. A trip for two to a tropical island was the bonus. I had all staff compete for the cash prize. The person who collected the most sold bottle tops won. I simply gave the trip to the two women and said thanks for your help, have a great week. It cost me nothing, and cost the liquor company very little. They already had a strong affiliation with the resort, so the trip was free. All the company had to pay for were the airfares and the cash prize. It cost less than $600, but massively increased sales of their products and made two of my key staff very happy. BE CREATIVE!

Keep in mind that Generation Y are the immediate generation; they want it now. So make the incentives immediate if possible. Generation Y will take 'good' now over 'great' later every day of the week. Don't believe me? Check this out. It is not just Generation Y who do this. We all do. Survey researchers have found that if you send a $5 cheque with the survey versus offering a $50 cheque on receipt of the survey, the $5 now survey returned twice as many responses as the $50 reward later. Crazy? No. Human nature! The laws of conditioning are well researched, and one of the major keys is the timing of the reward. Try to catch them doing something right and then reward them on the spot. Maybe it is with $20 cash. Maybe

Get together a storehouse of small but effective rewards you can give on the spot, which won't cost an arm and a leg.

movie tickets, maybe an extended lunch break or an early finish that Friday afternoon. Get together a storehouse of small but effective rewards you can give on the spot, which won't cost an arm and a leg.

Incentivise everything. It is essential to tie bonuses to performance. AKA Incentives. **Stop spending all your time and energy with poor performers. Reward and recognise top performance**. The others will soon catch on. And don't just limit it to your managers. What about the ones who do the actual work? Your managers and supervisors don't sell your products or keep your customers happy. It is your staff. Focus on them. Incentives can be so very simple. In fact, the most powerful incentive of all costs nothing. NOTHING! It is called recognition.

The key to incentives is to make your success their success. Do not reward mediocre performance. Reward only good performance. In order to do this, you must make it clear to your Generation Y staff what is expected of them and what they need to do to earn their incentives. Incentive programs can go horribly wrong and have the reverse effect on motivation if expectations are not clear. You do not want someone working towards goal posts that do not exist or exist in a different location in your mind. Be sure everyone knows where they stand. This is the directing part of the management process.

Try to make the incentives fun. There is a group of Pizza Huts in the United States who have 'bonus bucks', which staff get given on the spot. At the end of the month, or quarter, at the staff meeting (turned social event) some great prizes are auctioned off using the 'bonus bucks'. Perhaps if you are a sales call centre you could have a small basketball ring mounted on the wall of the call centre, and next to it a bell. When staff make three sales in a day, or five in a week or whatever is appropriate, they ring the bell. When they ring the bell everyone knows that someone has made target, and with that comes the opportunity to have three shots at the hoop from a pre-determined distance. If they get three out of three they win movie tickets, or an early mark or something else inexpensive. Also, for each shot they get in, they get a ticket into the major draw (say every three months) where they can win a holiday. Don't just have the holiday, though. Be sure to have the instant reward as well. It will be as effective, if not more so, than the major prize. This kind of incentive is a double bang for your buck. Not only does it tie incentive to performance it is also fun. I can see the staff gathering around for what would be no more than three minutes to witness the three shots, and cheering and cajoling the person who has earned the right to shoot. Simple, inexpensive and great for staff morale.

Regular Recognition

We all crave recognition. Generation Y can't live without it. Their whole life they have been played up to and supported. Hence, the self-esteem on steroids. Even in schools now, teachers are not allowed to give what would in many ways be referred to as constructive criticism to their students, because it may be damaging to the self-esteem of the child. Catch 22! But what it means for you is a workplace full of prima donnas who expect to be stroked for every good deed. In other words, if recognition is not already a part of your culture. Make it one. FAST!

What it means for you is a workplace full of prima donnas who expect to be stroked for every good deed.

Recognition is not always what you think. It does not have to be elaborate (and expensive) awards presentations. Simple congratulations will suffice. Or a thank you. Try to do this publicly; we know that Generation Y crave the limelight so make them stars in front of their peers and they will love you for it. This kind of simple recognition for a job well done is more important than Friday massages, or an espresso machine in the kitchen. It is about people feeling valued and acknowledged for the contribution they make.

As a manager, you need to be on the constant lookout for your staff doing something right. And then in the moment, seize the opportunity and express your gratitude for their efforts. In management books it is called managing by wandering around. As a manager, of anyone, you should be out there in the war zone, not cooped up in an office doing paperwork. If your upper management swamp you with paper work, revolt. Not with disdain, but through brilliant performance of your team. The only way you will get brilliant performance from your team is if you become a part of it. It has long been known that what is recognised and rewarded will be repeated. So get out in your teams and start catching people doing things right.

Make your recognition personal. Don't send an email every time. Take them aside and shake their hand. Take them out for lunch. You will learn so much about these people in the process. Make it public. Not just in the way I have mentioned above. Maybe you could use your top Generation Y staff in your next advertising materials. Maybe you could put on every aisle 'prepared and maintained by Tommy Smith'. Let the world know how great your staff are. (After you have let *them* know first of course.) By doing this, and making a bit of a fuss about your staff, you turn the receiving of the reward into the reward itself.

A few words of caution. Keep recognition and rewards proportionate, otherwise you will raise the bar to levels you cannot sustain, and disappointment will result.

Be a little creative in how you recognise your staff. If you have particularly young Generation Y staff, perhaps a letter home to their parents telling them what a delight their son or daughter is to have in your workplace. Maybe you could purchase concert tickets to a forthcoming gig by a popular band. Choose carefully! Popular in the eyes of Generation Y. Remember, what is a reward to you may not be to them.

As with everything Generation Y, keep it authentic. Recognition by giving them a fancy business title for their position will last about a day. If that long. They are not bluffed by such activities. All this will do is raise the expectations of your Generation Y staff to a level that will only ever result in disappointment, and then of course, poor performance.

When I said recognise top performance I was not just talking about profit and sales. If you and your company are serious about your values and culture, reward staff who are exemplars of such values. Perhaps one of your younger staff members organises a great social function (let them do this sort of thing). Reward that. Maybe you saw them handle a customer complaint with empathy and understanding. Perhaps they brought to your attention an anomaly that staff could have exploited, or maybe they were truthful about theft that was occurring. **What is recognised and rewarded is repeated.**

Challenge Them

There are few more difficult tasks for a manager than to keep their staff 'challenged'. It is a fine line. I recall one of my sales staff in my seminar business complaining that she was not challenged anymore. When queried, she said she needed a new challenge, something more difficult to sink her teeth into. As far as I was concerned she was far from mastering the first challenge yet (very far). I think she wanted some variety, not more challenge. There is a difference. BIG difference. I think her need to be more 'challenged' was really a need for some variety and for her ego to be stroked. I mean that in a good way. Sort of. I think she wanted to feel like a more important part of the business, which is admirable. The trouble was explaining that she first needed to display her competence in her current areas of responsibility before being given more. I will talk more later about creating variety in the workplace, but first here are some ideas for challenging your up-and-coming stars.

'We take risks on people. If you sit around and wait until they have been around long enough to make it "safe" they will leave. People want to be challenged.'

Linda Botter,
Lion Nathan Australia

Whet their appetite for bigger and better things by inviting them to key meetings. Ask them to do some research in preparation for such a meeting. Ask their opinion where possible and relevant (even when it isn't relevant). Set them mini tasks and projects like a competition website review, or a product report. Ask them to survey some of your customers. Make sure it is not trivial. It better be of consequence or they will feel even less challenged, or worse, less valued.

Put them on new project teams regularly. Give them

'When given the chance Generation Y are brilliant. They add so much to the matters they are engaged in.'

Deborah Stonley, Henry Davis York

some responsibility on these teams. Perhaps they are responsible for coordinating everyone to be at the same place at the same time. Maybe they are responsible for selecting the meeting venues and organising some catering. Generation Y are not averse to risk. If you engage them in projects that are a little left of field and potentially will fail, but have a huge upside, Generation Y will go into battle for you.

Involve Generation Y in decision-making. Tom Peters says, if you do not have a board member under 30, get one. (I am available by the way ... Seriously.) He also says if you do not have someone in IT/IS under the age of 25 you are kidding yourself. And he isn't joking. Tom Peters never jokes. You don't become one of the most influential management thinkers of our time by joking. DON'T make it window dressing, though. A Foundation for Young Australians survey showed that 'window dressing' was the number one dissatisfaction expressed by Generation Y regarding their involvement in decision-making processes. Their research, titled 'Sharing a New Story: Young People in Decision-Making', reported that Generation Y want three things:

1> **Meaning:** They want to be doing something that has a bigger purpose and that they believe in.
2> **Control:** They want to be making real decisions, be heard, and having the resources to see the task through.
3> **Connectedness:** They wanted a team approach to decision-making.

Don't be afraid of including them in decision-making. Thankfully, they are well versed and experienced in making decisions. While they are over-parented in many ways, they are under-parented in others. They are the first real latchkey generation. They are often left to their own devices, have access to their own finances, and thus have the power to make decisions. Not only that, but infinitely more choices are available to young people nowadays, which means they have had to become skilled in the art of making decisions.

Generation Y value a collaborative approach. They just want to be involved. Oh, and ensure they get some recognition for their involvement.

It is essential that you manage this prudently. I have said repeatedly that it is not uncommon for Generation Y's confidence to exceed their competence. Don't throw them in too far over their heads because they may not swim. If you keep a collaborative approach, you can ensure you will seldom cross that line. This is mentoring, as opposed to just coaching. Another little piece of advice here is not to play all your trump cards at once. Always have some other project or responsibility up your sleeve for your Generation Yers if they continue to perform admirably.

The Employability Factor

It is all about the resume. No longer are people even thinking of staying with a company for life. They are thinking of where to next. How do I build my career? If you want to motivate Generation Y, keep this in mind. What are you offering that will enhance their resume? What exciting new projects will you make available to them? What new skills are they learning? The employability factor is a key motivator for Generation Y. If you can make them more employable, they will pledge their allegiance. Remember, your job is to transform!

Given the nature of today's workplace, particularly the white-collar workplace, there is less room for vertical movement. Organisations are getting flatter and flatter. Build into your program opportunities to move laterally. Have interdepartmental, and even international exchange programs. Not only does this enhance your image as an employer of choice, it will generate unique innovations in your own team and division. Major innovations can come from people outside of your industry. This is because they are not caught up in the day-to-day grind that ultimately causes blinkers. Plus, they are not conditioned to be limited in their beliefs about what is possible and what is not possible in your organisation. Swap talent with other departments and relish the fresh new perspective this brings.

Variety

Variety is the spice of life and, given that boredom is enemy number one of young talent, this is potentially your source of most leverage in motivating your Generation Y staff. This is particularly relevant for those in more mundane jobs, which is where most of your young talented individuals start. Here are some thoughts on adding variety to your workplace and to the jobs themselves, so you don't kill the flair you so desperately want from these people.

Fun

All managers of Generation Y should be allocated a 'Play Budget'. Money devoted to activities like a group social event, an inclusive (versus exclusive) competition, or even a surprise tray of doughnuts on a Monday morning. You may even like to ask Generation Y what they think your Play Budget should be spent on. Again, a simple technique that involves your Generation Y staff, and one that makes your decisions more effective.

'Fun won't happen unless it is in your budgets. It won't happen if managers don't plan for it.'

Rosemary Kirkby

Generation Y, despite their inbuilt desire to be grown up, are still kids at heart. WE ALL ARE! Everyone enjoys fun for fun's sake. Imagine the culture that would be created in your organisations if the primary role of your managers and supervisors was to be Play Makers. People who make the job fun. The increases in retention and performance would mean massive increases in profit. I like that term, PLAY MAKERS! Stop taking yourself so seriously. None of us are that important. Add some play to your workplace and watch not only how much better a time your staff are having, but how much better a time YOU are having.

Fun does not have to be unproductive. Even if at first some activities may seem as though they are. It is the improvement in morale and staff satisfaction (I hate that word) that will be productive.

Rotation

When surveyed, some Generation Yers say they would rather experience personal injury than be bored. So keep it interesting. HOW? What about rotating staff between roles for a bit of variety? Not only will it increase their skills, it will make their job more interesting. Plus, it will help you, and them, identify their strengths and weaknesses.

Let people do different sorts of projects. While I understand that you need good people in every position, and you can't keep moving and training and moving and training, if you don't offer some variety in people's roles then they will go elsewhere eventually, and in the meantime be disengaged.

Environment

I have a little task for you. Go to the break room, or kitchen that your staff go to, and give me three words to describe the environment. Is it a happy place? What about stimulating? Or perhaps engaging? If you thought of dull, boring and dirty then do something about it. Get a working bee happening and ask your staff what colour to paint the walls. Then have them do it.

What about this: do your Generation Y staff have any control over their environment? Do they have their own desk, or locker, or at least some place to put their stuff? Do they have the opportunity to personalise that space? Maybe put some pictures up? Such an activity, trivial as it may seem, is very powerful psychologically. To have some personal space, or at least adding a personal touch to a communal space, can create a tremendous sense of belonging and a team. Both very desirable in the culture of your organisation. A recent trend, which I hope will die FAST is 'hot desking', where you don't have a desk because you are often on the road or with clients; you have to book desk space when you need it, and then when finished you need to take everything home or away with you. I could not think of anything more clinical and transient. Where is the sense of belonging in such an environment? Try NOWHERE! I had a conversation with a Generation Yer in one of the big four accounting firms recently and the thing he said he hated most about his job was the hot desking set-up. I know when I worked at what was then Coopers & Lybrand that I chose that company over a similar firm. I chose them because they were the only ones that offered me a desk of my own. Go with PERSONAL, or better still, STIMULATING!

Build a Workspace that Motivates

In my work with Australian companies I have found that the design of the workspace is crucial to engaging and motivating staff. In fact, some would argue it plays a huge part in retaining them, too. It is no secret that our mood and performance reflects our environment. If you don't believe me, take a walk around your local hospital and tell me how it makes you feel. There is energy in our environment and unfortunately most Australian companies create the wrong energy in their work environments. In the new world economy the new model for doing business is Leverage Talent for Profit. Period! This requires talented people. Is your workspace attractive to highly talented people? Does it allow them to collaborate in the ways they need to give your company a competitive advantage in the marketplace? If not then it should. If you want a motivated and creative team, then the workspace needs to facilitate this.

Rosemary Kirkby, one of Australia's leading managers of organisational change, knows implicitly how to help generate positive cultural change in even the largest corporations. Part of how she does this, though not necessarily the first place she starts, is by changing the workspace. Check out Rosemary's tips for designing workspaces – drawn up specifically for this book!

Rosemary Kirkby's Seven Tips for Designing Workspaces that WORK!

1> **Design for Functionality**
Effective work environments arise from a deep understanding of the way in which work is done and life is

lived. Beware the designer who would promise you a funky space. It's not about a 'look' which can be copied from one organisation to another, or from the latest design magazine. Before you worry about how it looks it needs to work! Design your work environment to support the needs customers have of your people, and the personal and professional aspirations of the generations in your organisation.

It is not about being funky or modern. It is about being functional. Your workspace should facilitate work. Sure, play and pleasing aesthetics are a part of this, but at the core of the issues is productive work. Your workspace should be functional for your people, not for your output per square metre calculation.

2> **Design for Choice**

In any organisation there will be different work styles, depending on the work being done. Individuals also have preferences for the way in which they work.

In the same way a teacher must design lessons for students with different learning styles, we must also build workspaces knowing that people have different work styles, and that these styles will change depending on the time of day and the nature of work to be completed. You must design with choice in mind. Include quiet rooms, rooms for collaboration, hide-aways, relaxing spaces, stimulating spaces. Make it possible for all your people to find places to do quiet, concentrated work as well as places to collaborate, relax, share a coffee, celebrate achievement. It doesn't have to cost more. Think laterally!

3> **Design Laterally for Collaboration**

If you want an organisation which is fast and responsive to changes in the external environment (and who doesn't?) you need to make it possible for people to share ideas and work together effectively. Many work environments make connection with others very difficult. Make it easy and watch the ideas flow! The power structures in organisations are changing. We are seeing flatter and flatter management structures, and our workplaces should mirror this. Gone are the days when the higher your position the higher the floor you worked on and where your little blue plastic key allowed you to visit only your floor. It is time to crack the organisation right open, and to allow ideas to flow up and down and sideways, too.

4> **Design for a 24/7 World**

Also gone are the days when workplaces were designed for a mostly male workforce, working 9 to 5 in an organisation whose industry was shaped only by movements in the domestic economy. Yet many workplaces are still designed for that world.

At the same time, many of our most talented employees are demanding more flexibility to meet personal commitments and lifestyle goals. As talented workers begin to demand more and more flexibility, our workspaces need to mirror this. Different industries have different cycles, as do different departments. Be realistic about the way work is evolving in your organisation and plan to support it. Sometimes seriously long hours are required to get things done. Ensure your workspace facilitates this. Having the facilities to cook a healthy stir-fry will alleviate the reliance on takeaway pizza and will signal your care for the health and wellbeing of your project teams if they are staying late. Or if your call centre staff start work early, you might want to include breakfast cereal with their morning papers. A hungry consultant dealing with a difficult customer at 11am could be a recipe for disaster! Little things like this make a job all the more functional for the worker.

5> **Design Multi-Sensory Workspaces**
You want your people inspired and stimulated when they come to work. The physical environment, as much as the work itself, plays a part in this. Visually appealing environments are especially important for Generation Y. Don't stop at visual. How does it smell? How does it sound? Most importantly, how does it feel to be in that space? Humans are emotional creatures, and we trigger our emotions through our senses. Appeal to them in as many ways as possible. Good design doesn't have to cost more!

6> **Design for Life**
Nowadays people spend as much time, if not more, at work as they do at home. Stop talking about work–life balance and start talking about Life Balance. Is your workspace livable? And I don't mean can people sleep there. I mean, are there places where, depending on mood and circumstances, people can escape somewhere for privacy, or come together to socialise and collaborate if required. In the same way we would be able to in our homes. James Grose, Principal, Bligh Voller Nield architects and the architect for National at Docklands and Campus MLC, is a medium-density house designer. It was knowledge of how people live that allowed him to design workspaces that WORK!

7> **Use a Multi-Disciplinary Approach to Design that does not try to Create Culture Change**
Too often people try to use physical design in the workspace as a way to instigate change. Research has shown that the WOW factor of a new workspace lasts just six weeks. If the management styles and work practices do not support the new space, it will simply be funky, not functional. Workspace design is just one part of cultural change. It needs to be a part of a much bigger initiative. You do not need designers, you need experts in cultural change.

Social Workplace

We all want to work with people we like and trust. Period. If you want your staff to work better as a team then take a close look at what level of social interaction you encourage. Do you have staff drinks on a Friday night? Do you have a regular monthly staff social event? This is not a Year 8 classroom, where people don't talk or even look at the person next to them. We all know that approach does not even work in education, let alone in business. If you don't talk to the other people you work and learn with in business, you will no longer even be in business. Encourage social interaction. In fact, facilitate it.

'Don't give us a new workspace, with new desks and bright colours if when I get here in the morning I still can't service the customer properly.'

Focus Group response prior to building Campus MLC

If you get out of their way, they will probably create it themselves. Why not appoint someone to be the social director? Better still, appoint more than one. Give them a budget and a suitable time and have them come back with a proposal. You may even go out on a limb and make it during work time. Two or three times a year in the hotel I managed, we would close, on a normal trading night, and have a staff party. Sometimes we would go on a cruise, other times we would just have a meal together. Paid for by the hotel on hotel time. For a smallish business, this can be an expensive thing to do but the rewards were worth it. Six months later, people were still talking about the cruises and the nights. It gave my managers and supervisors a chance to let their hair down a little with their staff, making them much more personable and approachable when work resumed as normal.

Balanced Outlook

The concept of work–life balance is not new. Many people I talk to are sick of hearing about it. Well, bad news. It is not a fad and it is not going away. The only thing I think ought to be different is that we should stop making the distinction between work and life. They are one and the same thing. It should be life balance.

Generation Y, as we have already discovered, are lifestyle centred. This, by the way, does not mean that they only want to work 9 to 5 three days a week (although some certainly will). Rather, it means that they will either make work a fully integrated part of their life and part of their identity (good for you), or they will treat it as a means to achieving what they really want out of life. The key is not to get them to go one way or the other, but to realise that they are fully functioning human beings with wants and desires, who cannot, and never will be, fully satisfied by work. Happy people produce professional results. **Personally developed people produce professional results**. Look at employees beyond the walls of their cubicle and treat the whole person.

Personally developed people produce professional results.

In medicine, it has long been known that the most effective forms of treatment deal with the whole person, not just the symptom. Your staff are no different. You will often find the cause of poor workplace performance not to be a lack of competence, or lack of empowerment, or lack of resources, but often some personal challenge that is eating away at your staff member from the inside out.

Try getting to know your staff. Have lunch with at least one staff member each week. Ask them how they are. But be genuinely interested in their response and LISTEN! They will give you plenty of cues on what might be going well or not so well for them. I am often told after presentations that you should not get personal because business is business, not personal. That is the biggest load of crap I have ever heard. Business is all and only personal. People design, make, sell, distribute, and buy our products. I repeat, People. Persons are PERSONAL! Ask the PEOPLE who work for you if business is personal!

I no longer offer sick leave to my staff. I give them personal leave. It is basically the same entitlement of leave as traditional sick leave except I give them the right to take it for other personal issues. Perhaps they have a wedding to attend, or want to take an extra-long weekend. It is better to create an environment of honesty where people can be truthful, as opposed to someone calling in sick when they are not really sick. I found this had two profound effects in my business. Firstly, people continued to use almost their full allocation of days off (they were using them as sick leave anyway). Secondly, the number of actual days taken off for sickness was reduced dramatically (hmmmm) and it became very rare that I would be caught offguard by a call or SMS first thing in the morning saying someone would not be at work that day. You see, if it is personal leave they can give you warning, but if they have to fake being sick they certainly can't say 'by the way I just thought I should let you know that I will be sick on Monday next week'. Can you believe they SMS in sick? I love it (sort of).

Now I do get that this could cause chaos in some organisations and could be very, very expensive. But if it is a problem because of managers' attitudes to the concept, do it anyway and start to educate your managers on what sorts of culture fully engage people in the workplace. If the problem is because of metrics, then we have a conversation. Here is what you might do. Find out what the current sick leave requirements are per person, and assuming they do not accrue annually, work out the average number of days taken per 12-month period. Say the average is 8.2 out of 10 days, giving the extra 1.8 days off per year might in fact be quite profitable. Although you are losing 1.8 days per year per person, the improvements in organisation, morale and just the message it gives to your staff could far outweigh the 1.8 days lost. If, on the other hand, it is more like 3.7 out of 10, think very carefully before looking at a system like this. I like it because of its 'softness'. You know, treating people as people. If your company's sick leave accrues year after year, it would not make a difference so you might as well do it.

Offer your staff opportunity, even on work time, to be involved in some sort of charity activities. Many companies are beginning to do this as a part of their general work schedule. This will be particularly effective for Generation Y. They genuinely want to make a difference in the world, and volunteering, as we have discovered, is higher for their age group (27% for Generation Y) than it has ever been in the past

(17% for Generation X), so why not incorporate this into your workplace. It not only shows that the company truly has values other than profit, it will also make a significant contribution to the level of personal satisfaction your staff feel.

Look for extraordinary learning opportunities. Legal publishing house Thomson Publishing recently took their entire team to an Indian Seafood Cooking course, followed by a Health and Lifestyle workshop. A survey of Generation Y by Look-Look Marketing Consultancy found the ten things that Generation Y were most interested in learning about:

1> **Other languages and cultures**
2> **Computers and technology**
3> **Music, including playing and DJ'ing**
4> **Investing in the stock market and real estate**
5> **History and art**
6> **Literature**
7> **Politics**
8> **Spirituality**
9> **Law, and knowing your rights**
10> **Psychology**

From my work with thousands of Generation Yers, I would put investing, psychology and DJ'ing right up the top. Why not do some out-of-worktime courses on some of these topics? I especially like the idea of teaching your staff to invest. If they are building wealth working for you, it is less likely that they will be on the lookout for more lucrative employment opportunities.

Find travel opportunities to use as incentives for Generation Y. While this is usually best suited to those in more professional, white-collar fields and to larger companies, there is no reason that interstate conferences could not be included in the mix. At Woolworths Limited, for instance, each year they fly in some of their best people from all over Australia to be a part of the AGM and other fun and educational opportunities. By the way, some of the 'best people' include apprentice butchers and checkout operators.

Engage Them

Engaging Generation Y may seem at first to be more of the same, but I assure you it is not. Including Generation Y in decision-making, and inviting them to key meetings, as well as putting them on interesting projects, is part of engaging them, but not all of it. Essentially, when I talk about engaging your staff, I am talking about keeping them in the loop and creating for them a vested interest in the performance and goings-on of your business.

For instance, I think it is essential for you to be upfront and honest with your Generation Y staff about the company's performance. But don't *just* do that. Illustrate to them what role they play in that performance and how together you can improve it even further. Or, if there are challenges, talk and brainstorm about how you (use WE) intend to address them.

Inspire them to see the vision (you do have one, don't you?) of the company. Be sure you live by it. When you do, you will get Generation Y to buy-in, provided that vision is powerful. They will want to be a part of it and will genuinely become engaged. All of a sudden their job won't consist of photocopying for cases already closed, numbering audit documents or cranking out code on a computer. Rather, it will be part of a healthy system that ensures the growth and development of the company and the other organisations you work for. A much more inspiring thing to be doing, wouldn't you agree?

It does not need to be this abstract, either. Why not conduct a meeting with your Generation Y staff and ask them how can you do this same job, just as well and just as fast, in a way that is more fun and engaging. They are likely to come up with a way to make their jobs not only more fun, but possibly even more efficient. For example, I know of a smaller supermarket that asked their staff exactly this, regarding packing shelves, and Generation Y came back with the suggestion of using two people. One to break the boxes, hand the products and man the ladder, and the other to actually pack neatly onto the shelves. Not only did it massively increase the speed of packing, more so than the extra cost of labour, but it also made packing the shelves a more social, and therefore fun task. Or at the beginning of every shift in a call centre, get the staff into a huddle and set the clear objectives for the day: 'Let's focus today on delivering insanely great customer service. Great job yesterday on the upsell focus – sales were up by 11%.'

This is a key theme throughout this chapter, and in fact, all the tactical chapters. **ENGAGE Generation Y in the process. All processes. Ask their opinion. Seek their advice.**

Your Quest!

Consider these questions:

> Is your compensation fair or above?

> What sorts of non-cash benefits could you offer your young staff?

> Are there opportunities to implement performance-based incentive programs in your division? What about incentives for people to be 'culture champions'?

> Do you regularly recognise your team members, both formally and informally?

> If I were to ask your staff if they felt challenged, what would they say? What would you say if I asked you if they were challenged?

> Do you involve your Generation Y talent in key decision-making processes?

> Are you constantly increasing the 'employability' of your Generation Y staff?

> Is there any way you could put some cooperative competition into the day-to-day running of your division? How could you make that competition FUN?

> Do you ever rotate your staff between roles?

> What three words would you use to describe the environment within which your Generation Yers work? Are those three words conducive to creating the results you want to see from your team?

> When was the last time you and your team did something together, socially?

> Would you say that you and your company take a balanced stance in regards to work–life issues? Have you considered things like personal leave instead of sick leave?

> Could you instigate an opportunity for some of your staff to donate some time to charitable causes?

> Is your Generation Y talent kept in the loop? Do they know what is happening in the business, from a strategic and tactical standpoint?

Day-to-Day Management

Generation Y are a chaotic generation, raised in chaotic times. They do not resist change, they revel in it. They want self-expression, and won't allow people to treat them like dirt. They are impatient and want everything, NOW! It must be the latest, fastest and best or else it is just 'sooooo yesterday'. All of this makes them a very challenging generation to manage. But there is hope. Lots of it. They can be managed, though perhaps not in the traditional ways, and if managed in the right spirit, they will be extremely valuable and profitable members of your team.

I keep harping on the positives. It is to re-ground you. It could be easy to get overwhelmed by all the things that are suggested and by the nature of Generation Y, but I firmly believe in the self-fulfilling prophecy. You get what you expect. If you expect younger talent to be more difficult to manage than your current, older workforce, then they will be. If, on the other hand, you expect Generation Y to be energetic and valuable members of your team, they will be.

Even if you only have time to read one thing about managing Generation Y, this is what it should be. **The key to managing is about understanding that everyone sees the world their own way**. Managers need to accept the fact that there is more than one way to do things. Those who are able to embrace this will benefit greatly because Generation Y will not want to be passive in their role. They want to be engaged and to participate in the formation of their role. In order for this to happen, the manager will need to be more concerned with what is useful than with being right. In other words, be open-minded.

Coaching versus Directing

A new paradigm of managing has emerged: coaching. Coaching, as we have already discussed, is a very open, empowering and flexible style of management. I believe coaching to be a very powerful tool of the manager, as opposed to being the ideology for management. Particularly for Generation Y. Not only are Generation Y a very coachable generation, being both open to and wanting it, they will resent and shy away from being 'told' what to do. The traditional 'my way or the highway' is just not going to work. And to tell you the truth, this 'directing only' style of management is so far from what managing should be for any generation it is not funny.

'We don't just manage. We coach.'

Edward Kaleel,
Marc Edward Agency

The most talented of your young recruits will have a tendency to want to do it themselves. So, coaching means giving them the opportunity to explore this desire, and to even make mistakes in the process. Then they will be open to guidance and some direction which, when balanced with coaching, becomes a kind of mentoring.

A good mentor will guide when they need to, be there to correct them when they need to and most importantly, will keep their mentees accountable for what they do. To use a sporting analogy, this is also what a sporting coach does. They are the third party with an independent eye. They see what the player cannot see. They may not have ever been as good at the game as the player, but they are a student of the game. An experienced campaigner with insights and experience about what works and what does not work. The steady hand.

Perhaps the lesson here for HR is that managers in business are the same. Managers don't do the work, their staff do. So managers need to be master motivators and students of the game. Constantly seeking out new and improved ways of doing things. Ensuring their staff (players) have all the resources they need to get the job done right.

A good sporting coach never treats his or her players like idiots, knowing full well their team is only as good as the players. A key lesson here, too. Coaches demonstrate and then help, rather than just control and direct. They get the individuals working together for a common goal, or in this case a common vision.

In sport, you don't go to an all-in-one training camp for four days and then get left to your own devices for the entire season, although in business you often are. In sport, the players receive coaching and training and direction consistently. And the more important your role, the more training and coaching you receive. For some reason, business seems to be different. We seem to immerse our hot new talent in training for a few days and then expect peak performance all year. Not only that, but it seems that the higher up in an organisation you get, the less you are expected to learn. Hmmm!

I have read that more than 60% of Australian executives employ a coach to keep them accountable. I believe it. This is what managers need to do, or at least provide for all their players, if they want peak performance. I have people that fill these roles for me. I call them mentors and I pay some of them. Both personal and business, and the lines between the two are getting more and more blurred as time goes on. I also have coaches, who purely help draw out of me what already exists but I just can't harness. They employ a very powerful questioning process.

'They are very responsive to nurturing, provided it is personalised.'

Deborah Stonley, Henry Davis York

If a manager were to begin viewing their staff as players this would have a tremendous impact on performance because they would realise that players are the talent, it is they who get the job done. The manager's job is to make their good players great and their great players outstanding. As opposed to making players do it management's way or the highway.

Genuine Empowerment

I can hear you sighing. Empowerment has been done to death. I KNOW! But let's talk about what empowerment really means. It means giving your staff the resources they need to do the job. Generation Y have never had to 'make do with what they have', which is going to make your life very difficult. They will demand that you provide them with resources, including equipment, information and power, to get the job done. Ask yourself, does your IT/IS infrastructure do this? Does your training program do this? Do your managers do this? By 'do this' I mean 'give your staff the resources they need to do the job'. No matter how motivated and enthusiastic they are, if they are trying to do a job they are not equipped to do, they will soon become disenchanted.

I want you to think deeply about that last statement, and apply it beyond technology and time and other obvious factors. What about culture? Water will always find its level. If you put a bright, bubbly Generation Yer into a dead, stale and boring environment and leave them there, it is only a matter of time before they join the troops. If you are serious about innovation, creativity and ground-breaking ideas, ask yourself, are you creating an environment conducive to this? If your workplace lacks energy and flair, don't expect your staff to be innovative and creative at work. If your manager is rude, arrogant and impersonal, why should the employee be any other way to those customers that call in to make and order or to make a complaint? Generation Y will do as you do not as you say.

Model Performance

The last statement from the last paragraph is as old as the hills but as true today as it has ever been. You must lead by example. Or as Mr G said, 'Be the change you wish to see in the world.' (Mr G being Mahatma Gandhi.) Demonstrate versus tell. Do versus say.

It is easy to forget, as you move further along in your career, just what you knew and did not know when you started out. You would be surprised how few Generation Yers actually know how to dress for an interview. Even fewer would know what excellent customer service looks like. Never assume they know. What really should be commonsense seldom is.

Start with the way you speak directly to Generation Y. I call it the puppy dog test. Think about how you talk to your puppy dog and compare that with how you treat your staff. I once heard Geoffrey Gittomer, US-based consultant and expert in sales, put one of his audiences to the Grandma test. He suggested adding 'Grandma' to the end of your sentences to see if they are still suitable: 'Four sales a day, and this is not negotiable, Grandma.'

I like the line I heard in the Hollywood movie *Remember the Titans.* When scolded by his captain for having a bad attitude, a player responded with, 'Attitude reflects leadership, captain.' Great line, and so true. If you want a good team working for you, start working on yourself first. Realise that the culture in your team is driven by you, the leader.

Model integrity, ethics and values> Generation Y have been brought up watching television that convinces them to be as loud, contrary and obnoxious as possible. It says 'Look after number one because no-one else will'. If you want genuine cooperation, you will also need to be cooperative. If you want your Generation Yers to be motivated by their work, you had better be motivated by your own. Generation Y will not 'follow the rules' like generations have done in the past. And 'because I said so' won't cut it either. If you say 'We value our customers' and then at a morning huddle close by saying 'Leave them broke in the aisles', Generation Y will see the anomaly instantly and begin to question your integrity, and while they respect competence, they respect integrity equally. You cannot successfully lead a team of people who do not respect you.

I am big on this integrity and ethics thing because communication and cooperation hinge on trust. If you keep your word and treat people with respect, then your team members will be more likely to come to you with their concerns, share their ideas, and cooperate with you to achieve company goals. If you are going to keep the channels of communication open, you must foster a culture of trust.

It will often come down to the little things. Like doing

what you say you will. Being on time for meetings. Keeping promises. When you said way back in April that you would have a performance review for them in August, you had better schedule it because I assure you they won't forget. Keep your promises and usually, by default, Generation Y will start to keep promises to you and their customers. They will know that when they say 'I will have that to you by Thursday', they will. No excuses.

I love the policy taken by Brett Godfrey, CEO of Virgin Blue, who makes his top managers, himself included, spend one full day in the trenches every quarter. They load baggage onto planes, check people in at the counter, serve as a steward on a flight. There could not be a better way to get involved and set a good example. Not to mention gaining a real sense of what your staff go through, daily. Hyatt Hotels do a similar thing. You would not know it, but the next room service person who brings you your food may be the global CEO or HR Director of Hyatt Hotels.

Flexibility

Another essential key to good managing is behavioural flexibility. This is the ability to adapt and change on demand to better handle a situation. Management Consultant Ken Blanchard, author of *The One Minute Manager*, has a famous management course, based around Situational Leadership, which teaches managers what style of management is required for certain employees in certain situations. But rather than rehash some well-versed and well-documented management theories, I would like to focus our attention on two issues, potentially the most talked about regarding the new workforce: uniform and scheduling.

Uniform> If we are concerned with what is useful then we are concerned mainly with performance and culture. To be concerned only with performance and culture can shed new light on uniform. Is it necessary? Is your work uniform out of date? Do your staff like it? Does it improve performance? Does it enhance your customers' experience? Does it reinforce your brand? There are many issues to look at in regards to uniform, but essentially I am asking you to consider your company's dress code and see if it is really necessary and if there is scope for variation.

If it is necessary and there is no scope for variation, fine. Ensure that this is not compromised. If it is necessary, but scope is allowed, then communicate what is acceptable to your staff. If it is unnecessary, dump it altogether. Maybe your entire uniform is necessary, but could be updated and made more modern, still achieving the same objective. Have you thought about that? My image consultant told me I am what I wear. To some degree, I believe this. I know when I dress sharp I feel sharp. I also know when I dress fashionably I feel modern.

Here is an interesting test. Compare your dress code to what appears in *Business Review Weekly* (not *Cleo* or *Men's Style* but *Business Review Weekly*) and see if you are up-to-date. Interesting, huh?

So am I pro-uniform or not? Of course I am pro-uniform. When necessary.

Work Schedule> My stand on working hours is no different from that on uniform. If there are essential and logical hours that staff should be at work, enforce them. However, if roles are more outcome orientated, and do not require staff to be in the office everyday, don't make them. Keep them accountable and ensure that they are getting the job done, but don't enforce 'rules' just for the sake of enforcing rules.

If you are going to allow flexible work routine and locations, you had better be ready for it and you had better manage it properly. Firstly, your people must be M-Powered. (Kind of like Empowered.) M-Powered is a word I am borrowing from Tom Peters' book *Re-Imagine* (read it!). It means that, particularly in white-collar jobs, staff need to be empowered while mobile. M for mobile. Hence M (mobile) Powered (empowered with what they need to do the job).

Clear expectations will need to be SPELT OUT, and certain performance indicators created and monitored if this is to work. It is key here to be sure that any staff member, young or old, who is going to be operating in a more self-administered and -governed way, needs to realise what outcomes are expected from them, and how their performance against those outcomes will be assessed.

For those of you offering shiftwork, do Generation Y have any say in the roster? Do you allow them to give their preferences each week? What about during the shift? Who dictates when they need a break? All I am saying is this: enforce and make rigid what needs to be rigid, but allow some flexibility in other areas.

'To manage Generation Y properly you need to set very clear boundaries and expectations and enforce them. You need to also make sure within those boundaries there is room for the individual to develop themselves and employ their creativity.'

Edward Kaleel,
Marc Edward Agency

Accountability

This is a huge issue when managing talented people. Once you have clearly outlined expectations, including rules and performance, then you had better keep your Generation Y staff accountable. If they sense that not all rules are enforced, they will begin to test you in more ways than one: 'Well if that is not a real rule, then perhaps neither is this.'

To keep people accountable, you will need to keep only the most relevant rules. In order to do this you will need to audit policies and procedures and ask a big fat WHY? after each one. More specifically:

> **Take an inventory of all not negotiables**
> **Identify the scope for the negotiables**
> **Eliminate the unnecessary**
> **Enforce. If it matters it matters**

Remember that as far as Generation Y are concerned everything is negotiable. They will attempt to push the limits. As a manager you must set the limit, explain the WHY (rationale) behind it, and then ensure it is not breached. Having said this, you may find it surprising that research in the United States has found that Generation Y thrive in a structured environment. I agree, they do thrive. The key is to create structure where necessary and where it enhances performance and sales and customer satisfaction. Where structure does not matter so much, give your staff the space and opportunity to think a little left of centre; you will be pleased with what comes up.

In summation, do an audit of all your rules and regulations, checking which are relevant and which are not. The key word is relevant!

Drive Change

Embrace change. No, I take that back. Drive and create it. Generation Y do not resist change they thrive on it. They have never known the stability that Baby Boomers once knew, or that Generation Xers at least got a taste of. For Generation Y, change is normal, or to use a cliché, 'Their only certainty is change'.

One of my favourite things about Generation Y is that they will expect you to use technology to the fullest. They feel technology in their gut. Some even talk about the 'spirit' of computers. So be willing to go along for the ride. I should add here that there comes a point where the job just needs to be done. You have to make do with what you have. If we were to seriously try to keep up with every advancement made in technology, we would never get anything done. Less than a month after buying my top of the range laptop, a new model was introduced that superseded it. Getting Generation Y at times to just do the work will be a challenge, but if you have trust and clearly set expectations, this should not be a problem.

Use Generation Y, and their openness to change, to test new technologies, and new ways of doing business. Generation Y will relish the change of scenery and you will get a low-cost pilot program for something that may potentially add millions to your bottom line.

Embrace Team

We have already referred to Generation Y as a connected generation. They thrive in a connected environment. We also mentioned inclusive competition. So much of what makes Generation Y interested in what they are doing hinges on whether they're doing it with other people, preferably people they like and trust. They have been brought up watching different television than previous generations. Baby Boomers and Generation X had heroes such as Superman, Batman, Spiderman and other rugged individuals. My generation (Generation Y) on the other hand, were raised worshipping the Teenage Mutant Ninja Turtles, Power Rangers and Pokemon. All of which worked in teams to destroy their formidable, evil opponents. Like Superman and friends, they were working for the good of everyone, but they were doing it as a group. And, mind you, most of these groups had an all-wise and all-knowing mentor. Like Splinter for the Ninja Turtles, a rat who was skilled in the teachings and wisdom of the Ninja. It is little wonder that Generation Y respond so well to coaching and love to work as a team. The actual motto of the Power Rangers was 'The power of teamwork overcomes all'.

Enough of me reliving my strange, video-game crazy childhood. As a manager, you should be focusing on creating cooperation (inclusive competition), rather than exclusive competition between staff. Generation Y may never bleed and die for your company, but they will go to the wall for their friends. If you build a team of friends and colleagues in the workplace, they will lift each other and your division or crew to a new level.

Lion Nathan Australia In Focus

According to Lion Nathan, the real key to managing young talent is the leader. They use the word 'leader', and never the term 'manager'. In fact, this careful choice of words is used in all four profiled companies. At Lion Nathan, a leader must be able to ensure their team can say 'yes' to the following questions, when asked about their leader:

- **Are they interested in me?**
- **Are they interested in my development?**
- **Do they provide me with opportunities when they are available?**
- **Do they support and encourage me?**
- **Do they engage me with an exciting vision of my future?**
- **Do they give me a sense of belonging?**

When I made the comment to Linda Botter that Generation Y come to work for companies but they leave bosses, she replied, 'Exactly. Absolutely right.'

The major leadership development at Lion Nathan right now is to better equip their leaders with coaching skills, because this is seen as the true way to engage and develop talent.

Lion Nathan are famous for their 'One on One's'. This is where, once per month, each team member gets to sit with their leader and express concerns, make requests, and look at opportunities for development. It is completely acceptable in a One on One for a team member to say to his or her leader, 'You are my leader and I expect more from you'.

Your Quest!

Brainstorm a few answers to these questions, and choose three things to begin working on straightaway:

- Do you find yourself focusing on being right as opposed to focusing on what is useful?
- Are the managers in your company directors or coaches?
- If I were to ask your people, would they say that they are empowered to do their jobs? What more could you do to make them even more empowered?
- Do the managers in your organisation say one thing and do another, or do they lead by example? What is one thing you could do better in your work as a leader of people?
- Is there any room for flexibility in the way you do business? Perhaps you are holding onto uniforms or dress codes that no longer serve a positive purpose.
- Do you set very clear expectations and then keep your young talent accountable for living up to those expectations?
- Do you resist change and seek the status quo? Is there any way you could drive change and improvement in your workplace? In what areas would this be most beneficial?
- Do you embrace the concept of team?

Communicating

Over the past decade a new paradigm has emerged: that business is about people, not processes. A shift to the 'soft' side of business, so to speak. Well there is little doubt that survival in a business world solely dependent on the talent of your people is going to be as much about the soft things, like work–life balance and communication, as about the hard stuff like numbers, budgets and share price.

So what does this mean and what has it got to do with a book on Generation Y? Let me deal with the latter first. Not only are Generation Y a connected generation who thrive in environments of open communication, but with them they bring new challenges for business. Firstly, they communicate differently, and through different mediums than just verbal and written. They call email 'snail mail'. And secondly, they make it necessary for you to acquire some skills in cross-generational communication. Many adults don't even understand the jargon of their Generation Y staff (lol).

This cross-generational thing is more serious than you think. Firstly, we have the obvious problem of older managers and supervisors trying to deal with young employees. Tougher still is the emerging reality that we will have people from Generation X and Baby Boomer generations reporting to Generation Y supervisors, managers and project leaders. Scary stuff. My number one challenge as the general manager of Molly Maguire's Hotel was that I was among the youngest people on the staff of 30. And I mean in the

'I believe that being completely honest and upfront in the way you communicate with Generation Y is the best way to gain their respect and get them to buy-in.'

Edward Kaleel,
Marc Edward Agency

youngest seven or eight, and I was the boss. The buck stopped with me. Great learning experience for me, but I found that staff reporting to me took it two ways. Either they thought it was awesome that I had managed to climb to such a level at such a young age, and used it as inspiration, or they resented it and came up with all the reasons under the sun why they would have been better for the job. The fact that I was brought in from the outside certainly did not help the situation.

Consider even the death of traditional etiquette among the new workforce. Titles, and addressing people as 'Sir' or 'Madam', are not only not used, but are resented by Generation Y. Some don't even use the words 'Mum' and 'Dad' anymore when speaking directly to their parents. This will be a bitter pill for some older people to swallow; worse if the Generation Yer is the boss.

This chapter on communicating with Generation Y should help you bridge the cross-generational challenge.

As far as moving to the soft side of business, we have already dealt with many aspects of this. It means to be concerned with people, with their emotions, needs, feelings and to gear your strategy around making them happy and productive, rather than to focus solely on numbers and share price. (That was a very soft explanation I might add.) Generation Y simply will not respond to, or even put up with, management by numbers. They want to be treated as individuals. As someone who matters. For a manager, remember:

- **Get to know your team**
- **Be personable not clinical**
- **Your staff are people not cogs**
- **Do not patronise. Generation Y will run a mile**

Sounds generic, I know. That is because it is. Don't brush over this stuff, because this is the main (read ONLY) thing. It is a manager's number one job. Keep the players happy.

The Seven Keys to Successful Generation Y Communication

I recommend at this point that you review the chapter on training Generation Y because many of the techniques for trainers are relevant to managers. Just a few additions here. To jog your memory, the tips included for trainers are:

1> Come out blazing
2> Leave your ego at the door
3> Ramp it up!
4> Shoot straight
5> Weave your magic
6> Don't be something that you are not
7> Don't judge a book by its cover

The Essence of Communication

I believe that the quality of communication, not just in the business world, but in homes and in schools as well, is poor. And while this is not a book on communication, in a generic sense, some of the basics of good communication are essential if you want to get through to Generation Y. I also believe that Generation Y will highlight poor communication because of their unwillingness to put up with much of it.

1> Know your objective At the most basic level, it is important to realise that the effectiveness of your communication is not what YOU say but what THEY hear. It is how the message is interpreted. What makes perfect sense may be completely incomprehensible to them. The goal of communication is for them to leave with an accurate understanding of what you were trying to say. And if you are going to do that, you had better be very clear on what it is you are trying to say. I call this being purposeful in your communication.

2> Get to the point The second thing to understand is that what you have to say should be communicated in as few words as possible to avoid any distortion or misperception.

3> Communicate from within their frame of reference If someone is to understand what you say, then say it as much as possible in their words, not yours. And it is at this point that communication becomes much more difficult with Generation Y. Again I suggest rereading the chapter on training Generation Y, because the points covered there about using metaphors and relevant stories apply also to management style communication.

4> Use your sensory acuity (notice if it is working) Neuro Linguistic Programming, of which I am a certified practitioner, studies human communication. A term used in NLP is 'sensory acuity', which simply means take detailed notice of how people respond to what you are saying. Essentially, you want to know if they understand what you are saying.

5> Receive feedback Ask Generation Y if they understand what you have just said, and ask them to explain what they have understood. This does not mean repeat what you said, but to genuinely explain what they have understood from the conversation. Given the power of what we now know as viral marketing, as well as what we already know about office gossip, this step is crucial. Are you on the same page?

6> Exercise behavioural flexibility (change your approach) If feedback indicates that the communication is clearly not working, meaning their understanding is very different from your intended understanding, then you will need to change your approach. This requires behavioural flexibility. Change what you are doing until it works.

Additional pointers for communicating with Generation Y, or anyone for that matter, include:

> **Be honest. We surely know by now that Generation Y have an enormous bullshit detector on their forehead and they can detect a hidden motive or insincerity a mile away. Keep it real.**

> **Try to understand their world. I am not suggesting that**

you listen to Eminem, or attend a Beyonce concert, but you should at least try to stay clued into what is going on in the Generation Y world. This book is a great start for you, so well done.

- **Be authentic. While it is important to try to communicate from within their frame of reference, I think it is even more important that you don't try to be something that you are not.**
- **Don't judge. This generation have a different set of values from yours. They are neither right nor wrong, just different. Trying to force them into changing to be more like you is management suicide with these guys. People will defend their beliefs and values when challenged. Recall, move away from being right and focus only on what is useful. When you open yourself up, you will find that they have as much to teach you as you them.**
- **Don't suck up. Ever!**
- **Never dull down. Be yourself. Always! You need to be someone they look up to.**
- **Listen twice as much as you talk.**
- **Be courteous.**
- **Smile.**

Use Technology

Use SMS, email, or ICQ messaging when communicating with Generation Y. If you have the facility to do so, use video-streaming through email or something similar. Having made this point, nothing, even for Generation Y, beats real face-to-face communication. Even in the training room. Despite some awesome results for companies training their staff online, and IBM have published some excellent results, most often these results were achieved teaching technological applications. A computer program, no matter how brilliant, will not be effective in teaching communication skills or customer service. At least not as effective as a high-touch training environment.

Watch your language – long live the associate!

Generation Y do not like to be patronised; they are human beings and as such, see themselves as your peer. This is a key point for managers to understand. So often I am introduced to someone who is described by their boss as one of my staff members, or subordinate or employees. Try exchanging such terminology for colleague, team member or associate. Add 'friend' to that list as well.

Get over it! Things are not, and never will be, the way they used to be

As a Generation Yer I was never taught proper grammar at school. I never studied phonetics (whatever they are) and my younger peers were even taught that if it sounded right, that meant it was spelt right. For example 'fone' instead of 'phone'. My childhood is littered with memories of being corrected for leaving the 'g' off my words when speaking, and I have had to pay my Generation X sister to edit this book to ensure the grammar is at least tolerable. Shake your head all you want about this situation; things will not change. So get over it! Generation Y will use a much more colloquial tone, they will write emails in Gen'y'nese and they will write using incorrect grammar.

Get over it! Things are not, and never will be, the way they used to be.

Therefore, do your best not to let this bug you when you are communicating with Generation Y. The second you focus on these 'minor' issues (I know that my just saying they are minor issues will bug some of you) you will stop focusing on the message. Some Generation Yers interviewed for the research for this book even said I should use their language in the title.

Open, Regular, Structured Communication

Managers should always provide a forum for their staff to share ideas, vent frustrations or just talk. They can be team meetings, but should also be one on one. How else do you propose to build a relationship with your Generation Y staff? Quarterly performance reviews are not enough. I repeat, not enough. So few managers ever stick to them anyway. Make regular appointments to meet individually with your staff and communicate. Keep them in the loop with what is happening, coach them, and allow them the space to talk to you.

In property it is all about location, location, location. In managing Generation Y it is all about communication, communication, communication. Even communicate the bad news. Generation Y are not going to run and hide at the sound of bad news. Quite the opposite. They will want to tackle the problem head-on and, with you and the rest of the team, solve it.

I cannot emphasise enough the importance of keeping these appointments. Failure to do so equals feelings of not being valued. Remember that manager job number one is to keep the players happy and producing. After all, they, not you, do the work.

The Marc Edward Agency in Focus

Allow me to quote and relay the events of a recent meeting with MEA staff in Melbourne. It starts with Managing Director Edward Kaleel saying: 'You guys are lacking energy and your grooming sucks. In fact, some of you look like a bag of shit.'

The meeting went for three hours and was a session of complete honesty, where expectations were clearly laid out, and there was no regard for etiquette and political correctness. It was raw, to the point and backed up by actual examples of the above concerns.

It resulted in a standing ovation from the 60-plus attendees, with one young woman saying, 'On behalf of my three girlfriends, I just want to say thanks. We have never had someone be so upfront with us about what they expect and what they will and won't tolerate. It is really refreshing.'

I know few, if any, people with the ability to get the message across as loud and clear as Edward Kaleel. But when you consider he is responsible for managing the performance of 1000 Generation Y staff in very unpredictable and difficult to monitor environments, it is no wonder he is good at it. When interviewing Edward, he kept coming back again and again to the importance of being upfront and honest with Generation Y. He is quite adamant, as am I, that they actually do not resist boundaries and limitations, providing they are practical. His team leaders are the same. Here is what Trish says to her new promotions teams: 'I have enough friends. I do not need more. Yes I will be your friend. Yes we will have fun and it will be great. But don't cross me. Don't think just because we get along and have a good time that you can push the boundaries and breach the working code of ethics.'

Your Quest!

Take the time to carefully answer the following questions. Remember, the more effort you put into answering them, the more insight you will gain into areas for improvement in the way you manage.

> Evaluate the cross-generational communication in your team. Do people of all ages get on well together? Is there any likelihood that one of your Generation Yers will be promoted to a position of authority anytime soon? If yes, what strategies will you put in place to ensure they receive the opportunity to build the respect of their new team, regardless of age?
> How well do you know the individuals you employ?
> How do you refer to people over whom you have some formal authority?
> Do you provide formal and informal opportunities for you staff to communicate freely with you and the rest of their colleagues?

Developing

All good companies will be actively developing their core talent as a part of their succession strategy. It is essential that you are constantly developing your people because:

- **People leave**
- **You can't do everything yourself**
- **Business in the new economy is about talent**
- **A coach is never as good as the player**
- **By recruiting and developing young talent, you have the ability to mould them into the style of managers and leaders you need to survive in today's business worlds. This sure beats hiring someone else's rejects.**

Most companies I come across have very sophisticated development models and tools, but if for some reason you don't, here is a very simple diagnostic tool to help you decide what is the best way to develop some of your young talent.

Talent Development Matrix

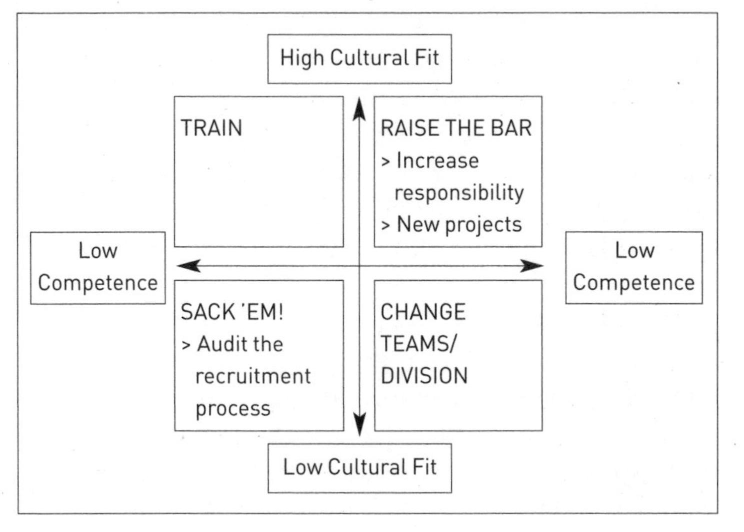

Train> If someone has good cultural fit, but is lacking in competence then the best thing is to train them up. Give them more skills.

Sack 'em> If a person in your organisation is lacking in skills and lacking in cultural fit, then trying to improve them will be like flogging a dead horse. Get rid of them because they are dragging the whole team down. If this is happening regularly, then you should audit your recruitment and selection process.

Change teams> If you have a highly competent member of staff but they are just being stifled in their current team due to poor cultural fit, you do not want to lose this person. Move them to a different team or department where they will fit in better.

Raise the bar> If you have someone who is a great fit for your culture, and also has the skills, nurture this person. Develop them by giving them increased responsibility. It is time for them to be challenged.

A simple diagnostic tool like this, mixed with some open and honest communication, will help you to decide on the best moves to develop your young talent. I so often see training and development mixed together, which may be correct, but I think development is so important it needs its own chapter and should also be very much the responsibility of the talents manager, not just people in the HR department.

Let's look at a few of the issues.

The Great Dilemma: To Train or Not To Train

In some cases, attrition rates have gotten so high (100% annually) that employers are reluctant to train and develop their Generation Y staff. The fact that retention is so low to me says train more. Look at the way you manage as well, but definitely train more. There are a number of reasons why I think this is the case.

Firstly, Generation Y value training and development. Highly. And the less you train, the more likely they are to see that you are not adding to their resume, which increases chances of them leaving. Remember, your job is to transform.

Secondly, even if they are going to leave in six months, you had better get them trained and productive as quickly as possible, or else you will not get a positive return on investment. You want them skilled and producing as soon as possible, and the more you retract training the longer this will take. It blows my mind when companies cut their training budgets first, before anything else, when times get a little tough. In the new business world where talent is king and people buy from you not because of your product (commoditisation) but because of your people and their expertise, then the tougher the times are, the more training your people should undergo. Why? Because how else will you differentiate yourself in the marketplace.

80/20 Rule

Don't spend 80% of your time fixing the bottom 20%. Like Jack Welch, former CEO of General Electric, and named CEO of the Century did, SACK 'EM! Maybe that is a little harsh, but you know what I mean. Spend your time with the performers. The top 20%. By doing this, you not only nurture and keep your top talent, but it shows the rest of the staff that excellent performance is rewarded handsomely and that non-performance is not. Then try to catch the other 60% doing something right, because what is rewarded and recognised will be repeated

Don't spend 80% of your time fixing the bottom 20%.

Mentoring

We have already discussed influences on Generation Y such as Teenage Mutant Ninja Turtles and the Power Rangers, and as trivial as such examples may at first seem, these were all the rage, and among the most watched television shows and then movies for young Generation Yers in their formative years. Both of these groups relied heavily on the influence and advice of their mentor. I have worked in some of the toughest schools in Australia, with some of the toughest students, and in the hundreds of programs I have been a part of, I am yet to see one as effective as Plan-It Youth, which is a New South Wales Department of Education program where students from tough backgrounds, who are identified as being 'at risk', are teamed with volunteer mentors from their local community. This program has proved time and time again to be extremely effective at either keeping the students in school, or helping them to gain long-term employment that offers future career prospects. Generation Y respond well to mentoring.

Organisations should have, if they do not already, a formal mentoring program where new Generation Y employees are teamed up with older, more experienced staff members. The benefits professionally for the new employee are huge, but add to that the improvement in the mentor's cross-generational communication that will result. It will be a rewarding relationship for both. It will help the new employee settle in faster, and thus become productive sooner. I also suggest that the mentor be from a different department or at least a different team. This way, there is little threat of 'word getting back to their boss' were they to share a frustration they are having in their team.

I have a program called 360-Degree Mentoring, where the process allows for both parties to be mentored. Adopting a more youthful mindset in your organisation can be very profitable, and mentoring should never be seen as a one-way thing.

A variation of this could be a buddy system, where a new Generation Y employee is teamed with another Generation Y employee who already knows the ropes and can be like a friend. Someone to spend lunch with in the first few days. Someone to ask work-related questions like how do I use the photocopier, or how do I fill out my time sheet.

Recognise and reward staff members who volunteer to become buddies and mentors. This is a generous act and will be beneficial to them in their communication and leadership skills.

Active Career Planning/Management

It is the role of the manager to be proactive in the career planning and management of members in their team. This, although an investment of time, is a very effective activity. It allows you to know more about your staff, find out what drives them and what their goals are, and also allows your company to meet that employee's needs in the best way possible. Or as I would say, to transform them into who they want to be. I developed a tool that allows a manager to do just this. Not as a product, but as something I wanted to use for myself. When I began using it with my staff, it became clear that it was a valuable process for any manager, or individual. It is called the Strategic Success Plan.

It would be a shame if one of your Generation Yers left your organisation to pursue an opportunity elsewhere that you could have provided yourself, had a little foresight been employed. Essentially, here is what you need to do with your Generation Y team member:

- **Establish personal goals**
- **Map a clear and achievable career path**
- **Identify what skills and experience they would require to get there**

> **Develop a plan, including formal and non-formal education, in-house training and projects that will help the team member develop such skills or acquire such experience**
> **Help them build their resume by identifying key learning and competencies gained on different work assignments**

As a manager, you should have a personal file on everyone in your team. Collect as much information as you can about their goals and aspirations. It will help you to achieve much of what we have talked about previously in this section on managing Generation Y.

Have your Generation Y employees present themselves to project managers with whom they could potentially work. Like a mini sales presentation or interview. This will not only increase the opportunities to develop this team member, but will also help to improve their communication skills.

By playing such an active role in the career development of your people (don't leave it all up to HR), you will avoid costly mistakes such as overcommitting people too young. We have spoken previously about the great divide between Generation Y confidence and competence. It would be easy to throw a Generation Yer the ball before they had the ability to catch it if you were playing a more passive role in their development.

Coaching versus Directing (AGAIN)

I am choosing to revisit the point about coaching your Generation Y staff versus just directing them. I am reminded here of the famous saying of Management Guru Dr Stephen Covey: 'You can't hold someone accountable for results if you supervise their methods.' Give Generation Y the space to make mistakes. Allow them to take on new and challenging roles, and if needs be, fail. It is part of working life. But be there to coach them through the challenge, not always giving them the answers but rather coaching them to uncover the answers themselves. And when required, shift back to giving clearer direction.

I can think of nothing more powerful in developing talent than taking the role of coach instead of director.

Merit-based Promotion

Promotion should not, and never should be, based on age. It should be based on performance and ability. Nor should a promotion be based on longevity, not if you want to survive in an increasingly competitive marketplace. Promote the dynamos, whether they be 23 or 53. Who cares how old they are? I think the three biggest opportunities facing business today are Young Talent, Old Talent and Women. Model the best managers of talent and follow their example. Let me name:

> **Delta Goodrem**
> **Lleyton Hewitt**
> **Ian Thorpe**

Just to point out that you don't have to be old to be good. These three are all class and not one of them is over the age of 25. Generation Y will expect that if they are good enough, they should be given the opportunity. At 19 I was put in charge, literally, of a four-million-dollar business. I wrote the cheques, did the hiring and firing, reported to the directors, dealt with accountants, lawyers and government agencies. At 19. I not only survived, the business thrived. I was responsible for the entire implementation of GST in the business and its systems, a challenge I know many experienced business people struggled with even years afterwards.

Why not try this on for size? Have your Generation Y staff review their own performance. Seriously. You will get a better view of how they are going and I think will be pleasantly surprised at their maturity, their ability to see their weaknesses but also their acknowledgement of their strengths.

Cool Projects

You should get your Generation Yers doing cool things. Things that are different. Perhaps you want to use them as guinea pigs for new CRM software. Maybe you see potential but for some reason, they are not fitting in well with their current team. Move them. Consider international (if available) or at least inter-departmental transfers. Not only will it add variety for them, but it will enhance their skills and performance as well.

Engage them in brainstorming new ideas, decision-making and all these other things we have mentioned previously. By doing so, you rapidly increase their skills and ability. There is no better way to develop someone than to give them a first-hand experience doing something.

Move Sideways

I have already made mention in this book that there are less and less opportunities to climb the proverbial corporate ladder. Knowing that, we must actively seek out lateral opportunities if we are to develop and more fully engage our young talent. Ask yourself, what other positions could a particular Generation Yer move into that would further develop their skills and proficiency? Do you have good working relationships with other managers who are also looking for similar opportunities for their staff? Does your organisation have an interdepartmental or even overseas exchange program in place? If not, could you put one in place?

Stretch Opportunities

A stretch opportunity is anything that will force a member of staff to improve and grow. Not only is it essential for this to happen from an employer point of view because it means you are maximising your return on investment, it is essential to keep your key talent engaged and motivated. Look for stretch opportunities everywhere. What jobs do you currently perform that would represent a stretch for your younger talent and free up some of your time to develop them and other members of your team?

High Leverage Generation Y Development Opportunities

There are, I believe, some unique opportunities for employers of Generation Y. Development opportunities that will give a handsome return on investment. These are the areas that businesses and managers of Generation Y should focus on if they want to turn their young potential into profit:

Communication Skills

Research report after research report on employer expectations says the same things. Graduates lack communication skills. It seems as though the development of such skills has been left for the workplace, so heed the call and let's do it. Generation Y are bright, creative and motivated. They sometimes lack the finesse and ability to communicate that is required to turn potential into results. So train and develop them in these areas:

- **Public speaking**
- **Business writing**
- **Relationship building**
- **Negotiation skills**
- **Conflict resolution**

Business Etiquette

I mentioned finesse was required to turn Generation Y potential into results. It never ceases to amaze me how well-educated people just don't get it. By get it I mean how to dress, how to eat, how to behave in public places, what is appropriate and what is not. Given the fact that Generation Y are the custodians of your brand, I suggest you invest heavily in bringing them up to speed in these areas.

Time Management

Self-confessed Generation Y challenge number one. Poor time management. Week in week out, when I ask Generation Y what skill would make the biggest difference to their life at school or at work, and the answer is almost always Time

Management. Baby Boomers and early Generation Xers have gone off the time management thing because it has been hammered to death in the literature, but truthfully, do you think people really get it?

We are getting busier and busier and there are more distractions than ever before. Getting organised and focused is essential if we are to meet our obligations and get things done.

Business Know-How

Teach Generation Y about business. Just generally at first. Focus particularly on marketing and sales, and then on things like reading a balance sheet and understanding a profit and loss statement. This will allow them to feel more in tune with what is happening in your business and give them a better understanding of why certain things are important. Take brand for instance. If your Generation Yers truly understood the power of branding, do you think they would question the importance of the uniform/dress code?

Think Commercially

In response to the calls and needs of my clients, I developed a program called Think Business. It was aimed at addressing the six major areas of commercial reality that many young talented Generation Yers had either not considered or just couldn't quite grasp. The six paradigms taught in Think Business are:

1> **Think Ownership. You are accountable for your own actions and results.**

2> **Think Strategy. Your goals and actions need to be aligned with the corporate objectives.**

3> **Think ROI. The company makes an investment in you and fiscal reality demands a return on that investment. Your salary is not an appearance fee. And nor do promotional opportunities and payrise come just because you show up, and don't leave.**

4> **Think Brand. You as an individual are the creators of the company brand. People judge the company based on their interactions with you. Therefore, your performance and behaviour should be aligned and live up to the promise of the company brand.**

5> **Think Relationships. People do business with people they know, like and trust. It is about integrity, quality communication and building lasting and mutually beneficial relationships with customers and clients.**

6> **Think Innovation. In this highly competitive business world we must always be on the lookout for new and exciting opportunities and for new and improved ways of doing what we do.**

These are powerful lessons for Generation Y, which will ensure they develop faster and become more effective.

Personal Development

Personally developed people produce professional results. Generation Y want more than just material satisfaction out of life. They want the perfect life (as seen at the movies). They want the perfect relationship, fulfillment, adventure and more. The key to all of these things is an in-depth understanding of yourself, what you value and what you want to achieve. Motivation is an intrinsic thing, and if you truly want to create a team of dynamos, you had better get them working on themselves. One of my most popular programs involves working with teams on an ongoing basis and engaging them in a formal process of self-development. The results are always positive for the business and for the individual.

Let me give you an example. One of my clients owns a chain of real estate agencies. I was working with his staff, one of whom had all the ability but for some reason was just not producing. No-one could understand why. After working with her individually for less than five sessions, we (she did not know either) discovered that it was her fear of being more successful than her husband (from a very traditional background) that was preventing her from performing. After resolving the issue with her husband, and more so with herself, she tripled her results the following month, and continues to go from strength to strength.

At Ford Australia, they use the term 'personal development' rather than 'professional development'. Every individual in the organisation has their own designated Performance Development Committee who they meet with regularly to discuss and progress their 'Individual Development Plans', and look for new opportunities to further their career and develop themselves as people.

Beware, don't send employees to a seminar where the speaker will ask them to buy a time share in Queensland or an apartment at Dockside in Melbourne. Also be aware that personal development may cause some of your people to leave. They may discover that working for you is not what they need. GOOD! They would have never produced significant results anyway. So a win win if you ask me. Most importantly, find someone who can relate to your Generation Yers to run your self-development programs. An over-the-hill sports star who could not get a gig commentating on television is probably not the best choice.

A final point on development. The chances are your organisation already has all of the development opportunities your staff require; they just don't know about them. If managers and HR and anyone else pivotal in developing talent in your organisation were to genuinely spend their time developing individuals, rather than creating blanket approaches, then you will more fully engage your Generation Y talent and be able to take better advantage of the opportunities that already exist. It will be key to have a communications strategy that ensures all staff are aware of the various opportunities that exist, and that managers be on the lookout for these opportunities for their staff.

Your Quest!

There are few more important things than developing the talent in your organisation. Answer these questions and look for opportunities to profit further from your people:

> Using the Talent Development Matrix, plot each individual in your team and sketch out a rough plan for their development. Make the tough decisions and remove people from your team who really should not be there.

> Do you have a Career Management Plan for each of the people in your team? If not, start one.

> Are you investing the training into your people that you should be? The ABS reports that the average time spent in employer-paid training is only 16.5 hours per person per year. If you are not at four times that number then you are not serious about developing your people.

> Do you find you are spending your time with the non-performers rather than the high achievers? Do you take your high achievers for granted?

> Is there a formal mentoring program in your workplace? If not, get one. If yes, is it 360 degrees?

> Do you team new talent with a buddy to help the smooth settling in of these people?

> Do you promote based on merit, potential and performance, or longevity? If it is longevity, ask yourself do you prefer performance or longevity? Then promote based on whichever you want to see more of, because what is rewarded is repeated.

> What cool projects have you in the pipeline that some of your key Generation Y talent would relish the opportunity to be involved in?

> Are there lateral opportunities in your company? Are there vertical opportunities? There had better be one or the other or both if you want to engage young talent in your workplace.

> Is it time you stretched some of your talent? Push their comfort zones and force them to grow and develop?

> Are there people in your organisation with all the ability and all the skill but just aren't performing? Do they, perhaps, need some personal development?

Part Four >
Retaining Generation Y

>

Retaining

Retention is not a Generation Y thing, it is an *everybody* thing. Challenges relating to retention are rampant at all levels of any organisation. Take the 2003 study by International Management Consultancy Booz Allen and Hamilton, which showed that 22% of the Australian companies surveyed had replaced their CEO in the past twelve months. In 2003, the average tenure of a CEO was 4.4 years, down from 5.8 in 2001. Where is the loyalty you might ask? Chances are, in the CEO's case, they had no choice but to leave, if you know what I mean. At a time when companies are not showing their people loyalty, shedding people when signs are tough, why on earth would people show their companies loyalty? In a world of options, it is not as though employees have limited choices or limited job prospects. Generation Y particularly, though, are what I call permi-seekers. They have their resume on <www.seek.com> or <www.careerone.com> and anywhere else like it ALL THE TIME. They have bookmarked these sites and visit them regularly. As I explained right at the beginning of this book, Generation Y are on the constant lookout for new, exciting opportunities.

An online poll conducted by www.seek.com showed that 96% of responders said they would leave their current position if a better offer came their way. Bear in mind, they might have already been on the seek website, looking for other jobs most likely, but this is still a frightening response. Is loyalty dead? No! Not dead. But certainly diminished, at least in the traditional meaning of the word. In the United States for example, the estimated time Generation Yers in their 20s will stay in the same job is only 1.1 years. Employees will not be pledging their life to any one organisation and nor will an employer be pledging a lifelong commitment to any one employee. The reality is, employee retention is not what it once was, and many industries are just going to have to live with that fact. The answer is not to slash training and development, as some companies are doing. And the reason for this is twofold. If you do not train and develop employees, your reputation as an employer of choice will be severely diminished and you won't attract quality candidates in the first place. Secondly, training and development is your key to getting a positive return on your human capital investment FAST! That is, before they move on elsewhere. Plus, a little auspicious I know, but you are attracting candidates that have been trained and developed elsewhere as well, so in reality what is going around is also coming around.

Perhaps we need a new definition of loyalty anyway. Perhaps we should not even measure loyalty at all. I would argue that a more effective measure of company performance in this area would be engagement. That is, measure the degree to which we engage our employees, be they CEOs or Generation Yers working the cash register. I think engagement is a better measure not only because it is a more accurate measure of return on investment, but because in reality, a reduction in retention does not have to mean reduction in productivity. A certain level of rollover is usually a good thing. I should note here, however, having said that some turnover can be a good thing, most studies do reveal that as employee turnover rises, customer loyalty decreases. Hardly a good thing.

Perhaps we should not even measure loyalty at all.

There are ways, at least for Generation Y, that you can maximise retention. Let me warn you, though, there are no quick fix formulas here. Retention is soft. It is about culture, people skills, management and much more. To tell you the truth, much of this book has been about retention. If you follow the advice outlined in Part 2 – Attracting Generation Y, such as creating your Employment Brand, as well the advice on excellent orientation programs and, most importantly, the chapter on Management, you will maximise your retention rates. Most of the issues talked about are 'soft' because people are soft. But soft will ultimately be hard. People directly impact the bottom line. First, I will review some key areas that will be essential to getting maximum engagement, and maximum retention as well.

Challenging Work

Exit interviews in a large Australian bank of Generation Y talent indicated that a lack of challenging work was the number one reason they left. If your young talent do not feel challenged, their interest will wane quickly, and with it their level of engagement. The result is that they leave.

Employability

You need to continually ask yourself in what ways are you increasing the employability of your staff? As long as you are enhancing their employability, you give them no reason to leave. Not only that, but in order to enhance such a thing you need to be employing them (a resource) fully.

Balanced Approach

Are you implementing policies that recognise the importance of your staff's personal lives? Do you have a good maternity and paternity leave program? Do you offer leave without pay? What about carer's leave? Do you allow some flexibility in scheduling? As a manager, are you sensitive to the personal challenges some of your staff might be facing?

Ford Australia in Focus

Let's take a look at the record of Ford Australia. Ford Australia put on over 30 new Generation Yers each year, and in 2004 actually put on more than 50. Let us look at their retention over the last few years.

Year started	Ford attrition
1995 – 1999	20%
2000	6%
2001	6%
2002	3%
2003	4%
2004	0%

When asked why their retention was so good, David Cvetkovski gave the following reasons:

> **Real work–life balance programs. We don't just talk about it**
> **Promoting internally**
> **Exceptional development program**
> **Non-financial benefits including gym, banking and drycleaning on site**
> **Providing real work**
> **Embracing the social nature of Generation Y and even making it part of our culture**
> **We have passion**

Note, too, Ford Australia's Individual Development Programs and People Development Committees. Ford Australia are clearly committed to developing and treating their people as individuals.

Henry Davis York in Focus

Like Ford, Henry Davis York have an enviable retention rate, especially for their industry.

Year Started	Total number recruited	Number currently employed
2001	10	8
2002	7	7
2003	16	16

Deborah Stonley gives the following reasons for their success:

> **We treat everyone as individuals with their own unique needs and desires**
> **We work with our partners on helping them to be better leaders**
> **We give our Generation Yers work that actually matters**
> **We put them on interesting cases**
> **We allow them to rotate between different functions**
> **We go out of our way to be flexible and are prepared to do the work required to make flexible work arrangements work for us, our people and our clients**

I have interviewed Deborah Stonley in depth, and it is little wonder people want to work there. She is passionate about people and about treating everyone as an individual. This attitude can't help but rub off on the partners who deal with their young lawyers.

The role of the manager

To avoid rehashing what has already been covered in the chapter on Management, let me just say this: retention is about good management. Actually, retention is about good management aligned with outstanding leadership, but the number one reason a Generation Yer will leave their job is that they don't like their boss. In the seek poll mentioned above, 60% of respondents sited 'management' when asked what they hated about their job. A corresponding study done by Right Management Consultants in the United States, asked managers what they thought was the key to retaining talent, and 89% said money. I wonder if Australian managers would have had similar replies. Are today's managers really that out of touch? I hope not. ALL studies I have ever read or seen quoted state that money is never the number one motivator for retention. I know people who have resigned from their job who were offered an extra $10,000 to stay (even though they were only on $60,000) and they still said NO! *Business Review Weekly* did a report on some of Australia's top Generation Y performers in the corporate world. They surveyed 50 working for blue chip Australian companies, and found that 10 were presently at risk of leaving and a further 10 were very likely to do so, despite the fact that all of them were already on six-figure salaries, some in excess of $250,000 including bonuses. Providing compensation is fair, Generation Y are not going to stay just because you offer them more money, and even if they do, it won't be for long. Retention is not a simple problem. It is a complex one. A problem filled with all the 'soft' intricacies of dealing with people: management!

Be it their supervisor, manager, project leader or whoever, Generation Y will usually blame management for their leaving a job. To use their words: 'My boss was a loser.' Power trips are out. Respect is in. If, as a manager, you implemented even 10% of what was covered in the Management chapter, you would see immediate improvements in retention. But what if you are not actually a manager. What if you are in HR, and retention is your project, but you have hundreds or even thousands of managers that need to do this, but think this 'people stuff' is a load of rubbish. Well, you can start by buying all of them a copy of this book. Why? Because education will be the key. What you are facing is a cultural challenge. The most difficult of all. In many of our largest organisations, particularly those that have always employed large numbers of young people, there is a culture of 'I got treated like dirt when I was starting out, so now it is my time to start dishing it out'. This is what I call a circular problem. Meaning it reinforces itself, and gets more and more entrenched as time goes on. What you need to do is find an entry point. Somewhere that you can penetrate and create a shift in perception, because it requires such a shift to break the cycle of the problem. We need to create a change in direction, and the key to doing this is education. Not of the employee, but of the manager and supervisors. Start managing poor retention instead of blaming 'kids these days'. Start educating your managers in the psychology of people

Power trips are out. Respect is in.

and in communication skills. Send them all a copy of *Emotional Intelligence* by Daniel Goleman, or stick them in one of my workshops. Do something!

People get treated poorly as they progress through the ranks, and as such, when they hit management they too treat new young talent the same way. After all, they were treated this way. And the process continues and feeds on itself. In order to make a change to something as deep rooted as this sort of management culture, we need to pick a specific piece, a wedge where we know we can make a difference. By doing this, we slow the momentum of the problem and, as we then make changes to another wedge, we eventually see a reversal of the problem where a better culture creates better results, which leads to an even stronger culture that allows for the process to work in reverse.

Managers should also be trained in effective delegation. Obviously, delegation is based on trust (a very soft issue) but managers need to be able to delegate, and delegate effectively. The reason for this is twofold. Firstly, delegation provides opportunities for staff members to gain valuable new experience. It makes them feel important and adds variety to their role.

Secondly, and maybe even more importantly, it frees up managers to do what managers are supposed to do. We have already said that Talent Development is manager job number one. At present, in many of the organisations I work with, managers are so busy just trying to keep up with the pace of change in their own responsibilities that the time left for their people is negligible. Suicide! Delegate and spend time with your team. **Generation Y will thrive working for a manager who is there as a coach and mentor, not just a hired hand.**

While we're at it, let's bring up the issue of manager insecurity. I recently quizzed a Generation Yer about why he hated his boss and he replied that he thought his boss was insecure. When I asked him to explain, he replied, 'He won't teach me anything. It is as if he is scared I will do it better and take his job.' Do you (or your managers) know that the quality of a coach (AKA manager) is measured by how great they make their players? Management is never about you. It is about them. This kind of manager insecurity will cost organisations big time.

So stop promoting technicians to managers. Pay them manager's wages and leave them where they are. Start hiring and promoting coaches. Why not send your manager on a management course to beat all other management courses. That is, make them coach an under-six cricket or soccer team. That will get their management skills up to scratch. And I am not joking.

It is a value thing

Your employee retention rate is a reflection of how valued your staff feel in their position. Even more so than the position itself. Sure, you have to add variety and fun, and be flexible, but most of all, your staff need to feel valued. How?

Start with the managers and the way they treat their team members (enough on this already). Then move onto the workspace and environment they perform in. Is it dull and boring? Is it old and in desperate need of a makeover? If a worker's workspace is old, dirty and in need of a makeover, they see this as a reflection of what they are worth to you and your company. Think about that. Once you have done this, move onto the common room, and finish with what social events and other such activities you engage your staff in. This will give you more than a good starting point.

Your level of staff retention is directly proportionate to how valued your staff feel. It is as simple as that. The chapter on Management was devoted to what a manager would need to do to make sure his or her staff felt valued. We have outlined what Generation Y want from a job and from an employer. Start there and do a piece-by-piece audit of how you do things in your company. Sure, you will never be able to do and implement all my suggestions, but you certainly could do some. Start with the one you think will make the biggest impact on how valued your staff feel and begin there. Maybe recognition is the easiest place, and the one with the most leverage.

After that, move on to the amount and quality of internal communication that you engage in. Do you keep your staff in the loop? Or do you send out mass-produced propaganda that basically says nothing? I am serious about this. Generation Y will want to be 'in the know'. And the best thing is, you don't have to be afraid to tell them bad news. They are far more likely to pledge their allegiance to you if you treat them like they matter by telling them what is going on and how they can help the situation.

How about listening to them for a change? Never assume you know how they feel or what they want. Do you have formal processes where all staff, not just Generation Y, can share their ideas, thoughts and challenges? If not, GET ONE! You can use a suggestions box, weekly or monthly brainstorming sessions or regular employee/manager evaluations. Seek their input.

Companies obsess about communication, but they think all too often that this is about 'what should we say'. Sometimes it is better to just listen. Say, for example, you are currently undergoing a significant restructure; you would be well advised to set up a formal communications policy that revolves around formal and informal staff feedback sessions and then goes forward. You should feed back to your staff what you have learnt from such sessions and what, if anything, you can do to resolve such issues.

A survey by the People Report in the United States into the restaurant industry showed restaurants that surveyed their employees twice annually had significantly better staff retention. Interestingly, the same survey showed that providing four or more hours of orientation reduced turnover by 30% in some organisations in the trial period of employment. It is all part of feeling valued, and orientation can create a sense of being a part of something bigger. You should also be aware that the third factor associated with excellent retention in this traditionally high turnover industry was active involvement in community projects.

Turn a Light on

If you want your Generation Y staff to hang around and produce, then you had better light a path for them. A path to something bigger. What are their career prospects? Sit down and talk to them about their aspirations. How can you and your company help them to achieve this? What lateral opportunities are available? With organisations getting flatter and flatter, there is less scope for Generation Y to move up the ladder, so we had better come up with other ways to enhance employees' skills than just traditional promotions. Generation Y want career development. Refer back to the chapter on Career Management.

A Genesys study of 28,000 call centre employees showed that 64% nominated 'lack of career opportunities' as job dissatisfaction number one. In an industry not known for good salaries and remuneration, only 24% said pay was their main reason for leaving a job. To reiterate my point about adding variety to the workplace, 44% said that the boring and repetitive nature of the work would be a big reason for leaving.

Remember, too, that you don't have to train all your Generation Y staff, only those you want to keep.

We must show Generation Yers, particularly those in entry-level positions, how what they are doing enhances their resume and employability. It almost seems counterproductive to use that sort of language – enhance their resume – but I can assure you that as long as you are enhancing the employability of your Generation Y staff, they will stay. That is, of course, assuming you are treating them like human beings. Remember, too, that you don't have to train all your Generation Y staff, only those you want to keep.

Take the call centre for instance. The call centre should be a gateway to bigger and better things in your organisation. Think about it this way. Companies pay millions to have consultants survey their customers and find out what they like and dislike about doing business with them. Just ask someone in your call centre, and they can tell you. And it won't cost you millions. The knowledge of the customer, not to mention their in-depth product knowledge as well, makes a call centre operator an excellent prospect for talent development in your organisation. Just ask Suncorp, which has five call centres with about 1400 staff. In *Business Review Weekly* (December 2003), General Manager Andrew Mulvogue was quoted as saying they are 'a breeding ground for the rest of the organisation. It is an ideal place for employees to become experts in our various products'. He goes on to say that they have a system in place which maps an agent's life in the call centre, as well as certain trigger points indicating time for a change. He also says that 'it is better for someone to come from the call centre, rather than straight from university, into the marketing department'.

By the way, the same Genesys study showed that annual turnover was higher than 50% in some of the call centres surveyed, but that the average was 28% in Australian call centres. Given industry estimates that it costs $35,000 to replace a phone agent, poor retention is costing BIG money. And considering that labour costs consist of upwards of 60% in this environment, and that over 240,000 employees work in call centres, the improvements to the bottom line could be massive. There is nothing 'soft' about that. Using Suncorp numbers of 1400 staff (although I know Suncorp would be performing better than the average) 1400 x 28% x $35,000 = $13,720,000. Therefore, an improvement of just 1% point in retention rates would mean savings of $490,000 for Suncorp Metway. What if you could get 5%? Call me!

Active career management and planning for your staff will be the key to retaining them long term (whatever long term means). It not only shows you care, but truly lights a path for them. They can see where they are going. They can see WHY they need to do what they are currently doing. And being Generation Y, it is all about WHY! Give them a reason to stay, be the reason training opportunities, promotional opportunities, lateral movement and cool new projects, a great boss, a fun work environment and so on. The key question is: what is it about your company, your team, your retail outlet that will make them want to stay?

Do you have young talent in key leadership positions?

Do you have young talent in decision-making positions? Do you promote based on merit or on age? A few things for you to think about.

What about the aspirations and vision of your company as a whole? Recall the 11,000 Generation Yers surveyed and asked why they would join the army in a time of war, and their reply, 'To be a part of something bigger'. Does your company stand for more than shareholder value and share price? Does you CEO talk about passion, culture, people and making a difference? Or just P/E ratios and dividends? Are the managers themselves inspired by the company and where it is going? If the CEO isn't inspired, and the managers aren't inspired, why do you keep expecting the rest of the company to be inspired? **Retention, and real buy-in starts at the top and filters down. NOT THE OTHER WAY AROUND!**

Churn baby Churn

For those of you convinced that there is nothing you can do about your alarmingly low retention rate, let me first say there is always room for improvement. I will also, however, concede that there are industries known for burnout and bad employee retention. Perhaps you're an insurance sales call centre. Maybe a customer complaints call centre. Perhaps it is entry-level retail. Whatever it is, some jobs by their very nature do not keep employees engaged and satisfied long term. While I believe there is always room for improvement (see the Suncorp Metway attitude), the reality is, in some of these industries the retention rate will never be brilliant. So prepare. Prepare well. Have streamlined (try online) recruiting processes. Find inexpensive ways to advertise (try in-house). Have an interview process that is not long and arduous, and employ fast.

You must be set up to deal with this. There is no point keeping your head in the sand hoping that one day it will get better. Aggressively work on the areas where you can see opportunity for improvement, and also work from the other direction, making it as efficient as possible to hire and replace those that go AWOL.

Let me repeat that having given advice on preparing for the worst, there is always room for improvement. Say, for example, you are in retail and you require large numbers of staff over the Christmas period. Here are a few ideas for keeping your staff for the entire period, even though they know they will laid off after the Christmas rush:

> **Be upfront about expectations**
> **Offer a grant/bonus for finishing the season. This may be as simple as cash bonuses or as intangible as a huge staff party**
> **Offer return positions the following year to those who finish the season.**

Negotiate

Good talent is hard to find. Very hard. So when you get it, do your best to hold on to it. Reward and acknowledge talent. Spend your time with your most talented individuals and the rest will get the message. Remember, what is rewarded is repeated.

Confusion Management

Survey after survey shows that employees want, and value, clear objectives for how they can contribute to the success of the organisation. Poor definition of roles and goals will be tolerated only so far. Make sure your Generation Y staff know their role.

Coaching and mentoring, by someone other than the manager, can help with managing the confusion. People need a rock. A sounding board they can go back to and get re-grounded. Coaching and mentoring can offer this. I have spoken in detail about formal mentoring, and also about the manager's role as coach and mentor. Let me add here that there is growing evidence professional coaching is a valuable tool for maximising the productivity of your people as well as improving retention.

Actively Fire

I am serious. Get rid of the tail. If you want to keep your good staff, get rid of the bad. They are poisonous to your organisation. They suck energy and passion from the workplace. Don't waste time with them if they belong somewhere else. Just hit Control Alt Delete. It is not fair to those who perform to be surrounded by people who aren't there to contribute.

I would also suggest you don't aim for 100% retention. Some turnover is good. I have heard it said that 15–16% is healthy. Jack Welch made active 'churn' part of his strategy and something to which he credits his phenomenal success. You should be happy to lose some of your people each year because it gives you an opportunity to inject some fresh new talent into your organisation. Your job, however, is to make sure it isn't your top performers who do the leaving.

Know the mood cycle

Most industries have a peak time. A time when stress is at its highest, and when turnover is most detrimental. Sit down with your team and identify these times. Then brainstorm ways that will make them more 'tolerable'. Maybe during tax time for accountants there could be dinner for the staff for two weeks because they will be working back late most nights. Perhaps in hospitality, it is a carefully planned roster over Christmas, trying to ensure that the big public holidays are shared among all the staff and not one person has to work all the days that the rest of the world takes off.

You should also be able to identify the warning signs of a disgruntled team member and act immediately when you see this coming. Don't wait for them to come to you. Instigate dialogue, get them talking. Don't wait until they are handing you their resignation.

Know what your competitors are doing

One of the biggest challenges with retention is that the people you want to retain the most are also the ones with the most options. They will be the ones that your competitors have their eye on. Be sure to know what other companies are doing. Not just companies inside your industry, but outside as well. What is considered fair compensation? What new perks and benefits are on offer? What training programs are they making available to their staff?

You might like to expand the benefits you are offering as well. Consider things like staff discounts. Or better still, staff family discounts. Staff family discounts mean your employees now have a whole army of people that want them to stay. A very good friend of mine worked at Kathmandu while studying for his degree. He stayed there for more than six months after he graduated because his family pressured him to at least stay until the following snow season so they could update their gear. Kathmandu offer huge discounts for their staff. There is nothing Generation Y likes more than being the person who can get you a good deal. Being connected, so to speak.

Good Selection = Good Retention

Without sounding too elementary, if you select the right person for the job in the first place, you have a better chance they will stay with you. The Department of Foreign Affairs and Trade lose only 4% of graduates over a five-year period. This is exceptional compared to the rest of the public sector, which some research has shown to be as high as 40% in some departments. When asked the secret of their success, the answer was careful selection. No, correction: *very* careful selection. They do, of course, offer extraordinary opportunities, including travel, but essentially, they credit their brilliant retention to good selection.

The Talent Zone Australasian Graduate Recruitment Benchmarking Study

This study showed, through correlation analysis, that the following factors positively impacted retention of staff in graduate programs:

- **Recruiting graduates from pre-graduate programs**
- **Lower overall graduate intake**
- **Steady graduate intake year on year**
- **Receiving less candidate applications**
- **Longer duration of graduate programs**

> **Rotational graduate programs across business units and departments**
> **Including salary reviews as part of the review process**
> **Offering higher than average graduate salaries**
> **Delivering greater financial benefits as part of the overall graduate package**
> **Installing a buddy/mentor system**

Dunn & Bradstreet in Focus

Mercer Human Resource Consulting were engaged in Australia to work with Dunn & Bradstreet to improve retention of Generation Y graduates. In the period from 30 December 1999 to July 2000, voluntary turnover had increased a massive 30%. Managing Director Christine Christian took this problem very seriously and engaged the international consulting firm Mercer to diagnose the specific problem and provide solutions.

Essentially, the research revealed that young recruits felt they had come to Dunn & Bradstreet with a false understanding of what their actual jobs would entail. They were led to believe that their roles would be more challenging and more aligned to their career aspirations. They felt the job advertisements and applications misrepresented the job. It was also discovered that managers were doing little to enable graduates to make use of their skills and qualifications. As well as this, quotas were seen to be unsustainable, which meant that pay levels would not be commensurate with expectations.

When managers began by responding it was 'too hard', it was clear to MD Christine Christian that something had to be done immediately.

With Mercer, they implemented the following solutions:

> **Created a profile of the ideal candidate**
> **Improved the screening process**
> **Changed the advertisement and interview process**
> **Clearly communicated career progression and time required in the role**
> **Redeveloped the job profile**

- **Focused on a realistic job preview during the interview process**
- **Democratised the planning process and gave management planning input**
- **Implemented a rotation program**
- **Implemented a mentor program**
- **Gave the task of career planning to the direct managers of the new graduates**
- **Introduced temporary projects to allow for graduates to develop their skills**
- **Introduced monthly meetings to communicate the company strategy**
- **Redesigned pay levels and structure**
- **Increased base salary**
- **Introduced reward systems for customer satisfaction, not just dollars**

Although this book was 90% written before I gained access to this case study, you will notice that it follows very closely the recommendations I put forward.

Turnover of key talent went to 0%. Customer satisfaction measures went up 14%, and productivity returned to desired levels.

Congratulations Dunn & Bradstreet and Mercer Human Resource Consulting. Much could be learnt from this case study. Use it as a model to begin an audit of your employment and recruiting process.

Your Quest!

More questions for you to answer:

> Should you be more focused perhaps on engaging your staff rather than retaining them?
> What is it about you and your company that would make your staff want to stay?
> What is it about your brand or your company that might make your staff want to leave? What can you do to improve these things?
> Is there a destructive management culture in your organisation, making retention poor? What small steps could you take now to begin to slow that negative momentum?
> How might you make someone in your team, division or store feel more valuable today?
> Do you actively fire those who create negative energy in the workplace, as well as the poor performers?
> What are your competitors doing that might lure key talent from your organisation to their organisation?

Exiting

I would love to put this chapter right at the start of the tactics section of this book, because having it here at the end might make some think it is not as important as the other chapters. Nothing could be further from the truth. I believe the Exit Process is essential for the following reasons:

- **Done well, it will not only protect, but could even serve to enhance your Employer Brand.**
- **Managed properly, it can minimise the loss of valuable intellectual property that so often leaves when a key member of your team leaves.**
- **It can be a valuable learning experience, regarding how your organisation could better serve its people, and what to do next with the exiting staff member's role.**

Let's start with protecting your Employer Brand. Nothing could be more damaging to your reputation as an Employer of Choice than an army of ex-employees spreading the word about town that you are not a very nice company to work for. But you 'looked after them so well while they were here' you may say. Sure, you probably did, but remember, last impressions linger! How did they feel treated as they left? A close friend of mine, an architect, recently left a very respectable Australian developer, where she was a key contributor to some of their biggest projects. She had been there for more than four years. On the Friday she was due to leave, there was no goodbye present, no staff drinks, and scarcely a word from her previous boss as she finished up. 'It must be a surprise party' she thought, as she packed her things. But nothing. Not a thing. To say that she was very upset about it would be an understatement. It has long been known in the hospitality industry that if someone has a bad customer service experience, they will tell ten times more people than they would if they had had a good customer service experience. Leaving a job is no different. I guarantee you that if the exit process is a negative one, that person will sing it from the rooftops, and knowing the power of 'word of mouth', the damage that this sort of thing can do to your Employer Brand is more than you can imagine.

Even the terminology 'Exit' is negative. Could we not think of something a little more personable? What about 'Farewell Strategy'? Or better still 'Farewell Experience'. To bid someone farewell is to wish them all the best with their new venture. You see, in the mindset of the leaver, they are going on to bigger and better things, to learn, grow and develop some more. Perhaps you should be happy for them. Maybe if you were happy for them, they might look to you as the destination for their next move, and come back bringing with them more skills and better practices. I like to say, 'You don't have to hate them.' Leaving is a good thing. Maybe they need to leave before they get too stale. Maybe they want to pursue other opportunities. By making it an unpleasant experience, you not only damage your brand, but you negate the likelihood of their returning. If your Exit Process became a Farewell Experience, it would become a future recruiting strategy.

'You don't have to hate them.'

Now for minimising the loss of valuable intellectual property. Does your Exit Strategy create the in-built desire in your exiting talent to ensure they leave behind all the knowledge they have gained in their role, and the will to ensure the smooth transition of their successor? If not, it should. For example, do you look at the exit interview as 'just another pain in the neck' when someone leaves your company? Or do you look at it as an opportunity for you, and other key members of your organisation, to retain some of their investment in the exiting talent and to capture the knowledge required to move your team forward?

What about the opportunity to learn from the exit interview? To learn how you could make your business an employer of choice. To learn how you could more fully engage your staff. To learn what are the most appropriate steps moving forward in that person's position. If you ask provocative questions and then listen, you might learn that you should not be replacing them in that position and instead, you should be investing in technology that may offer large improvements in efficiency in that specific operation. People are hardly going to suggest something like that while they are still working for you because they risk innovating themselves out of a job. There are countless examples of what you could learn. The key here is that you approach the interview, and in fact the whole process (call it experience), as an opportunity to improve what you do and how you do it.

Here are a few ideas that might get you thinking constructively about the Farewell Experience.

Say Thanks

I know it sounds trite, but it is very real. Be sure to say thanks. Thank the Generation Yer who is leaving for their time, effort and dedication. Thank them for coming to work for you and for being a valuable member of your team. Let them know they will be welcomed back if they ever wish to rejoin your company, and ask them to stay in touch so you can let them know of any unique opportunities that may suit them. I have already mentioned my friend who left a large Australian retailer to join Australia's leading airline. On her last day, a senior manager said to her, 'We would love to have you back, anytime. We will miss you.' Talk about last words lingering. What lasting impression do you think that made on my friend? A bloody good one, to say the least. Twelve words and three seconds to immortality in the mind of that one person. A very profitable investment if you ask me.

'We would love to have you back, anytime. We will miss you.'

What's next?

Why not ask the leaving talent what they recommend you do next? It is highly likely that they have a number of excellent ideas about how to better do what they have been doing, and how the whole team could be better organised. It is part of human nature that we pick up on all the little things that annoy us. Being aware of these little things will be extremely valuable to you as a manager when looking at how to raise the bar and improve what you do.

Refer a Friend

Here are two magic questions to ask at an exit interview:

- **Would you refer our company to a friend?**
- **Do you know anyone who may be interested in applying for your old position?**

Start with 'Would you refer us to a friend?'. Forget about a refer-a-friend program if your company is not the sort your employees would want to expose their friends to. The answer to this question could prove to be very valuable to you, as a line or HR manager. Consider this as a line of questioning:

'Would you refer us to your friends?'
'No.'
'Why not?'
'Because X, Y, Z ...'
'How would you suggest we improve?'
'X, Y, Z ...'

'How else do you think we could make our staff feel more valued? And what would we need to do in order to make ourselves the kind of employer that you WOULD refer to a friend?'

And then LISTEN!

Assuming that they are prepared to refer you, ask them straight out to give you the names of some people who may be interested in applying for their old position. Think about this; who would know better what sort of person would do well in that position and what sort of person is now needed in that position? Maybe that is a question you could ask, too. For example:

'What kind of person do you think we now need in this position?'

'What character traits should we look for? What about experience?'

'Is there anyone you know internally who might be a good candidate?'

I am sure you are getting the picture. And I am sure you are probably already asking some of these questions. I want to make sure you are listening to the answers, and that you see how valuable they could be. You may also consider attaching an incentive to this. Meaning, if the person referred from outside the company makes it through the recruitment and selection process and is employed, providing they stay at least three months, the referrer gets a cash bonus. Imagine that! Three months after you leave a company they are still sending you cheques. Cool company!

Schoolfriends.com your business

I love this concept. Have you been on <schoolfriends.com> yet (.com.au for Australia)? If you are not familiar with the site, here is how it works. It is a database-driven site with more than a million members sorted by where they went to school, TAFE or university; and their previous workplaces. You can then get online and search for someone you have not seen for four or even forty years and catch up with them. It is like a MASSIVE people search engine. Well, adopt that concept and merge it with the concept of an alumni group, and you potentially have access to a kick-ass talent pool. Imagine if everyone that has ever worked for your company became part of a club or alumni-style association and continued to enjoy some of the benefits they enjoyed while working for you, such as discount movie tickets, or some version of store discount, as well as being notified of internal jobs available and other opportunities. Can you see the scope? HUGE! Let us refocus this to Generation Y for a minute. Many of your key young talent will suffer from an attack of the travel bug and will pack up and head overseas. On their return, however, they will be looking for employment in Australia again. Not only that, but they will be wiser and more able when they return. It is like a year of free training and experience that you can now tap into.

The internet makes this a much simpler project than it would have once been. Create an online community. A hub where staff, past and present, go to share ideas, information and resources.

Ford Australia have a 'regrettable losses' list of anyone who leaves, and few do, who was a truly great contributor to the organisation. They are contacted regularly to see how they are and to discuss possible options of returning to Ford Australia. This has proven very successful, and many of the company's best people who left have eventually returned.

Your Quest!

Now for your Exit Interview.

> How do you perceive the exit process?

> Is the exit process in your business a clinical or a positive experience? How might you go about transforming it into a positive farewell experience?

> Are you learning from the ideas and suggestions of staff that are leaving your organisation?

> Do you make it a habit, not just when they leave, of saying 'thank you' to your staff for the contribution they make to the business?

> Could you start a company alumni?

Conclusion

I hope that your quest thus far has been insightful and rewarding. I hope that after reading this book you will begin to implement some changes within your organisation that will better utilise the talent you have, and allow you to attract even more young talent to your organisation. I hope you realise that Generation Y represents a unique and powerful opportunity if you are prepared to tap into it, as opposed to a frightening trend as you may have previously thought.

Sometimes in business we don't need to work harder, just smarter. I hope this book offers you some of the smarts to better attract, manage and engage your Generation Y workforce. If there is anything I can do to assist as you implement some changes in your organisation, please be in touch. Feel free to share with me your success stories, and even your not-so-successful stories. If you believe you are doing an outstanding job working with young talent, get in touch. I would love to know more about what you are doing that is working so well.

Remember, too, that this book is only the beginning of your quest. The real journey and the real rewards come from implementing what you have learnt. Nothing ever changes unless we do something. My advice to you would be to just pick one thing and act on that. When you have got that 80% right, select another and act on that. Just make sure you act on something, because then our time here together has been worthwhile.

Best wishes,

Peter Sheahan

Index